COOKING CREATIVELY
WITH
NATURAL FOODS

COOKING CREATIVELY
WITH
NATURAL FOODS

by Edith and Sam Brown

HAWTHORN BOOKS, INC.
Publishers
New York

COOKING CREATIVELY WITH NATURAL FOODS

DESIGN BY G. & G.

Illustrations by Hope Meryman

1 2 3 4 5 6 7 8 9 10

To the young people of America
who have initiated a return
to nature and natural foods

ACKNOWLEDGMENTS

Our sincere thanks go to Eugene Boe for his encouragement and expertise; without him this book would not have gotten off the ground and into the kitchen. Much appreciation is also due to those dear friends and relatives who not only helped to taste and test—but best of all, also often stayed to help clean up and put away!

E. B.
S. B.

CONTENTS

INTRODUCTION

This cookbook has been 35 years in the making. It really goes back to the birth of Brownies. That was in 1936. In the beginning we were just a sliver in the wall, hardly a soybean's throw from Union Square in New York City. The address hasn't changed, but *we* have.

Brownies began as a tiny shop selling natural foods to people who lived or worked in the neighborhood. Today we are a restaurant–bakery–country store complex sprawled across Siamese-twin brownstone houses. We feed and fortify an international clientele that comes to us from flattering distances.

Our Colonial-style restaurant is divided between a long counter with stools in the front and a charming dining room in the rear. We are open for lunch and dinner and serve an average of 750 meals daily. Our store has been called a Disneyland of natural food products.

In the beginning, Brownies was Sam Brown. Sam was only 19 years old way back then, but he was it: owner, operator, sales staff, handyman. Short in the tooth though he was, Sam already had under his belt 6 years' experience in a similar store uptown, where he worked days while going to school at night.

The expansion of Brownies began modestly in 1938. Sam acquired a vegetable-juice extractor and installed four stools in the shop. Vegetable-juice bars have long since become old hat, but the one on East 16th Street happened to be the first one in the country.

The juice bar won a warm welcome. Customers "dug" the oral vitamin shots being dispensed from the extractor. Soon people were coming from precincts far beyond the neighborhood to "get juiced." The word spread. There appeared a distinguished visitor in the person of the late Clementine Paddleford, the influential food editor of (alas, also the late) New York *Herald-Tribune*. Miss Paddleford came, sipped, and wrote rapturously about her discovery. That rave review really put Brownies on the map.

Business began humming along so well that Sam felt another expansion coming on; this time it would be a human one. He needed the services of a secretary-bookkeeper. Enter a 17-year-old girl named Edith Tucker. . . . The rest of that particular script you've read before: long hours of propinquity, business spilling over into romance, and the time-honored cliché of girl marries boss.

What babes in the woods we were back in that remote time! We were much too young to be experts at anything, but all of our customers looked to us as authorities on good nutrition, diets, and cooking. Determined not to disappoint, we boned up and invited the public to a series of evening seminars in the back room. We discoursed with bravado on the wonders of natural foods as the open sesame to good health, and we gave cooking demonstrations. To supplement our wisdom and expertise we also had the temerity to ask distinguished persons to come in and lecture—gratis!

Looking back, we seem to have been like a couple of spanking-new schoolteachers trying to keep a jump ahead of the class. Our customers who came from beyond the neighborhood thought they should get something more than a vegetable-juice cocktail for making the effort to get to Brownies. Edith met the demand by coming up with a salad menu. The salads were all originals. They used wholesome ingredients in unusual combinations, and they were created as much to arrest the eye as to satisfy the palate and the inner man.

So began our salad days. The next thing we knew, we were in the soup, so to speak. We woke up one morning to find ourselves a full-fledged health-foods restaurant.

In its premier phase Brownies admittedly attracted its share of eccentrics. We had dotty old ladies galore, clomping through the door in their Murray Space Shoes, clamoring for asparagus-fern salads dressed with essence of eucalyptus. And wall-to-wall hypochondriacs: "Oh, Mr. Brown, do you think if I put just ten grains of raw sugar in my rose-hip tea, my pancreas will become overstimulated?"

Today the whole world embraces the idea of good nutrition; everybody is anxious to rediscover the natural tastes of foods. So we have everybody lighting our doors: business people, publishers, secretaries, laborers, film producers and actors, television executives, housewives, photographers and models, professors and students, folk singers, rock musicians. Danny Kaye, David Brinkley, Julie Newmar, Gayelord Hauser, Helen Hayes, Anita Loos, Bea Lillie, Tony Perkins, Robert Merrill, Red Buttons, Andy Warhol, Rita Moreno. (We ourselves have become minor celebrities of sorts by having appeared and been talked about on network television shows, as well as on local New York programs. Everybody comes. And especially that vanguard of the whole ecology movement, the young!

And finally we have even been taken up by our own family! Our 3 children had always found the fare on the family table acceptable enough, but they had never exactly flipped over the magic of Brownies. How times have changed! Our daughter Gayle's conversion occurred on a train when she saw a much-admired young instructor of hers carrying a Brownies shopping bag. Our younger daughter, Karen, heard fellow students talking about Brownies when she was at Berkeley, and *she* suddenly started seeing us in a new light. Son Dennis is nothing if not a pragmatist; when he sized up the action at Brownies, he decided to get into the health-foods game.

On Earth Day in 1970 Karen came into the restaurant after an exhilarating stroll down a carless Fifth Avenue. "Mother," she said, "when are you going to write that cookbook so I can start making some of these dishes in my own apartment?" It was perhaps the sincerest compliment our cuisine had ever received—and the ultimate goad to get us cracking on the cookbook.

We are all growing wiser about the food we eat. Our eyes have been opened to the toll exacted by modern methods of agriculture and food-processing. At last we are becoming aware that we have been eating too much, enjoying it too little, and getting a poor return for the money spent and the calories consumed.

In pioneer times a family lived almost entirely on what it produced. It was a harsh, often meager life. Nutritionally, though, that family was better off than today's affluent classes, with their preference for brightly packaged, easy-does-it, plastic foods. This spoiled society, dependent on so many labor-saving conveniences, needs far less fuel to keep it going than our hard-working ancestors needed. For the amount of energy we are burning up, most of us should not be taking in more than 1,500 to 2,500 calories daily. We take in more, most of us, but of dead foods, nutritionally empty.

Natural foods are our best safeguard against empty calories. They are a refuge from the hideous array of TV dinners, cake and muffin and frosting mixes, breads with the taste and texture of cotton batting, pop-snap-and-crackle cereals, instant puddings, carbonated soft drinks, deep-fried horrors, and sugar-and-chemical-ridden pastries which have glutted supermarket shelves since the end of World War II. A whole generation of youngsters has come of age not knowing the taste of anything real. Time alone can tell the effect tons of ingested junk will have on their health, both psychic and somatic.

Essentially, natural foods are fresh, whole, unrefined, and unpolished foods grown in soils that have not been chemically treated. They are also free of additives, preservatives, and pesticide sprays. Nutritionists can point out how superior they are in value to foods that have been through the mills. The contents of this book will indicate their enormous variety and versatility. More important, any test panel anywhere would rate them superior in taste. You won't find too many of them in your local supermarket (someone has remarked that if a person would eat really well, he should follow the average housewife around a supermarket and be sure *not* to buy anything she's dropped into her shopping cart), but with the growth of organic farming and health-foods stores, they are accessible to almost everybody.

In following our recipes—indeed, in all your cooking—you should use organic, natural, unrefined, unprocessed, unadulterated foods: fruits, vegetables, eggs, cheeses, flours, nuts, and so forth. Although they are not essential for the success of the recipes (your cake will turn out if you use a supermarket egg instead of an organic one), they *are* important for anyone concerned with good-tasting, healthy eating. Therefore, every time we tell you a dish requires a sliced tomato, say, you are to translate that inside your head into "a sliced *organic* tomato," please! We assure you that you'll notice the difference. We are all for organic foods, as we've said. A word of caution, though: Unfortunately, not everything that is sold as organic is organic. Alas, there are a number of unscrupulous quick-buck artists peddling produce labeled organic which is no more organic than the stuff you find in any market. If you can't have your own organic garden, be sure that the vendor you deal with is trustworthy and that he knows *his* purveyors to be trustworthy. The same advice goes for health-foods restaurants; make sure you know what you're getting.

We readily concede that eating naturally, in a literal monetary accounting, costs more. Anything coming off a mass-production line will always be cheaper than the unprocessed item that requires individual care and handling. But unit for unit—when you compare the nutrients your money has bought—natural foods turn out to be the better bargain.

We are always pleased, of course, when our well-traveled friends tell us, "There's no place in the world like Brownies." (Having done a bit of traveling ourselves, we agree.) We smile when satisfied diners acclaim Edith as a born cook or a genius. How did Edith do it? She honestly doesn't know. Cooking interested her. She devoured cookbooks by the shelf and then put the books out of her mind. She had mastered the principles, and she had a knack. Her impulse was to move on, to reject imitation in favor of innovation.

That sweet sound of "Recipe, please" has been falling on our ears for a long time. For years hardly a day passed on which someone did not ask for one recipe or another, but we were always unable to oblige—and not out of coyness or because we didn't want to share a good thing.

The problem, simply, was that all the dishes had been created for institutional use, conceived in the proportions appropriate for the restaurant. There had never been time to break the recipes down for domestic consumption. (That is not as easy a task as it might seem: If you have devised a recipe that makes 100 servings, for example, for reasons too complicated to go into here you cannot just divide everything by 25 and presto! have a recipe that will serve a family of 4. Would that it were that uncomplicated!)

Now, at last, we have bowed to popular demand. We have taken a sabbatical and written a cookbook. The restaurant recipes have been broken down and carefully tested for home use. To those of you who encouraged this effort, we hope the recipes will make you remember us fondly. To those of you who have never been to our restaurant, we are happy to bring the best of Brownies to you.

Bon appetit! A votre santé!

IMPORTANT!

All ingredients used should be, as far as possible, organic, natural, unrefined, unprocessed, and free from chemical additives or preservatives.

Use either bottled spring or charcoal-filtered tap water.

All fruits and vegetables should be fresh and uncooked unless otherwise specified.

Dried herbs are to be used in all recipes unless otherwise specified.

Refer to Chapter 1, "The Natural-Foods Cupboard," for descriptions of any unfamiliar ingredients or appliances.

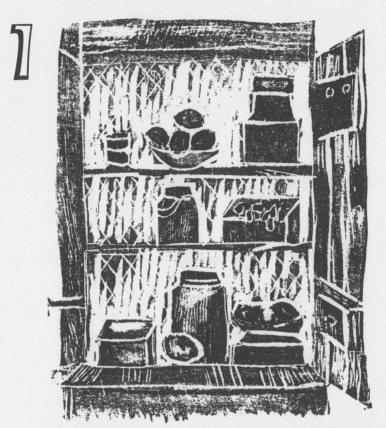

THE NATURAL-FOODS CUPBOARD

A Glossary

To anyone not yet "into" natural foods, some of the ingredients of the recipes in this book may seem exotic. Don't think of them as strange, however, but as friends-in-waiting. They aren't too remote or elusive: Most are available at your nearest health-foods store, and nowadays that is usually very nearby indeed.

Listed and described below are some of the less-familiar ingredients that appear throughout *Cooking Creatively with Natural Foods*. Also included are the names of some of the recommended appliances mentioned in the book. They too can be bought in health-foods stores.

APPLIANCES

Blender: A versatile electric home appliance that blends, purees, grinds, etc., and enables anyone to create unique and nourishing drinks, soups, desserts, and so forth in just minutes.

Grinder: A small electric appliance, also known as a mill, that is perfect for grinding all seeds, grains, nuts, and herbs into meals and powders.

Juice extractor: An electric appliance that provides a simple way to extract pure, delicious juice, a bountiful source of nature's vitamins and minerals, from most fruits and vegetables.

Mill: *See* Grinder.

Sprouter: The use of this makes an indoor garden possible the year round. Easy-to-follow instructions enable you to have the satisfying experience of growing your own fresh sprouts from the seeds or beans of alfalfa, mung, soy, wheat, lentil, etc. In 3 to 5 days you are rewarded with a bountiful crop of sprouts, delectable when used in salads, sandwiches, omelets, and so on.

Steamer: The superior choice of utensil for preparing fish and vegetables. Maximum flavor, color, and nutrition are retained by steaming. There are several stainless-steel collapsible devices available that fit any size cooking pot.

Water filter: When fresh spring water is not available, the activated-charcoal water filter is a must in every kitchen. Some styles can be attached to the sink faucet for simple filtering, or there are separate individual units that filter impurities from water in minutes.

Yogurt-maker: Converts homogenized milk, skim milk, soybean milk, or skim-milk powder into yogurt overnight, and permits you to enjoy this delightful food with ease. Various flavored yogurts can be made with the addition of fruits, nutrition boosters, honey, etc. Works on electricity.

FOODS

Agar: A seaweed with excellent thickening qualities, it is used very effectively in salad dressings, jellies, and soups. Used alone, it provides nonnutritive bulk.

Apple-cider vinegar: Generally made from whole tree-ripened apples. The preferable variety is made from unsprayed apples, aged in wood and unpasteurized.

Bakon Yeast: Yeast that has been hickory-smoked. A flavorful way to use yeast in cooking.

Barbados molasses: A West Indian import during Colonial days, made famous in the general store of yesteryear and by the perennial tonic of sulphur and molasses. Popularly used today in beverages, baking, and desserts.

Beans: Mung, soy, kidney, pigeon, pinto, lima, black turtle, lentils —a wonderful world of vegetable proteins. An economical choice for one-dish meals, soups, salads, and main dishes.

Big Franks: All-vegetable protein, seasoned and flavored like America's all-time favorite, the hot dog. Made from wheat, soy, yeast, and vegetables. Just heat and serve. The same "frankfurters," but smaller in size, are sold under the name Linketts.

Blackstrap molasses: The product of the last extraction of the sugarcane, it contains the least amount of carbohydrates of all types of molasses. It is particularly rich in minerals, especially iron, 1 tablespoon having ⅓ the daily adult requirement.

Brewer's yeast: Originally yeast was exclusively a by-product of the brewing of beer. Now most yeasts are specifically grown for nutritional use and are therefore known as primary or nutritional yeasts. These yeasts are valuable supplements to the diet—rich in good proteins, an excellent source of all known B vitamins, particularly nucleic acid, virtually free of fat and carbohydrates. Brewer's yeast is available in powdered, flaked, or seasoned forms. Potency of the yeast is determined by the broth or medium in which the yeast was grown: Check your label for potency.

Brown-rice flour: Popular with people who are allergic to wheat and rye. Excellent as a thickener in place of cornstarch.

Buckwheat noodles: Imported from Japan. Made of whole buckwheat, they have a wonderful nutty flavor and make unusual pasta dishes.

Carob bits: Carob is made from the fruit of the carob tree, grown in the Mediterranean area and the Middle East. It is also known as St.-John's-bread, honey locust, *carobi, boeckser,* and *Johannisbrot.* Carob bits resemble chocolate chips in both flavor, looks, and uses.

Carob powder: Looks and tastes like chocolate yet contains no chocolate or cocoa. It can be used in cakes, cookies, and puddings and in many other ways.

Choplet Burger: Rich in protein, this meat substitute resembling beefburger is made from soy, brewer's yeast, and whole grains. Ready to use right from the can.

Couscous: A traditional North African and Near Eastern wheat dish used like rice or pasta. The imported variety is called couscous; the domestic is also known as bulgur wheat.

Creamed Papaya: Tree-ripened, fresh tropical melon in a concentrated form, prepared without sugar. Rich in natural pepsin. May be used as is or diluted to make a drink.

Date sugar: Also called date sweetener, a natural sweet made from pulverized and crystallized dates. Use as you would sugar to sweeten cereals, cakes, cookies, salads.

Dulse: Dried seaweed obtained off the coast of Nova Scotia. Exotic flavor, rich in ocean minerals, superb when used in chowders and fish dishes.

Eggs, organic: Sometimes referred to as fertile eggs because roosters roam through the chicken flock. The eggs are produced on farms where the chickens still run free (free range) and are fed natural grain with no antibodies added. Since the chickens are not confined in cubicles as for commercially produced eggs, there is no need for D.D.T. spraying. These differences add up to happier, healthier chickens . . . and superior eggs.

Extracts and flavorings: As called for in several recipes: lemon, orange, vanilla, etc. Be certain to procure those extracts and flavorings that are pure and free from synthetics, artificial colors, and chemicals. Read your labels.

Fearn Soy-O Mix: A blend of soybeans and wheat flours richer in protein and lower in starch than most other flours. Ready to use for pancakes or your favorite baking recipe. Also available is a Whole Wheat Soy-O Mix.

Fruit and berry concentrates, pure: Strawberry, blueberry, blackberry, apple, grape, plum, cranberry. All natural and unsweetened, with a wonderful fresh flavor.

Fruits, dried: Apples, apricots, bananas, cherries, currants, dates (and date chips), figs, peaches, pears, prunes, Monukka raisins (plump, black, seedless), etc. Energy by the pound. These are now available organically grown, all rich in wonderful flavor and food value. By all means avoid sulphured and sugar-sweetened varieties.

Green-banana flour: Made from selected unsprayed bananas, it is an exciting replacement for instant mashed potatoes. We find it excellent for thickening.

Hijiki: An excellent-tasting Japanese seaweed. Easy to prepare, versatile in use, rich in minerals. Serve as a vegetable or use for seasoning.

Honey: Nature's most perfect sweet. Select your honey from apiaries that produce organically. Be sure that is is uncooked and unfiltered. Light honey is fragrant, delicate, and sweet, best for fruit, berries, and beverages. Dark honey is pungent and aromatic, ideal for baking or when the flavor of honey should dominate. Honey is also available in a crystallized form; with age, honey thickens and thus may be spread more easily.

Kelp: A seaweed that is the richest natural source of food iodine and ocean minerals. The granulated form is excellent as a seasoning.

Krisp: Krisp is a high-protein food product that has the rich hickory-smoked flavor of bacon. An ideal seasoning for low-fat and meatless dieters. May be used in rice, dips, eggs, soup, etc.

Laver: A popular dried seaweed from Japan. This particular variety is very tender and can be eaten right from the package or crumbled into soups, sauces, and dips. . . . Contains loads of minerals.

Lecithin: A pleasant natural food supplement derived from soy, rich in choline and inositol. It comes in granule form.

Lemon-juice mayonnaise: A superior mayonnaise made with soybean oil and fresh lemon juice, without preservatives. Preferable to commercial mayonnaise.

Linketts: *See* Big Franks.

Maple syrup: Pure sap from the maple tree, boiled down to syrup density; about 35 gallons of sap are required to make 1 gallon of pure syrup. Also available in crystallized and block-sugar forms. Use on cereals, toast, fruits, jams, pancakes, and in candy-making.

90% Protein: This is an excellent food supplement, providing a desirable balance of essential amino acids in easy-to-digest powder form. One heaping tablespoon contains 10 grams of protein.

Nuteena: A white smooth-textured meat substitute made from nuts, soy, yeast, and vegetables.

Nuts: Almonds, Brazil nuts, cashews, filberts, pecans, walnuts, pignolias (pine nuts), peanuts, to mention but a few. Best when natural, raw, and unsalted. Flavor enhanced by dry roasting.

An excellent source of protein, unsaturated oils, and vitamins. Also available as nut butters and meals.

Oils: Be sure all oils are cold-pressed and without preservatives. Should be kept refrigerated after opening. A wonderful variety available, such as soybean, safflower, walnut, almond, avocado, sesame, corn, peanut. May be used interchangeably or blended together. All indicated in low-cholesterol diets.

Papaya Syrup Concentrate: Made from concentrated tree-ripened papaya, raw sugar, honey, and lemon juice. May be diluted with water or milk. It also has many uses in making dressings, desserts, or drinks.

Pastas: Made with soy, artichoke, whole wheat, or buckwheat, they add variety and extra nutrition. Spaghetti, macaroni, and noodles made with these ingredients have a unique flavor.

Proteena: A vegetable protein made from wheat protein, nuts, and soy. Tastes like liver, comes ready to use.

Raw sugar: Generally called turbinado sugar, this is a washed sugar that has not been bleached. It is preferable to the common white bleached product. Use as you would regular sugar.

Rice Millet Cakes: Made from 100 percent whole organic brown rice, millet, sesame seeds, and sea salt. They taste like popcorn. Use as a substitute for bread, crackers, or toast.

Rice polishings: The outer coating removed from brown rice to make it white. Rich in the B vitamins and gluten-free. Superb food supplement.

Rice-wine vinegar: A delicate, mellow vinegar produced from rice, imported from Japan. Indicated where mildness is preferred; use in place of lemon or lime juice or cider vinegar.

Sea salt: Made from sun-evaporated seawater. Rich in the minerals of the sea. Preferable to mined salt, used the same way.

Seaweed, roasted dried: Thin wafers of dried seaweed, delicately seasoned with soy sauce. Ready to serve with soups, salads, rice. Rich in ocean minerals.

Seeds: Chia, pumpkin, sunflower, and sesame. Each seed is the new life of the plant, nature's storehouse of proteins, vitamins, and minerals. The raw material form is most desirable. Oven toasting often improves flavor. Great in baking, cooking, salads, or just for eating right from the bag.

Sesame seeds: Rich in protein, delightful in cookies, cakes, and confections. Sprinkle on foods to impart a rare flavor. Available in natural raw or toasted varieties.

Soyameat, Chicken or Beef Style: A vegetable-protein product made from soy, it has a unique texture closely resembling chicken or beef. Easily used right from the can.

Soybean granules: An economical high-protein food with a pleasant nutlike flavor. About 3 times as much protein as lean beef. Quick cooking.

Soybean powder: A select variety of soybeans, the richest source of vegetable protein, ground into a fine flour. Ideal for drinks, baking, or adding to your favorite recipe.

Soybeans (canned): Since soybeans require several hours' cooking time, it is advisable when time is of the essence to choose one of the superior canned varieties. The green type cooked in its own juice is a prime choice. Also available in Boston-baked style or with tomato sauce.

Soybeans (dried): An economical source of complete protein and lecithin. They take considerably longer to cook than ordinary beans and must be soaked overnight first. The results, however, are worth it.

Soy Nuts: Roasted soybeans, made with sunflower oil. A natural, wholesome complete protein without preservatives. Ready to eat.

Spike: A dee-licious seasoning created by Gayelord Hauser, containing 26 piquant spices, herbs, and exotic flavorings. It is sensational in salads, soups, sauces, and vegetables.

Spring water: Water from natural springs, free from chemicals and impurities. Available bottled.

Stripple Zips: Bacony, crunchy, smoky bits of vegetable protein made from soy and yeast. A wonderful meatless flavoring.

Sweet 'n Low: Granulated sugar-substitute for cooking, baking, canning, and table use. Without cyclamates.

Tahini: Sesame crushed into a delectable paste. It has all the virtues of the whole seed and is versatile in its use in cooking, baking, and desserts.

Tamari (soy) **sauce:** Made from soybeans, wheat, and salt, with no chemicals or preservatives. Aged for 18 months, it's rich in flavor. Excellent as a table seasoning or used in cooking.

Tartrate baking powder: Aluminum-free, preferable to the double-acting type. Available under the brand name of Royal Baking Powder.

TasteeCuts: Prepared from wheat protein, yeast extract, and vegetable seasonings. This has a veal-like taste.

Tea Nuts: A delightful Oriental specialty consisting of rice-coated peanuts, delicately flavored with soy sauce.

Tiger's Milk: A "nutrition booster" made from nonfat dry milk, concentrated high protein from soy, primary yeast, and milk caseinate. Can be added to almost every recipe for extra nutrition, or may be used in milk or juice as a drink.

VegeBurger: All-vegetable protein, made from soy, wheat, and vegetables. May be used directly from the can as you would chopped meat.

VegeChee: Like Oriental bean curd. Made of soy, it is cheeselike in consistency. An excellent protein in salads and hot dishes.

Vegelona: Lightly spiced meat substitute made from wheat protein, yeast, soy, vegetables. Excellent as a spread.

Vegetable-broth powder: Many excellent varieties are available. Look for those prepared from organically grown vegetables, fortified with yeast and wheat germ. Makes an excellent base for seasonings, soups, gravies, and party dips.

Vegetable Skallops: An all-vegetable protein that may be used as scallops would be.

Viobin Wheat Germ: *See* Wheat germ.

Wham: A vegetable-protein food that tastes like ham but has ⅔ less calories, more amino acids, and less fat. It's a power-house of protein. Available in frozen form only.

Wheat germ: Heart of the wheat, it is a rich source of the B-complex and E vitamins and protein. Available raw or toasted. Its uses are practically infinite. For fine-textured cakes use Viobin Wheat Germ; defatted and toasted, its very fine texture allows it to combine better for this purpose.

Whole grains: Wheat, rye, oats, corn, barley, and millet are all delicious and full of nutrition when used in their natural state. Can be used in various ways in cooking and baking. Also available as flours and meals.

SNACKTIME AS A WHOLESOME PASTIME
(Nibbles, Spreads, and Appetizers)

Snacking is the universal pastime. As we become more spectators than participants, more automated than self-propelled, we seem also to be nibbling and munching more and more—and benefiting from it less and less. We sit so much of our lives away—in front of the television set, around the card table or the swimming pool, in cars, at sporting events or the movies. And as we sit, our hands keep reaching for the inevitable tidbit. More often than not we reach for a "baddie" rather than a goodie . . . fried gastronomic horrors, and all kinds of hi-cal, lo-val (or lo-cal, no-val) beverages, both soft and hard. It needn't be so.

The operative word in our approach to snacks is *protein*. Start with a base of fish, cheese, eggs, or soybeans, and you are on to something of value. From such a base the innovative cook can take off in an infinity of directions and still arrive at a creation that qualifies as a "snack."

In these recipes snacks come together under a wide umbrella: They include hors d'oeuvres, appetizers, dips, spreads, tidbits, sandwich fillers, after-school pacifiers, and bedtime bribes. There are many that can be used as toppings to turn a salad into a robust meal. They also store well in the refrigerator. And for some delightful confections—as seductive as candy - but wholesome—see Chapter 13 (pages 213–225).

VEGETARIAN LIVER

1½ cups diced Spanish onions   3 hard-cooked eggs
¾ cup soybean oil   ½ teaspoon Spike
1 14-ounce can Proteena   ¼ teaspoon garlic powder

Sauté the onions in the oil until brown. Grind through the medium blade of a meat grinder the Proteena, eggs, and sautéed onions with their oil. Add the Spike and garlic powder and mix thoroughly. Refrigerate.

Serves 6.

COD-LIVER SUNFLOWER BALLS

1 4½-ounce can smoked cod
  liver in olive oil, mashed
¼ cup mashed avocado
1 hard-cooked egg, mashed
¼ cup toasted sunflower
  seeds
¼ cup toasted wheat germ

2 tablespoons sesame-
  sunflower meal
1 teaspoon Brownies
  Vege-C-Salt (see page 40)
¼ teaspoon garlic powder
½ teaspoon oregano
½ cup toasted sunflower
  seeds

Combine all the ingredients except the ½ cup sunflower seeds
and mix together thoroughly. Form into 20 balls and roll each in
the sunflower seeds. Refrigerate.
    Serves 6–8.

SPROUTED SOLE APPETIZER

12 large, thick tomato slices
1 cup flaked poached sole
⅓ cup alfalfa sprouts
2 tablespoons finely diced
  Spanish onion
2 tablespoons finely diced
  celery
¼ cup finely diced
  cucumber with skin
¼ cup lemon-juice
  mayonnaise

2 tablespoons sour cream
1½ teaspoons Brownies
  Vege-C-Salt (see page 40)
¼ teaspoon garlic powder
¼ teaspoon Italian Seasoning
  (see page 41)
¼ teaspoon oregano
Few grindings of pepper
2 tablespoons toasted
  sunflower seeds

Arrange the tomato slices on a serving dish. Combine the remaining ingredients except for the sunflower seeds and mix thoroughly. Divide among the 12 tomato slices. Sprinkle with the
sunflower seeds and refrigerate.
    Serves 4–6.

SALMON SCROD SEVICHE

1 cup bite-size cubes
  fresh salmon
1 cup bite-size cubes
  fresh scrod
½ cup fresh lime juice
½ cup fresh grapefruit juice
1 teaspoon sea salt
Few grindings of pepper
¼ teaspoon garlic powder

¼ teaspoon celery seed
2 tablespoons diced scallions
¼ cup diced sweet red
  pepper
1 tablespoon snipped fresh
  chives
2 tablespoons minced fresh
  dill

Combine all the ingredients in a bowl and mix gently. Refrigerate for several hours or overnight, stirring occasionally.
  Serves 6–8.

ZUCCHINI SALMON ROUNDS

½ cup shredded unpeeled
  zucchini
½ cup flaked fresh poached
  salmon
2 tablespoons diced pimiento
2 tablespoons diced Spanish
  onion

2 tablespoons lemon-juice
  mayonnaise
1 teaspoon Brownies
  Vege-C-Salt (see page 40)
¼ teaspoon garlic powder
⅛ teaspoon allspice
⅛ teaspoon turmeric
32 zucchini rounds

Combine all the ingredients except the zucchini rounds and mix thoroughly. Divide the filling among 16 zucchini rounds and top each with the remaining 16 zucchini rounds, making 16 filled zucchini sandwiches.
  Serves 4–5.

SARDINE CHEESE PUFFS

1 4⅜-ounce can Portuguese
  skinless and boneless
  sardines, mashed
2 tablespoons diced Spanish
  onions
¼ cup diced mushrooms
2 tablespoons diced pimiento
2 eggs
¼ cup shredded Cheddar
  cheese

½ teaspoon Brownies
  Vege-C-Salt (see page 40)
¼ teaspoon garlic powder
½ teaspoon Bakon Yeast
½ cup buttermilk
¾ cup Fearn Whole Wheat
  Soy-O Mix
¼ cup toasted sesame seeds
Soybean oil

Combine all the ingredients except for the soybean oil and mix
thoroughly. Drop mixture from a teaspoon into ½-inch-deep soybean oil on moderate heat and brown on both sides.
Serves 8.

TANGY TUNA SPEARS

1 cup tuna fish packed in
  soybean oil
¼ cup diced pitted black
  olives
⅓ cup toasted pumpkin seeds
2 tablespoons finely diced
  Spanish onion
1 teaspoon Brownies
  Vege-C-Salt (see page 40)
¼ teaspoon garlic powder
¼ teaspoon nutmeg
1 tablespoon *tamari* sauce

2 tablespoons sour cream
2 tablespoons lemon-juice
  mayonnaise
2 tablespoons sesame meal
2 tablespoons toasted wheat
  germ
1 tablespoon fresh lime juice
Few grindings of pepper
3 cucumbers with peel,
  quartered
12 pimiento strips

Combine all but last 2 ingredients and mix thoroughly. Divide
the mixture on top of the cucumber spears and top each with a
pimiento strip. Refrigerate.
Serves 6.

SCANDINAVIAN HERRING SALAD

1 8-ounce jar herring in sour-
  cream sauce
⅔ cup canned drained and
  very finely chopped beets
¼ cup very finely diced
  Spanish onions
¼ cup finely diced celery
2 tablespoons lemon-juice
  mayonnaise
1 tablespoon sour cream
3 tablespoons minced fresh dill
¼ teaspoon garlic powder

Combine all the ingredients and mix thoroughly. Refrigerate for several hours before serving.
    Serves 6.

COUSCOUS APPETIZER

2 cups couscous
2 quarts boiling water
½ cup fresh lemon juice
½ cup soybean oil
¼ cup finely minced fresh dill
¼ cup finely minced fresh
  parsley
2 teaspoons sea salt
¼ teaspoon garlic powder
Dash of pepper

Combine the couscous and boiling water in a large bowl. Soak for 2 hours, then drain thoroughly. Add the remaining ingredients to the couscous and mix lightly. Refrigerate.
    Serves 8.

FRANK FRITTERS

1 13-ounce can Linketts
1⅓ cups Vegetable Fritter
  Batter(see page 170)
Soybean oil

Drain the Linketts and slice into ½-inch slices. Dip each slice into the fritter batter and brown on both sides in ½-inch-deep soybean oil on moderate heat.
    Serves 6.

PIZZA SUPREME

2½ cups Fearn Whole Wheat
Soy-O Mix
½ cup yellow cornmeal
¼ cup toasted wheat germ
⅓ cup safflower oil
1 egg
¾ cup skim milk
2 tablespoons toasted sesame
seeds
2 cups Brownies Tomato Sauce
(see page 46)

1 tablespoon snipped fresh
chives
1 teaspoon oregano
¼ teaspoon garlic powder
½ teaspoon Bakon Yeast
¼ teaspoon celery seed
1 teaspoon Krisp
1 13-ounce can Linketts
1 cup diced Cheddar cheese
½ cup diced Muenster cheese

Combine the Soy-O Mix, cornmeal, and wheat germ and blend
together. Make a well in the center and add all at once the safflower oil, egg, skim milk, and sesame seeds. Mix thoroughly until
the dough forms a smooth ball, using a little more Soy-O Mix if
necessary. Roll out on a board sprinkled with a little Soy-O Mix
into a 16-inch circle. Fit dough into a lightly oiled 14-inch pizza
pan, making a high rim. Bake in a preheated 375° F. oven for
15 minutes. Set aside. Combine the tomato sauce thoroughly with
the chives, oregano, garlic powder, Bakon Yeast, celery seed, and
Krisp and pour onto the cooled prebaked pizza crust. Drain the
Linketts and slice thin. Arrange the slices on top of the sauce in
the crust. Sprinkle the diced cheeses over all and bake in a preheated 375° F. oven for 30 minutes.
Serves 10.

SOY-STUFFED MUSHROOMS

20 large mushrooms
¼ cup diced Spanish onion
2 cloves garlic, minced
2 tablespoons soybean oil
¼ cup finely diced zucchini
½ cup drained canned green
soybeans, mashed
¼ cup toasted sesame seeds

2 tablespoons toasted wheat
germ
1 teaspoon Brownies
Vege-C-Salt (see page 40)
½ teaspoon oregano
¼ teaspoon Bakon Yeast
¼ teaspoon garlic powder
⅛ teaspoon nutmeg
20 pimiento strips

Remove the stems from the mushrooms. Arrange the caps in a lightly oiled baking pan and set aside. Sauté the onion and garlic in the oil. Chop the mushroom stems fine and add together with the zucchini to the onion-garlic mixture, stirring until light brown. Remove from fire and add the remaining ingredients except for the pimiento, mixing thoroughly. Divide the mixture among the mushroom caps, mounding it high. Bake in a pre-heated 375° F. oven for 20 minutes, then put under the broiler to brown. Top each mushroom with a pimiento strip. Serve hot or cold.

Serves 5–6.

MARINATED MUSHROOM MEDLEY

2 cups sliced mushrooms
½ cup diced sweet red pepper
½ cup thinly sliced zucchini
½ cup halved pitted black olives
¼ cup diced scallions
2 tablespoons snipped fresh chives
⅓ cup safflower oil

2 tablespoons apple-cider vinegar
2 tablespoons rice-wine vinegar
1 teaspoon Brownies Vege-C-Salt (see page 40)
¼ teaspoon garlic powder
¼ teaspoon Italian Seasoning (see page 41)
¼ teaspoon celery seeds

Combine all the ingredients in a bowl and mix lightly. Refrigerate several hours before serving.

Serves 6.

CARROT PEANUT-BUTTER BALLS

½ cup cottage cheese
½ cup cream cheese
⅓ cup fresh-ground peanut butter
2 tablespoons date sugar
½ teaspoon cinnamon
1 teaspoon vanilla extract
2 tablespoons yogurt

2 tablespoons carrot juice
2 tablespoons Viobin Wheat Germ
⅓ cup shredded carrots
1 Delicious apple with skin, shredded
1 cup unsalted Soy Nuts

Blend together thoroughly all the ingredients except the Soy Nuts. Form into 24 balls and roll each one in the Soy Nuts. Refrigerate.

Serves 8.

SPECIAL STUFFED EGGS

6 hard-cooked eggs
½ cup cream cheese
¼ cup sour cream
¼ cup chopped watercress
½ cup cooked green peas
3 tablespoons diced pimiento
½ cup toasted sesame seeds

1½ teaspoons Brownies
  Vege-C-Salt (see page 40)
¼ teaspoon garlic powder
¼ teaspoon nutmeg
2 tablespoons Viobin Wheat
  Germ
Paprika

Halve the eggs lengthwise and remove the yolks. Arrange the whites in a serving dish and set aside. In a bowl mash the egg yolks, cream cheese, and sour cream to a smooth paste. Stir in the remaining ingredients except for the paprika and blend lightly. Divide the mixture among the 12 egg-white halves, mounding high. Dust with paprika and refrigerate.

Serves 4–6.

COTTAGE CHEESE 'N' CHOPPED OLIVES

1½ cups cottage cheese
¾ cup diced pitted black
  olives
¾ cup shredded carrots
¼ cup snipped fresh chives

¼ cup goat-milk yogurt
½ teaspoon Brownies
  Vege-C-Salt (see page 40)
¼ teaspoon garlic powder
¼ teaspoon oregano

Combine all the ingredients and mix thoroughly.

Serves 6.

EGG SALAD

6 hard-cooked eggs, mashed
1½ cups finely minced celery
¼ cup lemon-juice mayonnaise

¾ teaspoon Brownies
  Vege-C-Salt (see page 40)

Combine all ingredients and mix thoroughly.
  Serves 4.

STRING BEANS 'N' EGGS

½ cup finely diced mushrooms
1 cup finely diced Spanish
  onion
½ cup soybean oil
2 cups chopped cooked string
  beans

6 hard-cooked eggs, mashed
2 teaspoons Bakon Yeast
1 teaspoon Brownies
  Vege-C-Salt (see page 40)
2 teaspoons Krisp
½ teaspoon garlic powder

Sauté mushrooms and onions in oil until onions are tinged with
brown. Combine with string beans and eggs, add seasonings, and
mix thoroughly. Refrigerate.
  Serves 4.

MUSHROOM EGG SPREAD

¾ cup finely diced mushrooms
¾ cup finely diced Spanish
  onion
½ cup soybean oil
6 hard-cooked eggs, mashed

1 teaspoon Brownies
  Vege-C-Salt (see page 40)
1 tablespoon Bakon Yeast
1 tablespoon Krisp

Sauté mushrooms and onions in oil until onions are tinged with
brown. Combine with eggs, add seasonings, and mix well.
  Serves 4.

SAFFLOWER-SUNFLOWER SPREAD

½ cup safflower-oil margarine
½ cup orange-blossom honey
¼ cup sesame-sunflower meal

1 teaspoon strawberry
  concentrate
1 teaspoon orange extract
⅓ cup toasted sunflower seeds

Cream the margarine and honey together until smooth. Add the remaining ingredients and blend thoroughly. May be served with toast, crackers, or pancakes.
    Yield: 2 cups.

AVOCADO CHEDDAR DIP

1 cup mashed avocado
½ cup shredded Cheddar
  cheese
4 teaspoons fresh-ground
  cashew butter
½ cup goat-milk yogurt
2 tablespoons sesame-sunflower
  meal

⅓ cup finely diced Spanish
  onion
½ cup toasted cashew pieces
2 teaspoons Brownies
  Vege-C-Salt (see page 40)
¼ teaspoon garlic powder
¼ teaspoon Bakon Yeast
1 tablespoon Krisp

Combine all ingredients in a bowl and mix thoroughly. Cover and refrigerate.
    Serves 6.

BROWN-RICE RELISH

2 cups Basic Brown Rice (see
  page 150)
1 cup steamed green peas
1 cup canned whole-kernel
  corn
¼ cup onions, sautéed

¼ cup diced pimiento
¼ cup soybean oil
¼ cup rice-wine vinegar
½ teaspoon sea salt
⅛ teaspoon garlic powder
Dash of pepper

Combine rice, peas, corn, onions, and pimiento in a large bowl and mix thoroughly. Add the remaining ingredients and toss lightly. Refrigerate until needed.
    Serves 8.

START THE JUICES FLOWING

(Beverages)

As we said in our Introduction, Brownies was really built on a foundation of fluids. The fluids were blended or extracted fresh fruit and vegetable drinks. We were actually the first restaurant to serve them, and for a while they were all we *did* serve. Since then we have grown manyfold, but we have not outgrown our partiality to highly vitaminized cocktails. Old customers and new ones seem to regard us as a prime place for "getting juiced"—in the healthiest sense of the expression. Our menus give prominent billing to our natural cocktails, and we keep improvising new ones, giving them names that will sing a little.

These drinks are rich, concentrated drafts filled with natural vitamins and sweets, enzymes, amino acids, minerals, and trace elements. They are the distillations of plants grown in the good earth and cooked by the sun. They flush, cleanse, build, fortify, and rejuvenate the body. They give luster to the eye and a spring to the step. They are the elixir of life. Surely they were what gushed from Ponce de León's elusive fountain of youth!

Modern-day cooks have made almost a fetish out of speed and ease. With the greatest of ease they can create a whole arsenal of "instant" beverages of great potency. Now anyone can whip up a powerhouse concoction in a matter of moments with the help of a juicer, extractor, or blender.

The spectrum of drinks is as broad as the imagination of the person who's mixing them. For primary ingredients there are fruits and vegetables in all possible combinations. Then consider all the variations of those combinations that can be made by the addition of an accessory ingredient or two or three: milks, yogurts, flavorings, seasonings, honeys, molasses, seeds, nuts, dried fruits, herbs, spices, wheat germ, brewer's yeast, high-protein powders, eggs, cottage cheese, rice polishings, or carob powder.

Vegetable juices are best obtained by means of an extractor. Citrus fruits should be juiced, plausibly enough, in a citrus juicer. Soft, bulky fruits like pears and peaches and bananas should be cut up and fed to the blender, with a liquid base—some kind of milk, juice, or yogurt—to build on. Blended beverages are best drunk immediately.

Assimilation is almost as quick as preparation. The extracted juices of fruits and vegetables can provide us with the vital essences of whole mounds of produce that would be much too bulky for us to eat our way through. We all do need roughage to regulate our systems, but raw vegetables and fruits on the whole are digested slowly; eaten in large quantities, they produce traffic jams along the alimentary canal. Juices, however, move along smartly. Obviously they are a special boon to anyone who wants a quick meal in a glass, and also to convalescents, the elderly, and anyone with a delicate stomach.

The drinks we present here bring together a lot of goodies in offbeat combinations—novel and, we trust, pleasant taste sensations that can be anyone's in a jiffy just for the mixing.

BROWNIES COCKTAILS

DUBONNET COCKTAIL

1 McIntosh apple   Grape juice

Juice the apple in an extractor. Add enough grape juice to the apple juice to fill an 8-ounce glass.
    Serves 1.

HONI-LULU

2-inch wedge pineapple   Carrots
Juice of ½ orange

Juice the pineapple in an extractor. Add the pineapple juice to the orange juice in an 8-ounce glass. Juice enough carrots in the extractor to fill the glass.
    Serves 1.

ORANGE BLOSSOM

½ McIntosh apple   Carrots
Juice of ½ orange

Juice the apple in an extractor. Add apple juice to orange juice in an 8-ounce glass. Juice enough carrots in the extractor to fill the glass.
    Serves 1.

SUNSHINE

2-inch wedge pineapple
Juice of ½ orange
Carrots

Dash of Papaya Syrup
  Concentrate
Squeeze of lime juice

Juice the pineapple in an extractor. Add the pineapple juice to the orange juice in an 8-ounce glass. Juice enough carrots in the extractor to fill the glass. Add the papaya and the lime.
  Serves 1.

BEET BLOSSOM

½ cup orange juice
1 teaspoon Papaya Syrup
  Concentrate

Beets

Put the orange juice and papaya concentrate in an 8-ounce glass. Juice enough beets in the extractor to fill glass with juice.
  Serves 1.

RAINBOW

1 beet
4 leaves romaine lettuce

Juice of ½ orange
Carrots

Juice the beet and the lettuce in an extractor. Add the beet and lettuce juices to the orange juice in an 8-ounce glass. Juice enough carrots in the extractor to fill the glass.
  Serves 1.

VEGETABLE GARDEN

1 beet
3 leaves escarole
2 leaves chicory

1 scallion
1 radish
Carrots

Juice the beet, escarole, chicory, scallion, and radish in an extractor. Put the juices in an 8-ounce glass. Juice enough carrots in the extractor to fill the glass.
  Serves 1.

BLUSH O' BEET

2 beets   Buttermilk

Juice the beets in an extractor. Put the juice in an 8-ounce glass and fill the glass with buttermilk.
　　Serves 1.

HALF AND HALF

Pascal celery   Carrots

Juice enough celery in an extractor to half fill an 8-ounce glass. Juice enough carrots in the extractor to fill the glass.
　　Serves 1.

EYE OPENER

Clump of spinach   Juice of ½ lemon
½ cup California tomato juice   Pascal celery

Juice the spinach in an extractor. Add the spinach juice to the tomato and lemon juices in an 8-ounce glass. Juice enough celery in the extractor to fill the glass.
　　Serves 1.

CUCUMBER COOLER

½ cucumber   2 stalks celery
3 radishes with leaves   ¼ cup canned pineapple juice

Juice the cucumber, radishes, and celery in an extractor. Add the pineapple juice to the vegetable juices.
　　Serves 1.

OLD-FASHIONED GARDEN COCKTAIL

Clump of spinach   2 stalks celery
Sprig of parsley   Carrots

Juice the spinach, parsley, and celery in an extractor and put the juices in an 8-ounce glass. Juice enough carrots in the extractor to fill the glass.
  Serves 1.

BROWNIES BLENDER DRINKS

BROWNIES BLAST

1 cup canned pineapple juice   1 teaspoon lecithin
1 tablespoon 90% Protein   1 teaspoon wheat-germ oil

Whip all ingredients in blender for 30 seconds.
  Serves 1.

MOUNTAIN COLADA

1⅓ cups canned unsweetened   ½ cup Monukka raisins
  pineapple juice   2 tablespoons clover honey
1⅓ cups carrot juice   ⅓ cup toasted unsweetened
⅔ cup orange juice   shredded coconut
⅔ cup canned unsweetened   2 tablespoons lecithin
  pineapple chunks   2 tablespoons soybean powder
½ cup sliced bananas

Whip all ingredients in blender for 2 minutes.
  Serves 4.

TRINIDAD SHAKE

1 cup canned unsweetened
  pineapple juice
2 eggs
½ cup canned unsweetened
  crushed pineapple
⅔ cup skim milk
2 tablespoons *tahini*

1 teaspoon Barbados molasses
1 teaspoon date sugar
2 tablespoons soybean powder
2 tablespoons powdered
  nonfat dry milk
2 tablespoons sesame meal
½ teaspoon vanilla extract

Whip all ingredients in blender for 1 minute.
  Serves 4.

PAPAYA 'N' PROTEIN

1 cup ice water
½ cup powdered nonfat
  dry milk
1 egg

1 teaspoon lecithin
3 tablespoons Papaya Syrup
  Concentrate

Whip all ingredients in blender for 30 seconds.
  Serves 2.

STRAWBERRY SHAKE

1 cup ice water
½ cup strawberries
½ cup powdered nonfat dry
  milk

Honey or Sweet 'n Low
  (optional)

Whip water, strawberries, and powdered milk in blender for
30 seconds. If desired, sweeten to taste with honey or Sweet 'n
Low.
  Serves 2.

STRAWBERRY STINGER

1 cup buttermilk
1 cup goat-milk yogurt
1 cup sliced strawberries
2 tablesoons strawberry
concentrate

2 tablespoons tupelo honey
2 tablespoons lecithin
2 tablespoons soybean powder

Whip all ingredients in blender for 1 minute.
Serves 4.

BLUEBERRY BURST

1 cup ice water
½ cup blueberries
½ cup powdered nonfat dry
milk

Honey or Sweet 'n Low
(optional)

Whip water, blueberries, and powdered milk in blender for
30 seconds. If desired, sweeten to taste with honey or Sweet 'n
Low.
Serves 2.

BLUEBERRY CREAM

1 cup goat-milk yogurt
1 cup skim milk
1 cup blueberries
3 tablespoons tupelo honey

3 tablespoons soybean powder
2 tablespoons toasted wheat
germ
½ teaspoon vanilla extract

Whip all ingredients in blender for 2 minutes.
Serves 3.

CHERRY CHIRP

1 cup ice water
½ cup powdered nonfat dry
milk
1 teaspoon brewer's yeast

1 teaspoon lecithin
2 tablespoons cherry
concentrate
Honey (optional)

Whip all ingredients except for honey in blender for 30 seconds. Sweeten with honey to taste if desired.
Serves 2.

PEACHES 'N' CREAM

1 cup chilled apple juice
1 cup sliced peaches
½ cup powdered nonfat dry
milk

1 teaspoon brewer's yeast
Honey or Sweet 'n Low
(optional)

Whip all ingredients except for last in blender for 30 seconds. If desired, sweeten to taste with honey or Sweet 'n Low.
Serves 4.

PEACH FUZZ

1 cup canned unsweetened
pineapple juice
1 cup skim milk
1 cup diced peaches

2 teaspoons raw sugar
3 tablespoons powdered nonfat
dry milk
2 tablespoons lecithin

Whip all ingredients in blender for 2 minutes.
Serves 4.

APRICOT ANGEL

2 cups skim milk
½ cup canned unsweetened
  pineapple juice
½ cup cottage cheese
⅔ cup dried apricots

1 teaspoon Barbados molasses
2 eggs
2 tablespoons lecithin
2 tablespoons clover honey

Whip all ingredients in blender for 2 minutes.
  Serves 4.

MINTY APPLE CUP

1 cup apple juice
1 cup diced McIntosh apples
  with skin
⅔ cup buttermilk
2 tablespoons powdered nonfat
  dry milk

2 teaspoons toasted wheat
  germ
1 tablespoon Papaya Syrup
  Concentrate
1 teaspoon mint flakes

Whip all ingredients in blender for 1 minute.
  Serves 4.

BANANA SPRITZ

1 cup canned unsweetened
  pineapple juice
½ cup carrot juice
1 cup skim milk
1 cup sliced bananas
2 tablespoons lecithin

2 tablespoons powdered nonfat
  dry milk
2 teaspoons Barbados molasses
2 teaspoons clover honey
½ teaspoon vanilla extract

Whip all ingredients in blender for 1 minute.
  Serves 4.

COCONUT JULEP

1¼ cups skim milk
1¼ cups canned unsweetened
  pineapple juice
2 eggs
1 cup toasted unsweetened
  shredded coconut

2 tablespoons *tahini*
3 tablespoons soybean powder
2 tablespoons lecithin
2 tablespoons orange-blossom
  honey
½ teaspoon lemon extract

Whip all ingredients in blender for 1 minute.
  Serves 4.

CARROT ORANGE FLOAT

1 cup carrot juice
1 cup orange juice
½ cup sliced carrots
2 teaspoons orange-blossom
  honey

2 teaspoons rice polishings
2 teaspoons soybean powder
¼ teaspoon sea salt
½ teaspoon vanilla extract

Whip all ingredients in blender for 1 minute.
  Serves 3.

TROPICAL TREAT

1 cup canned unsweetened
  grape juice
1 cup canned apple juice
½ cup canned unsweetened
  pineapple juice
½ cup carrot juice

⅔ cup diced nectarines
⅔ cup diced oranges
2 tablespoons lecithin
2 tablespoons date sugar
1 teaspoon lemon extract

Whip all ingredients in blender for 1 minute.
  Serves 4.

IT'S THE SEEDS

1 cup chilled canned pineapple
juice
¼ cup sunflower seeds

¼ cup pumpkin seeds
2 tablespoons *tahini*
2 tablespoons clover honey

Whip all ingredients in blender for 1 minute or until smooth.
Serves 2.

TIGER'S MILK FLIP

Juice of 1 orange
½ cup canned pineapple juice
½ cup skim milk

2 tablespoons Tiger's Milk
1 tablespoon Papaya Syrup
Concentrate

Whip all ingredients in blender for 30 seconds.
Serves 2.

PEANUTTY POP

1 cup skim milk
1 cup buttermilk
⅔ cup fresh-ground peanut
butter
2 eggs
¼ cup unsalted Soy Nuts,
toasted

2 tablespoons Papaya Syrup
Concentrate
2 tablespoons lecithin
2 tablespoons toasted wheat
germ
½ teaspoon cinnamon

Whip all ingredients in blender for 2 minutes.
Serves 4.

CASHEW MILK

1 cup water
½ cup cashew pieces

2 tablespoons date sugar

Whip all ingredients in blender for 1 minute. If cashews are
not completely liquefied, blend an additional ½ minute.
Serves 2.

CAROB FREEZE

½ cup water
½ cup crushed ice cubes
½ cup powdered nonfat dry milk

¼ cup carob powder
1 tablespoon honey
1 tablespoon brewer's yeast

Whip all ingredients in blender for 1 minute.
Serves 2.

BROWN VELVET

2 cups skim milk
¼ cup carob powder
2 tablespoons soybean powder
2 tablespoons powdered nonfat dry milk

2 teaspoons rice polishings
2 teaspoons lecithin
2 tablespoons *tahini*
2 tablespoons clover honey
½ teaspoon vanilla extract

Whip all ingredients in blender for 1 minute.
Serves 3.

PROTEIN JUBILEE

1 cup skim milk
¼ cup powdered nonfat dry milk
1 teaspoon soybean powder

1 teaspoon brewer's yeast
1 teaspoon honey
½ teaspoon blackstrap molasses

Whip all ingredients in blender for 1 minute.
Serves 2.

VEGETABLE TINGLE

1½ cups carrot juice
1 cup California tomato juice
2 eggs
⅔ cup diced celery
¼ cup diced cucumber with skin
¼ cup diced red onion
2 tablespoons fresh chives

2 tablespoons vegetable-broth powder
1 teaspoon Sesame Salt (see page 40)
½ teaspoon Italian Seasoning (see page 41)
½ teaspoon Brownies Vege-C-Salt (see page 40)
¼ teaspoon garlic powder

Whip all ingredients in blender for 2 minutes.
    Serves 4.

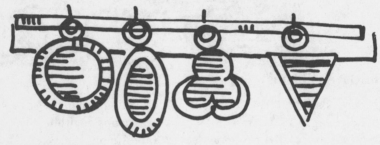

GARDEN LOVELY

1 cup goat-milk yogurt
1 cup buttermilk
⅔ cup skim milk
3 tablespoons powdered nonfat dry milk
2 tablespoons toasted wheat germ
½ cup sliced carrots
½ cup sliced celery

¼ cup diced cucumber with skin
¼ cup sliced radishes
¼ cup diced scallions
2 tablespoons fresh chives
½ teaspoon Brownies Vege-C-Salt (see page 40)
½ teaspoon celery seed
⅛ teaspoon sea salt
⅛ teaspoon garlic powder

Whip all ingredients in blender for 2 minutes.
    Serves 4.

CARROT ROYALE

1 cup skim milk
⅔ cup orange juice
1 cup sliced carrots
2 tablespoons Papaya Syrup
  Concentrate

1 tablespoon orange-blossom
  honey
2 tablespoons lecithin
2 tablespoons soybean powder
½ teaspoon vanilla extract
½ teaspoon cinnamon

Whip all ingredients in blender for 2 minutes.
  Serves 3.

CUCUMBER NOG

1 cup buttermilk
2 eggs
1 cup diced cucumber with
  skin
2 tablespoons powdered
  nonfat dry milk
2 teaspoons lecithin

2 teaspoons Krisp
2 teaspoons chives
¼ teaspoon dill
½ teaspoon Brownies
  Vege-C-Salt (see page 40)
⅛ teaspoon garlic powder

Whip all ingredients in blender for 1 minute.
  Serves 3.

TOMATO CRUSH

1 cup California tomato juice
½ cup diced tomato
1⅓ cups buttermilk
2 tablespoons diced scallions
2 teaspoons vegetable-broth
  powder

1 teaspoon lecithin
¼ teaspoon celery seed
¼ teaspoon dill
½ teaspoon chives
¼ teaspoon sea salt
½ teaspoon Krisp

Whip all ingredients in blender for 1 minute.
  Serves 4.

SOCKO SEAWEED

½ cup tomato juice
½ cup yogurt
½ teaspoon kelp

1 dulse leaf, cut fine
1 laver leaf, cut fine
1 teaspoon *tamari* sauce
  (optional)

Whip all ingredients in blender for 1 minute. May also be
served hot.
  Serves 1.

YOGURT MINT COOLER

1 cup goat-milk yogurt
1 cup skim milk
½ cup cottage cheese
1 egg
2 teaspoons mint flakes

2 teaspoons vegetable-broth
  powder
2 teaspoons fresh chives
½ teaspoon Sesame Salt
  (see page 40)
⅛ teaspoon sea salt

Whip all ingredients in blender for 1 minute.
  Serves 3.

4

DRESS UP SMARTLY
AND SEASON WITH REASON
(Seasonings, Dressings, and Sauces)

Dressings, sauces, and seasonings have their honored places at
the table. They can bring excitement to an otherwise ordinary
dish and very subtly—almost subliminally—they can boost the
food value of any dish they grace.

The French are certainly the first *sauciers* of the world. Their genius was to invent sauces to extend good foods that were in short supply or to camouflage poor foods. We have had somewhat different goals; we have aimed at tastiness *plus* built-in strength. With our sauces and dressings we turn a little sly and pour in the nutrients with a liberal hand: real enrichers like wheat germ, brewer's yeast, lecithin, kelp, and rice polishings.

We have tried to indicate throughout the book what sauce or dressing or homemade seasoning is best for various foods. (References in the book to Brownies sauces or Brownies seasonings, by the way, are not intended to hypo business in our retail store. As a matter of fact, no such products are for sale there. We make them only for use in our restaurant.) Here are the recipes, tailored to your own kitchen. Try them. When a cook produces something yummy, she will always be forgiven if it turns out to be healthful too!

SEASONINGS

BROWNIES VEGE-C-SALT

½ cup vegetable-broth powder
¼ cup Bakon Yeast

¼ cup sea salt
1 tablespoon garlic powder

Place all the ingredients in a small airtight container. Cover and shake thoroughly to blend.
Yield: 1 cup.

SESAME SALT

½ cup toasted sesame seeds
2 teaspoons sea salt

1 teaspoon kelp

Finely grind all the ingredients in a grinder or blender. Store in a closed container.
Yield: ½ cup.

ITALIAN SEASONING

2 tablespoons oregano
2 tablespoons basil
1 tablespoon rosemary

1 tablespoon thyme
1 teaspoon paprika

Place all the ingredients in a small airtight container. Cover and shake thoroughly to blend.
  Yield: ½ cup.

SALAD HERBS

2 tablespoons chives
2 tablespoons parsley
1 tablespoon basil

1 tablespoon savory
1 teaspoon tarragon
1 teaspoon mint

Place all the ingredients in a small airtight container. Cover and shake thoroughly to blend.
  Yield: ½ cup.

DRESSINGS

BROWNIES LO-CAL DRESSING

2 cups California tomato juice
1 cup apple-cider vinegar
½ teaspoon Sweet 'n Low
¼ teaspoon sea salt
¼ teaspoon garlic powder
2 teaspoons tarragon

½ teaspoon oregano
½ teaspoon basil
¼ teaspoon paprika
¼ teaspoon dry mustard
¼ teaspoon black pepper
3 tablespoons agar

Combine tomato juice, apple-cider vinegar, and Sweet 'n Low. Combine remaining ingredients, mixing well. Blend dry ingredients into liquid mixture, using a wire whip. (If desired, all ingredients may be put into a blender at low speed for 30 seconds.) Refrigerate until needed.
  Yield: 3 cups.

BROWNIES PUFA* DRESSING

2 eggs
¼ cup fresh lemon juice
¼ cup tomato puree
1 teaspoon paprika

1 teaspoon sea salt
¼ teaspoon garlic powder
2 cups soybean oil

Combine first 6 ingredients in blender at low speed for 1 minute. Add soybean oil in a thin, slow stream at high speed; keep blender going until all the oil is incorporated. Refrigerate.
Yield: 3 cups.

BROWNIES FISH DRESSING

1 cup soybean oil
½ cup fresh lemon juice
2 teaspoons sea salt
¼ teaspoon basil
½ teaspoon oregano

½ teaspoon garlic powder
2 teaspoons minced fresh parsley
2 teaspoons minced fresh dill

Combine all ingredients in a closed jar or container and shake until blended. Refrigerate. Use as needed.
Yield: 1½ cups.

WATERCRESS AND MUSHROOM DRESSING

1 cup sesame oil
⅓ cup rice-wine vinegar
½ cup watercress
½ cup sliced mushrooms
2 tablespoons soy sauce

¼ teaspoon sea salt
¼ teaspoon garlic powder
¼ teaspoon Italian Seasoning (see page 41)
Few grindings of pepper

Combine all ingredients in blender. Blend at medium speed for 30 seconds. Refrigerate until needed.
Yield: 2 cups.

* PolyUnsaturated Fatty Acids.

PINK AND PRETTY DRESSING

1 cup sour cream
¼ cup skim milk
⅔ cup sliced cooked beets
2 scallions, diced
¼ cup diced cucumber

¼ teaspoon sea salt
½ teaspoon savory
¼ teaspoon garlic powder
¼ teaspoon Brownies
  Vege-C-Salt (see page 40)

Combine all ingredients in blender at medium speed. Blend for 30 seconds. Refrigerate until needed.
  Yield: 2 cups.

AVOCADO EMERALD DRESSING

1 avocado, peeled and cubed
½ cup goat-milk yogurt
½ cup buttermilk
¼ cup chopped watercress
¼ cup chopped fresh *cilantro*
  (or fresh parsley)

2 scallions, diced
½ teaspoon Spike
½ teaspoon garlic powder
¼ teaspoon sea salt
¼ teaspoon dill

Mix all ingredients in blender at high speed for 1 minute. Refrigerate until needed.
  Yield: 2 cups.

LIMEY GINGER DRESSING

½ cup safflower oil
3 tablespoons fresh lime juice
Grated rind of 1 lime
1 tablespoon crystallized
  honey
¼ teaspoon powdered ginger

¼ teaspoon sea salt
⅛ teaspoon garlic powder
1 tablespoon beet juice
1 tablespoon minced
  crystallized ginger

Combine all but last ingredient in blender for 30 seconds at medium speed. Pour into storage container and add crystallized ginger. Blend thoroughly. Refrigerate until needed. Shake well before using.
  Yield: 1 cup.

PINEAPPLE CRANBERRY DRESSING

1 cup goat-milk yogurt
½ cup sour cream
½ cup lemon-juice
   mayonnaise
½ cup canned crushed
   unsweetened pineapple

¼ cup clover honey
½ cup toasted wheat germ
2 tablespoons cranberry
   concentrate
1 teaspoon vanilla extract

Combine all ingredients in blender at high speed for 1 minute. Pour into container and refrigerate until needed.
   Yield: 3 cups.

STRAWBERRY YOGURT DRESSING

1 cup goat-milk yogurt
½ cup buttermilk
1 cup sliced strawberries
¼ cup clover honey
¼ cup toasted wheat germ

1 tablespoon strawberry
   concentrate
¼ cup almond meal
½ teaspoon almond extract

Combine all ingredients in blender at low speed for 30 seconds. Refrigerate until needed.
   Yield: 2 cups.

SMOOTH-AND-LOVELY FRUIT DRESSING

½ cup cottage cheese
½ cup goat-milk yogurt
¼ cup sour cream
¼ cup orange juice

¼ cup Monukka raisins
1 tablespoon raw sugar
½ teaspoon cinnamon

Combine all ingredients in blender for 30 seconds at medium speed. Refrigerate until needed.
   Yield: 2 cups.

PEANUTTY DRESSING

1 cup sour cream
⅓ cup Papaya Syrup
  Concentrate
2 tablespoons strawberry
  concentrate

¼ cup fresh-ground peanut
  butter
¼ teaspoon almond extract
⅔ cup dry-roasted unsalted
  peanuts

Combine all ingredients except peanuts in blender for 30 seconds. Pour into storage container and add peanuts. Refrigerate until needed and then let stand for 10 minutes at room temperature before using.
    Yield: 2 cups.

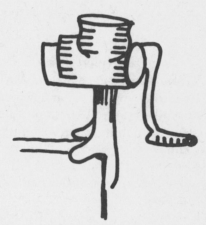

CRUNCHY CASHEW DRESSING

½ cup goat-milk yogurt
⅓ cup lemon-juice
  mayonnaise
⅓ cup fresh-ground
  toasted-cashew butter
½ cup buttermilk

⅓ cup chopped unsalted
  toasted cashews
1 teaspoon vanilla extract
½ teaspoon cinnamon
1 tablespoon clover honey

Combine all ingredients and mix until creamy. Refrigerate until needed.
    Yield: 2 cups.

SAUCES

BROWNIES TOMATO SAUCE

1 cup diced Spanish onion
½ cup diced celery
½ cup soybean oil
¼ cup finely chopped celery
    leaves
1 1-pound 12-ounce can
    whole California tomatoes
1 10½-ounce can tomato
    puree

½ cup California tomato juice
2 tablespoons minced fresh
    parsley
1 teaspoon sea salt
1 teaspoon paprika
¼ teaspoon garlic powder
1 teaspoon Italian Seasoning
    (see page 41)
1 teaspoon brewer's yeast

In a deep saucepan sauté the onion and celery in the oil until transparent. Stir in the celery leaves and add the tomatoes, tomato puree, and tomato juice. Cover pan and cook for 15 minutes on low fire. Remove cover and with a fork break up the tomatoes into small chunks. Add the parsley and seasonings and continue cooking 15 minutes more or until sauce is thick.

Yield: 2 cups.

POLYNESIAN SAUCE

1 cup dried apricots
3 cups water
1 cup canned crushed
    unsweetened pineapple
1 cup Papaya Syrup
    Concentrate
¼ cup orange-blossom honey

¼ cup fresh lemon juice
¼ cup rice-wine vinegar
½ teaspoon sea salt
½ teaspoon garlic powder
1 cup canned
    mandarin-orange sections

Combine the apricots and water and cook on low heat for 10 minutes. Place mixture in blender with the remaining ingredients except for the orange sections. Blend for 15 seconds at low speed. Pour into a storage container, add the orange sections, and stir thoroughly. Refrigerate. Serve hot or cold.

Yield: 4 cups.

NUTTY SAUCE

1½ cups skim milk
¼ cup ground walnuts
2 tablespoons soybean powder
½ cup fresh-ground peanut
butter

¼ cup toasted sesame seeds
2 tablespoons Sesame Salt
(see page 40)
¼ teaspoon sea salt
¼ teaspoon nutmeg

Combine all ingredients until smooth in a saucepan and cook on a low fire until warm, stirring constantly.
Yield: 2 cups.

STRAWBERRY BLUEBERRY SAUCE

1 cup orange juice
1 cup raw sugar
2 tablespoons brown-rice flour
2 tablespoons safflower oil

½ teaspoon lemon extract
1 cup sliced strawberries
1 cup blueberries

Combine first 3 ingredients in a saucepan and mix until smooth. Stir over low heat until thick and clear. Blend in the remaining ingredients and serve hot or cold over your favorite dessert, pancakes, or ice cream.
Yield: 2 cups.

RASPBERRY MAPLE SAUCE

1 cup maple syrup
1 cup raspberries
1 cup orange juice

1 orange with peel, quartered
and seeded
2 tablespoons safflower oil
1 teaspoon lemon extract

Combine all the ingredients in blender at high speed for 30 seconds. Serve hot or cold over pancakes or your favorite dessert.
Yield: 3 cups.

CARROT CURRANT SAUCE

1½ cups carrot juice
1½ cups orange juice
¾ cup raw sugar
4 tablespoons brown-rice flour

⅓ cup safflower oil
1½ cups dried currants
2 teaspoons orange extract

Blend the first 4 ingredients until smooth and cook in a saucepan over low heat, stirring, until thick and clear. Mix in the remaining ingredients. Serve hot or cold on your favorite dessert or pancakes.
  Yield: 4 cups.

CHERRY PINEAPPLE SAUCE

1 cup canned unsweetened
 pineapple juice
1 cup canned crushed
 unsweetened pineapple
½ cup maple syrup

2 tablespoons brown-rice flour
2 tablespoons safflower oil
1 cup pitted Bing cherries
½ teaspoon cinnamon

Combine the first 4 ingredients in a saucepan and stir over low heat until thick and clear. Blend in the remaining ingredients. Serve hot or cold over your favorite dessert, pancakes, or ice cream.
  Yield: 3 cups.

LEMON CRANBERRY SAUCE

2 cups raw sugar
2 cups water
½ cup fresh lemon juice
4 tablespoons brown-rice flour
1 cup cranberries

2 tablespoons safflower oil
2 tablespoons cranberry
 concentrate
1 teaspoon orange extract

Combine first 5 ingredients in a saucepan and stir over low heat until thick and clear. Blend in the remaining ingredients and serve hot or cold over pancakes, ice cream, or your favorite dessert.
  Yield: 4 cups.

SOUR-CREAM DATE SAUCE

1½ cups canned unsweetened pineapple juice
1 cup date sugar
⅓ cup safflower oil

2 tablespoons brown-rice flour
1 cup sour cream
2 teaspoons vanilla extract
1 cup diced pitted dates

Combine the first 4 ingredients and cook over low heat in a saucepan, stirring, until thick and clear. Stir in the remaining ingredients and serve hot or cold over your favorite dessert or pancakes.

Yield: 4 cups.

5

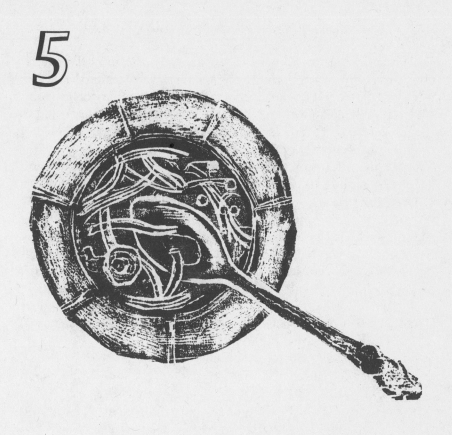

LADLES! TUREENS!... POTAGE!
(Soups)

Contrary to popular myth, soup is *not* synonymous with a can. Regrettably, soup-making has become a lost domestic art in this age of instant feeding. There was a time when grand dinners used to feature not 1 but 2 kitchen-made soups, one clear and one thick. Nowadays it is the rare home that ever serves even one soup made "from the roots up."

When Sam Brown bowed to the clamor for soups at Brownies, he recalled the wonderful taste and aroma of those that came from his mother's kitchen. His mother paid pennies for a pound of steel-cut oats, which, simmered together with stock and a nickel's worth of fresh vegetables off the pushcarts, made enough thick, nutritious soup to feed the whole family at least twice. Today the most economical dish we can prepare is a homemade soup containing things that usually go into the garbage can or down the drain: vegetable parings, unfinished salad, unserved dinner portions, unused cooking water. From such rejects are great soups made. A budget-conscious homemaker can turn a soup into a well-balanced meal by adding some low-cost, high-protein concentrates like skim milk or soybean powder to make it marvelously potent and more palatable. Economy aside, making your own soup is easy and fun. It gives you a safe product (no need to worry about botulism when you're eating your own) and one that is eminently health-enhancing.

In soup-making our basic premise is: Start from stock. Stock gives a rich foundation on which to build. The simmering of soup greens, celery, carrots, parsnips, and the like yields a zesty liquid that could be called Essence of Minerals. Whenever possible, we advise using organically grown vegetables and fruits. Unless you have a filter on your faucet, the chemical-free bottled spring water is preferable to plain water from the tap.

In the soups we present here we have been conservative with the fortifiers. We pour them in with a much freer hand at Brownies. In the restaurant we more often include Bakon Yeast and Krisp to give our soups that rich, smoky taste. Seasoning is such a personal thing that it is hard to be dogmatic about rules and measurements. One man's garlic is another man's gall and wormwood. Everybody should discover what he likes—and in what strength.

Aside from the things you usually find in soups, these recipes call for less-familiar ingredients such as couscous, millet, unpearled barley, lecithin, buttermilk, cottage cheese, yogurt, brewer's yeast, orange-blossom honey, pigeon and garbanzo and black turtle and mung beans, halibut and scrod, blueberries and peaches and cherries, and water chestnuts. The mere thought of soup and its enormous flexibility releases our inhibitions! Once you get into the soup habit, you too will probably be putting together new creations. Don't be afraid to go a little bit wild!

BROWNIES SOUP STOCK

3 large carrots, diced
5 stalks celery, diced
1 large Spanish onion with
  skin, quartered
1 large rutabaga, sliced

3 parsnips, sliced
1 bunch fresh parsley
1 bunch fresh dill
2 gallons water

Combine all the ingredients in a large kettle and bring to a boil, then simmer, covered, for 1 hour. Strain, discarding vegetables, and set aside till cool. Refrigerate and use as needed.
     Yield: 1 gallon.

BROWNIES CONSOMMÉ

3 quarts water
1 large Spanish onion with
  skin, quartered
2 large carrots, cut in
  large chunks
3 celery stalks with tops,
  each cut in 4 pieces
½ bunch fresh parsley

½ bunch fresh dill
2½ teaspoons sea salt
¾ teaspoon garlic powder
½ teaspoon savory
½ teaspoon rosemary
½ teaspoon tarragon
½ teaspoon nutmeg
⅛ teaspoon black pepper

Combine all ingredients in a large soup kettle. Cover and bring to boil, then cook on low fire for 30 minutes. Discard vegetables. Use as a clear broth or as a stock for soups and sauces.
     Yield: 3 quarts.

BROWNIES VEGETABLE SOUP

1 cup diced Spanish onion
2 cups diced celery
¾ cup soybean oil
4 quarts Brownies Soup Stock
(see page 53)
2 cups crushed canned
tomatoes
½ cup unpearled barley

½ cup dried black-eyed beans
1 cup diced carrots
1 cup green peas
1 cup shredded cabbage
1½ tablespoons sea salt
1 tablespoon Bakon Yeast
1 teaspoon kelp
½ teaspoon garlic powder

In a large soup kettle sauté onion and celery in the oil until the onion is transparent. Add the next 5 ingredients, cover, and cook about 45 minutes or until the beans and barley are tender. Add the remaining ingredients and cook 10 minutes more.
Serves 10–12.

SPRING GARDEN SOUP

1½ cups buttermilk
¼ cup goat-milk yogurt
½ cup sour cream
1 cup skim milk
1 cup diced tomatoes
¾ cup diced cucumber
with skin
¼ cup diced scallions
¼ cup sliced radishes
¼ cup diced green pepper

½ cup sliced canned
water chestnuts
2 teaspoons sea salt
1 teaspoon lecithin
1 teaspoon Italian Seasoning
(see page 41)
1 teaspoon dill
1 teaspoon paprika
Few grindings of pepper

Combine the first 5 ingredients in blender at low speed for 1 minute, then at high speed for 1 minute. Pour into large bowl, add remaining ingredients, and mix thoroughly. Serve cold.
Serves 6–8.

BOUQUET OF VEGETABLES SOUP

1 cup diced Spanish onion
1 cup diced celery
2 garlic cloves, minced
¼ cup safflower oil
1 cup sliced mushrooms
1 quart Brownies Consommé
   (see page 53)
2 quarts water
½ cup unpearled barley
½ cup pigeon beans
1 cup diced carrots
2 cups diced yellow squash
2 cups cauliflower florets
1 cup green peas
1 cup baby lima beans
¼ cup minced fresh parsley

1 tablespoon minced fresh
   dill
1½ cups tomato puree
2 teaspoons sea salt
2 teaspoons Brownies
   Vege-C-Salt (see page 40)
2 teaspoons Italian Seasoning
   (see page 41)
1 teaspoon garlic powder
1 tablespoon lecithin
1 teaspoon Bakon Yeast
½ teaspoon mace
2 tablespoons snipped fresh
   chives
2 tablespoons Krisp
Few grindings of fresh pepper

In a large soup kettle sauté onion, celery, and garlic in oil until light brown. Add mushrooms and sauté until brown. Add consommé, water, barley, and beans, cover, and cook for 30 minutes on low fire. Add remaining ingredients and cook for 45 minutes.
Serves 8–10.

SUNSHINE SOUP

¾ cup diced Spanish onion
½ cup diced celery
1 garlic clove, minced
¼ cup soybean oil
3 cups water
2 cups skim milk
½ cup powdered nonfat
   dry milk
2 cups canned corn kernels

1 cup green peas
¼ cup minced fresh parsley
1½ teaspoons sea salt
1 teaspoon Bakon Yeast
½ teaspoon Brownies
   Vege-C-Salt (see page 40)
½ teaspoon Italian Seasoning
   (see page 41)

In a large soup kettle sauté onion, celery, and garlic in the oil for 10 minutes. Add remaining ingredients, cover, and cook for 10 minutes. Cool to lukewarm and then pour 2 cups of the vegetables and 1 cup broth into a blender. Blend for 1 minute at medium speed. Return mixture to soup kettle, mix thoroughly, and reheat before serving.

Serves 6–8.

GREEN AND GREAT SOUP

½ cup diced red onion
½ cup diced celery
½ cup dried green mung beans
½ cup couscous
¼ cup sesame oil
2½ quarts water
2 cups tightly packed chopped spinach
2 cups green peas
1 cup tightly packed chopped escarole
⅓ cup minced fresh parsley

1 cup tomato puree
1½ cups California tomato juice
1 tablespoon lecithin
2 teaspoons sea salt
1 teaspoon dill
1 teaspoon Brownies Vege-C-Salt (see page 40)
½ teaspoon garlic powder
½ teaspoon oregano
½ teaspoon rosemary
¼ teaspoon nutmeg
Few grindings of pepper

In a large soup kettle sauté the onion, celery, mung beans, and couscous in the oil for 10 minutes, stirring occasionally. Add the water, cover, and cook for 30 minutes on a low fire. Add remaining ingredients and cook for 10 minutes.

Serves 6–8.

WONDERFUL WATERCRESS SOUP

3 cups water
1 cup Brownies Consommé
  (see page 53)
2 cups chopped watercress
  with stems
2 cups diced Idaho potatoes
  with skin
½ cup diced Spanish onion
½ cup diced carrots
½ cup diced celery
½ cup chopped fresh parsley
1½ teaspoons sea salt
1 teaspoon Brownies
  Vege-C-Salt (see page 40)

1 teaspoon vegetable-broth
  powder
1 teaspoon garlic powder
1 teaspoon dill
1 teaspoon Bakon Yeast
½ teaspoon Italian Seasoning
  (see page 41)
½ teaspoon rosemary
Few grindings of pepper
1 cup buttermilk
½ cup goat-milk yogurt
½ cup sour cream
Snipped fresh chives

Combine all but the last 4 ingredients in a kettle and cook on a medium fire for 30 minutes. Remove from fire and cool to lukewarm, then pour into a blender and blend for 1 minute at medium speed. Pour into a large bowl and blend in the buttermilk, yogurt, and sour cream with a wire whisk. Serve cold, with the chives as a garnish.
  Serves 8–10.

SEAWEED CHOWDER

1 cup diced Spanish onion
2 cups diced celery
¾ cup soybean oil
4 quarts Brownies Soup Stock
  (see page 53)
2 cups crushed canned
  tomatoes
2 cups diced potatoes
  with skin

¼ cup *hijiki*
¼ cup finely cut laver
¼ cup finely cut dulse
1 teaspoon kelp
1½ tablespoons Brownies
  Vege-C-Salt (see page 40)
1 tablespoon Bakon Yeast
½ teaspoon garlic powder

In a large soup kettle sauté onion and celery in oil until onion is transparent. Add the next 6 ingredients, cover, and cook over low flame about 30 minutes. Add remaining ingredients and cook 5 minutes more.

Serves 10–12.

AVOCADO SOUP

1 large avocado, peeled and diced
1 quart skim milk
1 cup powdered nonfat dry milk
1 tablespoon soybean powder
1 tablespoon minced fresh dill
1 teaspoon Bakon Yeast
¼ teaspoon basil
¼ teaspoon oregano
Few grindings of pepper

Combine all ingredients in a blender at medium speed for 30 seconds. Serve chilled.

Serves 6.

AVOCADO ESCAROLE SOUP

1 cup cubed avocado
1 cup chopped escarole
⅓ cup diced carrots
¼ cup diced scallions
1 cup goat-milk yogurt or regular yogurt
3 cups skim milk
½ cup powdered nonfat dry milk
¼ cup toasted walnuts
1 teaspoon sea salt
¼ teaspoon garlic powder
¼ teaspoon dill
¼ teaspoon tarragon
Toasted Soy Nuts

Combine all ingredients except for Soy Nuts in blender at low speed for 1 minute, then at high speed for 1 minute. Refrigerate and serve cold with garnish of toasted Soy Nuts.

Serves 6–8.

CUCUMBER POTAGE

2 cups diced cucumbers
  with skin
¼ cup diced celery
1 cup goat-milk yogurt
1 cup skim milk
2 cups chopped lettuce
¼ cup minced fresh parsley
1 tablespoon snipped fresh
  chives

¾ teaspoon sea salt
¼ teaspoon vegetable-broth
  powder
¼ teaspoon garlic powder
¼ teaspoon nutmeg
⅛ teaspoon powdered ginger
Snipped fresh chives

Combine all ingredients but last in blender at low speed for 1 minute, then at high speed for 1 minute. Refrigerate and serve cold, with garnish of chives.
  Serves 4.

MUSHROOM BARLEY SOUP

½ cup soybean oil
1 cup diced Spanish onion
2 cups diced celery
4 quarts Brownies Soup Stock
  (see page 53)
2 cups sliced mushrooms
2 cups diced carrots
1 cup diced canned tomatoes

1 cup unpearled barley
1 cup black-eyed beans
1 tablespoon sea salt
2 tablespoons Bakon Yeast
2 tablespoons *tamari* sauce
1 tablespoon · Krisp
½ teaspoon garlic powder

Heat the oil in a large soup kettle and sauté the onion and celery until the onion is transparent. Add the next 6 ingredients, cover, and bring to a boil. Cook on a low flame for 1¼ hours, stirring occasionally. Add remaining ingredients and cook for 15 minutes more.
  Serves 10–12.

BEAUTIFUL BROCCOLI SOUP

½ cup diced red onion
½ cup diced celery
2 tablespoons safflower oil
1½ quarts water
2 cups chopped broccoli
1 cup diced potato
2 teaspoons vegetable-broth powder
1 teaspoon sea salt
2 tablespoons *tamari* sauce

1 teaspoon Bakon Yeast
½ teaspoon Italian Seasoning (see page 41)
1 teaspoon dill
½ teaspoon garlic powder
¼ teaspoon allspice
¼ teaspoon nutmeg
1 tablespoon snipped fresh chives
1 tablespoon Krisp

In a large soup kettle sauté the onion and celery in the oil for 10 minutes. Add the remaining ingredients, cover the kettle, and cook on a low fire for 25 minutes. Cool to lukewarm. Pour 2 cups combined vegetables and broth into a blender and blend for 1 minute at medium speed. Return mixture to soup kettle, mix thoroughly, and reheat soup.
Serves 6.

SUPER SAUERKRAUT SOUP

¾ cup diced Spanish onion
2 garlic cloves, minced
¼ cup soybean oil
3 cups chopped cabbage
1 cup shredded carrots
1 tablespoon minced fresh dill
½ cup shredded potato
1 pound sauerkraut with its juice
1 cup diced tomatoes

1½ quarts water
¼ cup tomato puree
2 tablespoons raw sugar
2 teaspoons sea salt
1 teaspoon vegetable-broth powder
½ teaspoon oregano
½ teaspoon celery seed
¼ teaspoon mace
Few grindings of pepper

Sauté onion and garlic in oil in large kettle until onion is light brown. Add cabbage, carrots, and dill and cook for 5 minutes, stirring constantly. Add remaining ingredients, cover kettle, and cook on low fire for 20 minutes.
Serves 6.

TOMATO BROWN-RICE SOUP

1 cup diced Spanish onion
1 cup diced celery
¼ cup soybean oil
1 quart Brownies Consommé
(see page 53)
1 cup diced carrots
2 cups canned sliced tomatoes
2 cups tomato puree

1½ tablespoons Brownies
Vege-C-Salt (see page 40)
1½ tablespoons raw sugar
1 teaspoon paprika
1 teaspoon Bakon Yeast
½ teaspoon basil
½ teaspoon oregano
1 cup Basic Brown Rice (see
page 150)

In large soup kettle sauté onion and celery in the soybean oil until onion is transparent. Add the remaining ingredients except for the rice, cover, and cook about 45 minutes, stirring occasionally. Add the brown rice, mix thoroughly, and heat through.
Serves 8.

COLD CRIMSON SOUP

2 cups sliced cooked beets
1 cup chopped beet tops
1½ cups beet juice
½ cup goat-milk yogurt
½ cup diced pineapple
¼ cup diced celery
¼ cup sour cream
2 tablespoons minced fresh
parsley

1 cup canned unsweetened
pineapple juice
1 teaspoon sea salt
1 teaspoon dill
½ teaspoon Brownies
Vege-C-Salt (see page 40)
¼ teaspoon vegetable-broth
powder
Goat-milk yogurt
Snipped fresh chives

Combine all ingredients but last 2 in blender at low speed for 1 minute, then at high speed for 1 minute. Refrigerate and serve cold with a garnish of yogurt and chives.
Serves 4–6.

YOGURT BORSCHT

1 quart water
1 16-ounce can whole beets
    with liquid
⅓ cup raw sugar
1 tablespoon honey

¼ cup fresh lemon juice
½ teaspoon Brownies
    Vege-C-Salt (see page 40)
1 cup goat-milk yogurt

Combine water and beets in blender for 10 seconds. Add remaining ingredients and blend 10 seconds longer. Serve chilled.
    Serves 8.

COMBINATION BEAN SOUP

½ cup diced Spanish onion
½ cup diced celery
¼ cup soybean oil
2 cloves garlic, minced
3½ quarts water
½ cup dried black turtle beans
½ cup dried garbanzo beans
½ cup dried pea beans
½ cup dried lima beans
1 cup diced potato with skin
1 cup ½-inch pieces string
    beans

½ cup diced carrots
⅓ cup unpearled barley
1 cup tomato puree
¼ cup minced fresh parsley
2 tablespoons minced fresh dill
1½ teaspoons sea salt
1 teaspoon oregano
1 teaspoon rosemary
2 tablespoons Krisp
1 tablespoon lecithin
1 teaspoon Bakon Yeast
½ teaspoon celery seed

In a large soup kettle sauté the onion and celery in the oil until brown. Add remaining ingredients, cover, and bring to boil; then cook on low flame about 2 hours or until all the beans are tender, stirring occasionally.
    Serves 6–8.

CANNELLI-BEAN SOUP

½ cup soybean oil
1 cup diced Spanish onion
1 cup diced celery
1 cup diced carrots
1 cup crushed canned tomatoes
1 cup dried yellow split peas
1 cup dried *cannelli* beans

4 quarts Brownies Soup Stock
 (see page 53)
1 tablespoon sea salt
1 tablespoon brewer's yeast
1 tablespoon Krisp
2 tablespoons *tamari* sauce
½ teaspoon garlic powder

Heat the oil in a soup kettle and sauté the onion and celery until the onion is transparent. Add the next 5 ingredients and cook, covered, for 1¼ hours, stirring occasionally. Add the remaining ingredients and cook for 20 minutes or until the *cannelli* beans are tender.

Serves 10–12.

LENTIL SOUP

½ cup soybean oil
1 cup diced Spanish onion
1 cup diced celery
1 cup diced carrots
1 cup crushed canned tomatoes
2½ quarts Brownies Soup
 Stock (see page 53)

2 cups brown lentils
1 tablespoon sea salt
1 tablespoon Bakon Yeast
1 tablespoon *tamari* sauce
1 tablespoon Krisp
½ teaspoon garlic powder

Heat the oil in a large soup kettle and sauté the onion and celery until the onion is golden. Add the next 4 ingredients, cover, and cook for 35 minutes, stirring occasionally. Add the remaining ingredients and cook for an additional 15 minutes.

Serves 6–8.

BROWNIES SPLIT-PEA SOUP

1 cup diced Spanish onion
1 cup diced celery
¼ cup safflower oil
2 quarts Brownies Soup Stock
  (see page 53)
2 cups dried green split peas

1 cup diced carrots
1 tablespoon sea salt
1 tablespoon Bakon Yeast
1 tablespoon Stripple Zips
½ teaspoon garlic powder

In a large soup kettle sauté the onion and celery in the oil until the onion is transparent. Add the stock, split peas, carrots, and sea salt. Cook for 45 minutes or until split peas are disintegrated, stirring occasionally. Add remaining ingredients and stir thoroughly.

Serves 6–8.

SUPERIOR FISH POTAGE

1½ cups diced Spanish onion
1 cup diced celery
1 cup diced carrot
1 quart water
1 cup diced scallions
½ cup diced scrod
2 teaspoons sea salt
1 tablespoon lecithin
1 teaspoon Bakon Yeast
½ teaspoon garlic powder
¼ teaspoon powdered ginger

1 tablespoon snipped fresh
  chives
Few grindings of pepper
2 cups 1-inch scrod chunks
¼ cup minced fresh parsley
1 tablespoon minced fresh dill
1 1-pound can corn kernels
  with their liquid
1 cup skim milk
½ cup powdered nonfat dry
  milk

Combine first 7 ingredients in soup kettle. Cover and cook for 30 minutes on low fire. Cool to lukewarm, then pour into blender and blend for 1 minute at low speed. Return to kettle, add remaining ingredients, cover, and cook for 10 minutes on low fire, stirring occasionally.

Serves 8–10.

SCARLET FISH SOUP

½ cup diced Spanish onion
½ cup diced celery
2 scallions, diced
2 garlic cloves, minced
¼ cup safflower oil
1 quart Brownies Consommé (see page 53)
2 cups canned sliced tomatoes in tomato juice
1 cup diced new potatoes with skin

¼ cup minced fresh parsley
1 tablespoon minced fresh dill
1 teaspoon sea salt
1 teaspoon Brownies Vege-C-Salt (see page 40)
1 teaspoon oregano
1 teaspoon lecithin
1 tablespoon *tamari* sauce
1½ cups diced fresh halibut

In a large soup kettle sauté onion, celery, scallions, and garlic in oil for 10 minutes. Add all the remaining ingredients except halibut, cover, and cook for 20 minutes. Add the halibut and cook for 10 minutes more.

Serves 6–8.

YOGURT SOUP

1 quart buttermilk
2 cups goat-milk yogurt
½ teaspoon kelp

½ teaspoon Brownies Vege-C-Salt (see page 40)
1 teaspoon caraway seeds

Mix buttermilk and yogurt in blender for 5 seconds, add remaining ingredients, and blend 5 seconds longer. Serve chilled.

Serves 6.

MARVELOUS MILLET SOUP

½ cup diced scallions
½ cup diced celery
1 garlic clove, minced
¼ cup safflower oil
3 cups sliced mushrooms
2 cups cauliflower florets
½ cup diced carrots
¼ cup minced fresh parsley
1 tablespoon minced fresh dill
½ cup millet
2 cups Brownies Consommé
(see page 53)

2 cups water
1¾ teaspoons sea salt
1 teaspoon Italian Seasoning
(see page 41)
2 teaspoons paprika
1 tablespoon Krisp
1 teaspoon Bakon Yeast
¼ teaspoon celery seed
¼ teaspoon allspice
1½ cups skim milk
½ cup powdered nonfat dry
milk

In large soup kettle sauté scallions, celery, and garlic in oil for 5 minutes. Add the mushrooms and stir for 5 minutes. Add remaining ingredients except the skim milk and dry milk. Cover and cook on low fire for 30 minutes. Combine skim milk and dry milk, add to soup, stirring constantly, and mix thoroughly.
Serves 8–10.

STEEL-CUT OAT SOUP

1 cup steel-cut oats
2 quarts water
1 cup diced Spanish onion
1 cup diced celery
⅓ cup safflower oil
1½ cups sliced mushrooms
1½ cups thinly sliced carrots
1 cup green peas
1½ teaspoons sea salt

2 tablespoons *tamari* sauce
½ teaspoon garlic powder
1 tablespoon vegetable-broth
powder
½ teaspoon Italian Seasoning
(see page 41)
2 tablespoons snipped fresh
chives
½ teaspoon thyme

Combine the oats and water in a soup kettle. Bring to a boil, then continue cooking on a low fire. In a skillet sauté the onion and celery in the oil until golden. Add the mushrooms and brown. Add contents of skillet to the soup with the carrots and peas and continue cooking for about 45 minutes or until the vegetables are tender, stirring occasionally. Add more water if soup gets too thick. Add the remaining ingredients and stir well.

Serves 8–10.

COLD SWEDISH FRUIT SOUP

1½ quarts water
½ orange with peel, sliced thin
½ lemon with peel, sliced thin
½ cup Monukka raisins
¼ cup diced pineapple
½ cup raw sugar
2 tablespoons tapioca
¼ teaspoon sea salt
½ cup blueberries

¾ cup sliced peaches
¾ cup cherries, pitted
½ cup mandarin-orange sections
2 tablespoons fresh lemon juice
1 teaspoon orange extract
1 teaspoon lemon extract
¼ teaspoon cinnamon

Combine the first 8 ingredients in a large kettle and cook for 20 minutes. Remove from fire and let cool for 10 minutes. Add the remaining ingredients, mix thoroughly, and refrigerate. Serve very cold.

Serves 8.

APPLE FANTASY SOUP

1½ cups diced Delicious apples with skin
1½ cups canned unsweetened pineapple juice
½ cup skim milk
¼ cup powdered nonfat dry milk
⅓ cup sliced carrots

2 tablespoons orange-blossom honey
¼ teaspoon cinnamon
¼ teaspoon sea salt
¼ teaspoon nutmeg
Diced Delicious apple with skin
Blueberries

Combine all ingredients except for last 2 in blender at medium speed for 1 minute, then at high speed for 1 minute. Serve cold, with garnish of diced apple and blueberries.

Serves 4.

PEACH BLUE SOUP

2 cups buttermilk
1 cup goat-milk yogurt or
    regular yogurt
½ cup cottage cheese
2 cups diced peaches

1½ cups blueberries
2 tablespoons clover honey
1 tablespoon minced fresh mint
½ teaspoon orange extract
1 teaspoon sea salt

Combine buttermilk, yogurt, cottage cheese, 1½ cups peaches, ½ cup blueberries, honey, mint, orange extract, and salt in blender at medium speed for 1 minute, then at high speed for 1 minute. Pour into bowl, add remaining 1 cup blueberries and ½ cup peaches, and mix thoroughly. Serve cold.
    Serves 4–6.

PEACHY CARROT SOUP

2 cups apple juice
¼ cup skim milk
2 tablespoons powdered nonfat
    dry milk
1½ cups sliced carrots
1½ cups sliced peaches

1 tablespoon clover honey
½ teaspoon sea salt
¼ teaspoon mace
¼ teaspoon cinnamon
Sliced peaches

Combine all ingredients except last at medium speed in blender for 1 minute, then at high speed for 1 minute. Serve cold, with garnish of sliced peaches.
    Serves 4.

CHERRY PLUM SOUP

2 cups pitted and quartered
  blue Italian plums
1 cup pitted cherries
1 quart water
½ cup raw sugar
1 teaspoon cinnamon

1 teaspoon sea salt
1 orange with peel, quartered
  and seeded
Juice of 1 lemon
½ teaspoon lemon extract

Combine the first 6 ingredients in pot and cook for 20 minutes on low fire. Cool to lukewarm, then remove 1½ cups of liquid to blender and combine with the last 3 ingredients at high speed for 1 minute. Pour into cooked fruit and mix thoroughly. Serve cold.

Serves 4–6.

6

THE ENDLESS GARDEN OF DELIGHTS
(Salads)

Now let us pay homage to the noble salad. Millennia have not withered its charms, nor has custom staled its infinite variety. Its adaptability is truly extraordinary. In one form or another it turns up all over the place: as appetizer, relish, entrée, side dish, even dessert. Its repertoire embraces almost every edible thing short of butter, breakfast cereal, and soup.

Brownies has come a long way since those first days when we were making salads out of the pickings from our garden. Early on we unleashed our imaginations, introduced new elements, brought foods together in dramatic confrontations. As artists manqué we experimented with sculpted shapes and combinations of color to dazzle the eye.

Lunchtime is salad time at Brownies: We serve 63 varieties on any given day. They usually feature green soybeans, Vegetarian Liver (see page 12), Norwegian brislings, salmon, tuna, marinated herring, avocado, fresh fruit, Danish smoked sprats, cheese, anchovies, smoked cod livers, eggs, and stuffed tomatoes. But it's how you "get it all together," as the kids say, that separates the *salade distinguée* from the *salade ordinaire*. At dinner we serve everyone the bottomless salad bowl: greens on greens on greens, crowned with the bloodred of slivered beets and vivid orange of shredded carrots.

What is the secret of a good salad? Our own bias inclines toward seduction of the eye, arranging rendezvous between unlikely principals for that element of surprise. We like "bityness," freshness, texture, and the sensation of being close to Mother Earth. Here we'd like to share with you some originals from Brownies.

BASIC TOSSED-SALAD MIX

1 head romaine lettuce, coarsely sliced

1 head escarole, coarsely sliced

1 head chicory, coarsely sliced

4 cups shredded carrots

2 cups finely sliced red cabbage *

Toss all the ingredients together in a bowl. Refrigerate. Use as needed.

Serves 4–6.

* Omit when using recipe as a base for fruit salads.

SUNSET VEGETABLE SALAD

3 cups 1-inch pieces cooked wax beans
1 cup diced zucchini
½ cup sliced mushrooms
1¼ cups diced red onion
⅓ cup walnut oil
3 tablespoons apple-cider vinegar
2 tablespoons fresh lemon juice

1 tablespoon minced fresh dill
1 teaspoon sea salt
⅓ cup crumbled blue cheese
½ teaspoon Dijon mustard
¼ teaspoon allspice
¼ teaspoon garlic powder
¼ teaspoon Italian Seasoning (see page 41)
¼ teaspoon tarragon

Combine first 4 ingredients in a mixing bowl. In a small bowl mix together the remaining ingredients thoroughly to make dressing. Add dressing to vegetables and mix well. Refrigerate.
Serves 4.

ORIENTAL CHEW SALAD

1 quart thinly sliced Chinese cabbage
1 cup thinly sliced zucchini
1 cup shredded carrots
½ cup mung-bean sprouts
⅓ cup canned bamboo shoots
⅓ cup thinly sliced canned water chestnuts
2 scallions, diced

1 egg
½ cup safflower oil
¼ cup rice-wine vinegar
2 tablespoons *tamari* sauce
1 garlic clove, minced
1 teaspoon sea salt
¼ teaspoon powdered ginger
¼ teaspoon nutmeg

Combine first 7 ingredients in bowl. Make dressing with remaining ingredients combined in blender at high speed for 1 minute. Refrigerate vegetables and dressing separately and combine just before serving.
Serves 4–6.

KAREN'S "HEALTHY HANNAH" SALAD

1 Simpson lettuce
2 cups shredded carrots
1½ cups diced unpeeled
   cucumber
2 tomatoes, sliced

3 hard-cooked eggs, finely
   diced
1½ cups cottage cheese
1½ cups Dill Soybeans (see
   this page)
½ cup toasted sunflower seeds

Cut the lettuce in chunks and arrange in the bottom of a salad bowl. Layer the remaining ingredients except for the sunflower seeds on top of the lettuce. Top with the sunflower seeds and refrigerate.
   Serves 3–4.

DILL SOYBEANS

1 15½-ounce can green
   soybeans, drained
¼ cup sesame oil
¼ teaspoon Brownies
   Vege-C-Salt (see page 40)

⅛ teaspoon garlic powder
½ teaspoon Bakon Yeast
2 teaspoons minced fresh dill

Combine all the ingredients and mix thoroughly. Refrigerate.
   Serves 3–4.

JEWEL SALAD WITH COTTAGE-CHEESE DRESSING

1 unpeeled cucumber, diced
2 tomatoes, cut in chunks
⅔ cup chopped green pepper
⅓ cup chopped watercress
¼ cup diced Spanish onion
½ cup goat-milk yogurt
½ cup buttermilk
½ cup cottage cheese

¼ teaspoon sea salt
¼ teaspoon Brownies
   Vege-C-Salt (see page 40)
¼ teaspoon garlic powder
¼ teaspoon rosemary
¼ teaspoon marjoram
½ teaspoon paprika
Dash of pepper

Combine first 5 ingredients in a bowl. Combine the remaining ingredients in blender at medium speed for 30 seconds to make dressing. Pour dressing over vegetables and mix lightly. Refrigerate before serving.
   Serves 2–3.

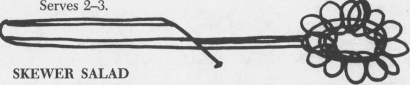

SKEWER SALAD

½ large head of lettuce
8 cherry tomatoes
8 pitted green olives
8 chunks Swiss cheese
8 pitted black olives
8 radishes
8 mushroom caps, brushed
   with lemon juice

8 chunks green pepper
8 chunks cucumber
Basic Tossed-Salad Mix (see
   page 72)
Avocado Emerald Dressing (see
   page 43)

Put lettuce-head half in center of a large, deep salad bowl. Thread each of 8 8-inch skewers with one each of the next 8 ingredients. Stick skewers into lettuce half, forming a circle. Fill the salad bowl with Basic Tossed-Salad Mix so that the lettuce half is completely covered. When serving, have each person take 1 skewer, some mixed salad, and some Avocado Emerald Dressing.
   Serves 8.

AVOCADO SALAD

2 avocados, cubed
1 cup diced pineapple
2 oranges, diced
¼ cup diced celery
2 tablespoons diced pimiento
¼ cup rice-wine vinegar
¼ cup safflower oil

¼ cup canned unsweetened
   pineapple juice
1 tablespoon fresh lemon juice
¼ cup Papaya Syrup
   Concentrate
¼ teaspoon Salad Herbs (see
   page 41)
½ teaspoon sea salt

In a large bowl combine avocados, pineapple, oranges, celery, and pimiento and mix lightly. For the dressing combine the remaining ingredients in another bowl and blend thoroughly. Pour dressing over fruit mixture and mix lightly. Refrigerate.
    Serves 4.

AVOCADO BEAN-SPROUT SALAD

2 avocados
1 cup alfalfa sprouts
2 tablespoons finely diced
   onion
¼ cup finely diced celery
½ cup goat-milk yogurt
2 tablespoons Brownies PUFA
   Dressing (see page 42)

1 tablespoon Brownies Low-
   Cal Dressing (see page 41)
1 tablespoon fresh lime juice
½ teaspoon sea salt
¼ teaspoon powdered ginger
⅛ teaspoon garlic powder
4 teaspoons toasted sunflower
   seeds

Cut avocados in half, remove seeds, and scoop out flesh, reserving shells. Cut avocado into small chunks and combine with alfalfa sprouts, onion, and celery in mixing bowl. Combine the remaining ingredients except for the sunflower seeds, and pour over avocado mixture; blend thoroughly. Divide among the 4 avocado shells and sprinkle each shell with 1 teaspoon sunflower seeds. Refrigerate before serving.
    Serves 4.

PERFECTION PEA SALAD .
(Dennis's Favorite)

1 cup green peas
¼ teaspoon sea salt
½ cup water
1 quart shredded romaine
  lettuce
1 tomato, diced
2 tablespoons diced red onion
½ cup diced celery

1 6-ounce jar marinated
  artichoke hearts
½ teaspoon sea salt
¼ teaspoon garlic powder
¼ teaspoon dill
2 tablespoons fresh lemon juice
¼ cup sesame oil

Steam peas in salted water in covered saucepan about 8 minutes. Remove from fire and cool. Combine remaining ingredients, add drained cooled peas, and mix lightly.
    Serves 4.

ZESTY ZUCCHINI SALAD

3 cups thinly sliced zucchini
1 large Delicious apple, diced
½ cup diced celery
½ cup sliced canned water
  chestnuts
1 cup goat-milk yogurt
½ cup Brownies PUFA
  Dressing (see page 42)

1 teaspoon sea salt
3 tablespoons toasted cashew
  meal
2 tablespoons toasted seasame
  seeds
½ teaspoon grated orange peel

Combine first 4 ingredients in a bowl. Combine remaining ingredients to make dressing, add to zucchini mixture, and mix lightly.
    Serves 4–6.

SUCCULENT SWISS-CHARD SALAD

1 cup Basic Lentils (see page
    133)
3 cups shredded swiss chard
2 cups shredded romaine
    lettuce
⅔ cup diced unpeeled
    cucumber
½ cup drained sauerkraut
2 tablespoons diced red onion

2 teaspoons Krisp
2 scallions, diced
½ cup goat-milk yogurt
¼ cup sour cream
3 tablespoons tomato puree
1 teaspoon sea salt
½ teaspoon oregano
¼ teaspoon garlic powder
Dash of pepper

Lightly toss cold lentils and next 7 ingredients together in bowl. Combine remaining ingredients for dressing. Refrigerate salad and dressing separately; mix just before serving.
    Serves 6–8.

COLORFUL CABBAGE SALAD

1½ quarts shredded green
    cabbage
1 quart shredded red cabbage
1 cup shredded carrots
½ cup diced green pepper
2 scallions, diced
½ cup sour cream
½ cup cottage cheese
½ cup lemon-juice
    mayonnaise

½ cup goat-milk yogurt
1 teaspoon sea salt
1 tablespoon fresh lime juice
1 tablespoon fresh lemon juice
¼ teaspoon garlic powder
¼ teaspoon allspice
¼ teaspoon turmeric
Few grindings of pepper

Combine first 5 ingredients in bowl. Combine remaining ingredients to make dressing. Mix vegetables and dressing together thoroughly and refrigerate.
    Serves 6–8.

HEARTS-OF-PALM SALAD

1 14-ounce can hearts of palm, drained and sliced
1 medium-size cucumber with skin, diced
¼ cup diced black olives
¼ cup diced pimiento
1 tomato, diced
3 tablespoons diced red onion
½ cup sliced mushrooms
⅓ cup almond oil

¼ cup rice-wine vinegar
2 tablespoons apple-cider vinegar
1 teaspoon sea salt
¼ teaspoon garlic powder
¼ teaspoon nutmeg
¼ teaspoon Italian Seasoning (see page 41)
Few grindings of pepper

Combine first 7 ingredients in bowl and toss lightly. Make dressing by combining remaining ingredients in covered jar and shaking thoroughly. Mix vegetables and dressing and refrigerate.
Serves 3–4.

SOPHISTICATED STRING BEANS

2 cups cold lightly cooked string beans, cut in julienne strips
1 cup shredded carrots
½ cup sliced canned water chestnuts
¼ cup shredded cauliflower
¼ cup diced pimiento
½ cup diced celery
2 hard-cooked eggs, diced

2 tablespoons diced onions
1 teaspoon sea salt
½ teaspoon Spike
Few grindings of pepper
¼ cup rice-wine vinegar
⅓ cup safflower oil
2 tablespoons *tamari* sauce
½ teaspoon Italian Seasoning (see page 41)
¼ teaspoon garlic powder

Combine string beans with the next 10 ingredients. Combine remaining ingredients in covered jar, shake thoroughly, and pour over vegetables. Serve cold.
Serves 4.

ROBUST BEAN AND CARROT SALAD

2 cups 1-inch pieces green
  beans
2 cups carrot rounds
1 cup water
1 teaspoon sea salt
½ cup goat-milk yogurt
⅓ cup sour cream
2 tablespoons diced pimiento
¼ cup mung-bean sprouts

1 scallion, diced
2 tablespoons grated Romano
  or Parmesan cheese
¼ teaspoon Spike
¼ teaspoon Italian Seasoning
  (see page 41)
½ teaspoon Dijon mustard
⅛ teaspoon garlic powder

Combine beans, carrots, water, and salt in covered saucepan and steam for 8 minutes or until vegetables are crisp and tender. Remove from fire, drain, put vegetables in mixing bowl, and refrigerate. When cold, combine remaining ingredients to make dressing, pour over vegetables, and mix thoroughly.
    Serves 4–6.

TRIPLE-TREAT BEAN SALAD

1 15½-ounce can green
  soybeans, drained
1 15-ounce can garbanzo
  beans, drained
1 16-ounce can kidney beans,
  drained
½ cup sliced mushrooms
⅓ cup diced celery
2 scallions, diced

½ cup sesame oil
¼ cup apple-cider vinegar
½ teaspoon Spike
½ teaspoon oregano
¼ teaspoon garlic powder
¼ teaspoon Italian Seasoning
  (see page 41)
Dash of pepper

Combine first 6 ingredients in bowl. For dressing combine remaining ingredients in covered jar, shake well, pour over vegetables, and mix lightly.
    Serves 6.

CRUNCHY SOYBEAN SALAD

1 15½-ounce can green
    soybeans
1 13-ounce can Chicken-Style
    Soyameat, drained and cut in
    julienne strips
½ cup diced zucchini
¼ cup diced celery
4 radishes, sliced thin
1 large scallion, diced

½ cup sour cream
¼ cup Brownies Lo-Cal
    Dressing (see page 41)
½ teaspoon sea salt
¼ teaspoon dill
¼ teaspoon oregano
¼ teaspoon Spike
Few grindings of pepper

Combine first 6 ingredients in bowl. Combine remaining ingredients to make dressing, pour over soybean mixture, mix thoroughly, and refrigerate.
Serves 4–6.

CREAMY CAULIFLOWER SALAD

2 cups cauliflower florets
1 large unpeeled cucumber,
    diced
½ cup diced green pepper
½ cup diced radishes
1 large scallion, diced
1 tablespoon snipped fresh
    chives
½ cup diced Swiss cheese
½ cup goat-milk yogurt
1 cup sour cream

¼ cup Brownies Lo-Cal
    Dressing (see page 41)
½ cup unpeeled cucumber,
    shredded fine
1¼ teaspoons sea salt
¼ teaspoon tarragon
¼ teaspoon savory
¼ teaspoon garlic powder
Few grindings of pepper
2 tablespoons chopped fresh
    parsley

Combine first 7 ingredients in bowl. Combine thoroughly the remaining ingredients except for the parsley to make dressing. Mix together lightly the cauliflower mixture and the dressing and refrigerate. Just before serving, garnish salad with parsley.
Serves 4.

SPEAR AND STICK SALAD

12 asparagus spears, steamed
3 cups carrot sticks, steamed
⅓ cup sesame oil
¼ cup rice-wine vinegar
2 tablespoons canned
  unsweetened pineapple juice
¼ cup canned crushed
  unsweetened pineapple

1 tablespoon fresh lime juice
Grated rind of 1 lime
1 tablespoon diced pimiento
¼ teaspoon Spike
1 tablespoon Krisp
½ teaspoon Sweet 'n Low

Place asparagus spears in center of large platter. Surround them with the carrot sticks in a circle. Combine remaining ingredients to make dressing, pour over the vegetables, and refrigerate. Serves 6.

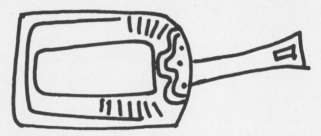

RED AND WHITE SALAD

8 cooked small white onions
2 cups sliced cooked beets
1 cup beet juice
2 tablespoons brown-rice flour
½ cup orange juice
⅓ cup canned crushed
  unsweetened pineapple

1 tablespoon *tamari* sauce
¼ teaspoon sea salt
1 teaspoon grated orange rind
¼ teaspoon powdered ginger
¼ teaspoon minced fresh
  mint

Cut onions in half and combine with beets in mixing bowl. Combine ¼ cup of the beet juice with the brown-rice flour and set aside. Combine the rest of the ingredients in a saucepan. Cook on low fire, and when liquid boils, add reserved thickened beet juice. Stir and cook for 10 minutes on low heat. Pour over vegetables. Serve hot or cold. Serves 4.

THE BEST OF BROCCOLI

4 cups cold lightly cooked
  broccoli florets
1 cup diced tomato
1 cup sliced mushrooms
⅓ cup unsalted Soy Nuts
1 tablespoon snipped fresh
  chives
1 large scallion, diced
1 teaspoon sea salt

1 tablespoon Krisp
Few grindings of pepper
¼ cup goat-milk yogurt
¼ cup Brownies PUFA
  Dressing (see page 42)
¼ cup Brownies Lo-Cal
  Dressing (see page 41)
¼ teaspoon dill
¼ teaspoon garlic powder

Combine broccoli with next 8 ingredients in mixing bowl. Combine remaining ingredients to make dressing, pour over the broccoli mixture, and mix lightly. Refrigerate.
    Serves 4–6.

EGGS IN THE NEST

8 leaves romaine lettuce
2 cups shredded carrots
1 cup mung-bean sprouts
2 hard-cooked eggs

2 tablespoons shredded beets
1 teaspoon minced parsley
Brownies PUFA Dressing (see
  page 42)

Arrange the lettuce leaves on a serving plate. Make a circle with the shredded carrots around the outer edge of the lettuce. Plump the mung-bean sprouts in the center and place the eggs on top. Garnish with the beets and parsley. Refrigerate. Serve with the dressing.
    Serves 2.

STUFFED TOMATOES WITH LIVER AND EGG

4 cups Basic Tossed-Salad
  Mix (see page 72)
2 tomatoes
½ cup Vegetarian Liver (see
  page 12)
½ cup Egg Salad
  (see page 20)

8 slices unpeeled cucumber
½ cup shredded carrots
½ cup shredded beets
2 sprigs watercress
1 teaspoon minced fresh
  parsley

Arrange tossed-salad mix in a salad bowl. Cut tomatoes in quarters but do *not* cut quite through to bottom, spread apart, and place on salad. Divide the vegetarian liver and egg salad between the 2 tomatoes. Garnish with the remaining ingredients. Refrigerate.

Serves 2.

BASIC FRESH FRUIT SALAD
(Summer Mix)

1 cantaloupe, peeled and cubed
3 peaches, cubed
3 oranges, peeled and cubed
½ pineapple, peeled and cubed
1 cup blueberries
1 cup seedless green grapes

2 bananas, sliced
¼ cup canned unsweetened pineapple juice
1 tablespoon fresh lemon juice
1 tablespoon orange-blossom honey

Combine the first 7 ingredients in a bowl. Blend the remaining ingredients and stir into the first combination. Refrigerate.

Serves 4.

BASIC FRESH FRUIT SALAD
(Winter Mix)

1 grapefruit, peeled and cubed
3 oranges, peeled and cubed
3 unpeeled McIntosh apples, cubed
½ pineapple, peeled and cubed
2 bananas, sliced

1 cup black grapes, seeded
¼ cup canned unsweetened pineapple juice
1 tablespoon fresh lemon juice
1 tablespoon orange-blossom honey

Combine the first 6 ingredients in a bowl. Blend pineapple juice, lemon juice, and honey and combine with the fruits. Refrigerate.

Serves 4.

SPECIALTY FRUIT PLATTER

6 leaves romaine lettuce
2 cups Basic Fresh Fruit
  Salad (Summer Mix)
  (see page 84)
1 cup cottage cheese
4 stewed prunes
4 stewed dried figs
4 stewed dried apricots
¼ cup stewed Monukka
  raisins

½ cup shredded carrots
¼ cup shredded beets
1 teaspoon minced fresh
  parsley
1 tablespoon toasted
  sunflower seeds
1 tablespoon toasted
  sesame seeds

Arrange the lettuce leaves on a serving plate. Place the fruit salad in the center and top with the cottage cheese. Surround with circle of the stewed fruits, alternating them. Garnish with the remaining ingredients. Refrigerate.

Serves 2.

AVOCADO 'N' FRESH FRUIT

3 cups mixed salad greens
1 avocado, cut in half
1 cup Basic Fresh Fruit Salad
  (Winter Mix) (see page 84)
½ cup cottage cheese
2 tablespoons stewed
  Monukka raisins

½ cup shredded carrots
¼ cup shredded beets
2 sprigs watercress
2 tablespoons chopped
  walnuts

Arrange the mixed salad greens in a salad bowl. Place the avocado halves on top and fill each cavity with the fruit salad. Top each with ¼ cup cottage cheese and 1 tablespoon raisins and garnish with the remaining ingredients. Refrigerate.

Serves 2.

BROWN-RICE KUMQUAT SALAD

8 preserved kumquats, sliced
4 cups Basic Brown Rice
  (see page 150)
⅔ cup canned crushed
  unsweetened pineapple
2 teaspoons minced fresh
  mint
1 tablespoon *tamari* sauce

4 teaspoons rice-wine vinegar
2 tablespoons almond oil
½ teaspoon powdered ginger
½ teaspoon cinnamon
1 teaspoon Papaya Syrup
  Concentrate
¼ teaspoon sea salt

Combine 6 of the sliced kumquats with the cold brown rice and the remaining ingredients in large bowl and toss together lightly. Garnish with reserved 2 sliced kumquats. Refrigerate.
    Serves 6.

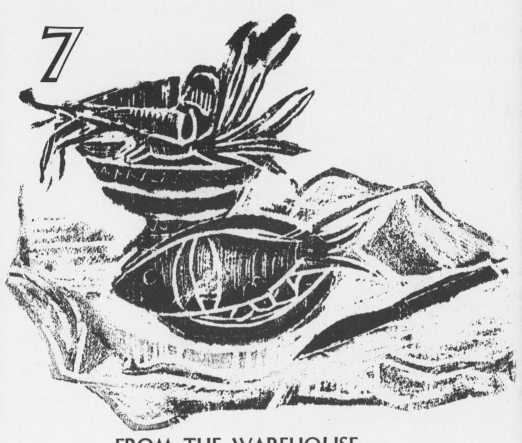

FROM THE WAREHOUSE
OF THE WATERS
(Fish)

Ocean, gulf, lake, stream, and pond make up our aqueous feed bag. The future will find us dipping deeper and deeper into the waters' rich depths for our food. To feed unborn generations, underwater "farming" must be widely practiced.

What we take from the waters of the world are mainly fish and shellfish. We love them for their delectability and their marvelous diversity. Although most of us eat only 3 or 4 kinds of fish, there are at least 300 or 400 edible varieties.

We love them because they are nutritionally superb. They have as much protein as meat—but only ½ to ⅔ the calories. Eating fish is preferable to eating the meat of most animals because the fish have not been given hormones and tranquilizers, nor have they been fed with plants grown on commercially fertilized soils poisoned with herbicides and pesticides. They have high phosphorus, iodine, and fluorine contents and a low fat count. The fats they do have are the polyunsaturated type, which do not raise the cholesterol level. No wonder the fish-loving Orientals stay so trim and avoid heart attacks!

Fish have the added blessings of being relatively economical and easy to prepare. They can be served in soups, salads, and casseroles, as a supplement to a meat dish, and by themselves as an entrée.

Fish are faster to cook than meat because they are usually flat (cooking time is increased by thickness) and because their lack of fat lets heat penetrate more rapidly. They can be sauced and seasoned with as much variety as meats and poultry. The basic methods of cooking are steaming, broiling, baking, or frying. *Absolutely verboten* is boiling. Stewing should be avoided too, as it tends to soak out the flavor. The basic Brownies approach to fish is to steam them first, which retains their succulence; then we baste them with Brownies Fish Dressing (see page 42) and broil briefly.

We feature fish in a number of presentation platters designed to seduce the eye, tickle the palate, and fortify the inner man. Scrod, sole, haddock, salmon, mackerel, and sea squabs are romanticized with colorful embellishments of cooked fresh vegetables, golden saffron rice, fresh herbs, exotic fruits, shredded coconut, toasted almonds or pignolia nuts, all surrounded with a scalloped wall of mashed yams.

"Fish dinners will make a man spring like a flea!" exclaimed Restoration poet Thomas Jordan. Amen.

Seaweed farmed from the garden of the sea is the lifeline of the fish. What feeds the fish so well is also beneficial to man. Seaweeds are a rich source of iodine and contain no less than 92 natural minerals of the ocean. Most seaweed comes from off the coasts of California and Japan. Kelp, dulse, laver, and *hijiki* are the seaweeds used in cooking at Brownies. We use them as seasoners and strengtheners for both fish and nonfish dishes, as well as in soups, sauces, and salads. Richest in iodine is kelp, which comes in powdered form and makes a potent seasoner. Dulse has a nice, pungent herringy taste; Nova Scotian young-sters chew it like candy. In its leafy state we scissor it and sprinkle it on top of fish or drop it into chowders, salads, or fish sauces. Dried laver, which comes in sheets from Japan, we crumple on fish. *Hijiki,* a treasured import from Japan, shreds like coconut and cooks up as a sublime complement to fish entrées.

What's for dinner? How about something fishy?

GOURMET FISH FEAST

1 pound red-snapper fillets, cut in 4 pieces
1 pound bluefish fillets, cut in 4 pieces
1 pound sole fillets, cut in 4 pieces
4 large sea squabs, cleaned
⅓ cup Brownies Fish Dressing (see page 42)
4 large tomatoes, quartered
1 teaspoon Brownies Vege-C-Salt (see page 40)
1 teaspoon paprika

4 cups Basic Wild Rice (see page 150)
2 tablespoons toasted sliced almonds
2 tablespoons toasted sesame seeds
2 teaspoons minced fresh parsley
1 orange with peel, cut in 8 slices and seeded
1 lemon with peel, cut in 8 slices and seeded

Brush the fish fillets with all but 2 tablespoons of the fish dressing and broil for 10 minutes. Sprinkle the tomato quarters with the Vege-C-Salt, paprika, and the 2 tablespoons fish dress-ing and broil for 5 minutes. Place 1 cup of wild rice on each of 4 serving plates. Arrange an assortment of the fish on the rice and garnish with the tomatoes and remaining ingredients.
Serves 4.

KETTLE OF FISH

1 quart Brownies Consommé (see page 53)
2 cups crushed tomatoes
1 cup diced celery
1 cup green peas
1 cup diced carrots
½ cup sautéed Spanish onions
1 teaspoon Brownies Vege-C-Salt (see page 40)

1 tablespoon chopped fresh dill
½ pound haddock
½ pound scrod
½ pound sole
Boiling water
Cottage-Cheese Dumplings
1 teaspoon paprika
2 teaspoons minced fresh parsley

In a saucepan bring the consommé to a simmer. Add the next 7 ingredients and continue to simmer until the carrots are tender —approximately 15 minutes. Steam the fish over boiling water in another pan for 8 minutes. Add the dumplings to vegetable mixture and heat well. Distribute consommé, vegetables, and dumplings among 4 decorative kettles and add the fish equally to each kettle. Garnish with paprika and parsley.
Serves 4.

Cottage-Cheese Dumplings

2 eggs
½ cup Brownies Consommé (see page 53)
1½ cups Fearn Soy-O Mix
1 cup stone-ground cornmeal
¼ cup cottage cheese

2 tablespoons chopped fresh parsley
¼ teaspoon Italian Seasoning (see page 41)
¼ teaspoon garlic powder
2 quarts Brownies Soup Stock (see page 53)

In a bowl beat eggs thoroughly. Add cooked consommé and continue beating slowly while adding the remaining ingredients except for the stock. Bring stock to a boil and drop in by teaspoonfuls the dumpling mixture. Cook dumplings for approximately 10 minutes in a covered pot, then remove them with a slotted spoon.

POLYNESIAN PLATTER

1 pound fresh salmon,
  cut in 4 pieces
½ pound scrod fillets,
  cut in 4 pieces
½ pound sole fillets,
  cut in 4 pieces
Boiling water
½ teaspoon Spike
2 cups Polynesian Sauce
  (see page 46)
8 Rice Millet Cakes
4 cups Saffron Brown Rice
  (see page 152)

1 cup canned unsweetened
  pineapple chunks
¼ cup unsweetened toasted
  shredded coconut
1 teaspoon minced fresh
  parsley
1 teaspoon paprika
12 Tea Nuts
1 orange with peel, cut in
  8 slices and seeded
1 lemon with peel, cut in
  8 slices and seeded

Steam the 3 fishes over the boiling water for 5 minutes. Sprinkle with Spike and 1 cup of the hot Polynesian Sauce. Broil for 5 minutes. Arrange four serving plates with 2 Rice Cakes on each and cover with 1 cup of rice per plate. Place an assortment of fish on the rice and drizzle the remaining cup of Polynesian Sauce over the fish. Garnish with the remaining ingredients.
  Serves 4.

LEMON SOLE IN CARROT SAUCE

6 8-ounce portions lemon sole
¼ cup diced Spanish onion
1 large garlic clove, minced
2 tablespoons safflower oil
⅓ cup diced sweet red
  pepper
½ cup diced yellow squash
1 cup carrot juice
⅓ cup skim milk
1 tablespoon brown-rice flour
1 tablespoon lecithin
1 tablespoon soybean powder

½ cup shredded Cheddar
  cheese
½ teaspoon Brownies
  Vege-C-Salt (see page 40)
1 teaspoon Sesame Salt
  (see page 40)
¼ teaspoon garlic powder
¼ teaspoon nutmeg
¼ teaspoon sea salt
½ teaspoon basil
1 tablespoon snipped fresh
  chives

Arrange lemon-sole fillets in a baking dish. Sauté the onion and garlic in the oil. Add the pepper and squash and cook for 5 minutes. Add the remaining ingredients and stir thoroughly until thickened. Pour over lemon sole and bake for 30 minutes in a preheated 350° F. oven.

Serves 6.

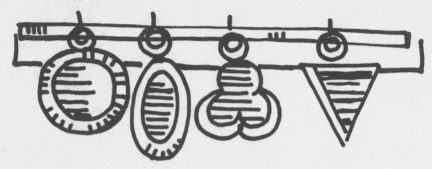

ROLLED SOLE IN ZUCCHINI SAUCE

8 8-ounce portions sole fillets
½ cup diced Spanish onion
⅓ cup diced celery
2 cloves garlic, minced
¼ cup sesame oil
1 cup sliced mushrooms
2 tablespoons tomato puree
2 tablespoons toasted sesame seeds
2 tablespoons toasted wheat germ
1 tablespoon lecithin
1 teaspoon Sesame Salt (see page 40)
½ teaspoon Brownies Vege-C-Salt (see page 40)
½ teaspoon caraway seeds
½ teaspoon oregano
1 egg
Zucchini Sauce

Arrange the fillets in a lightly oiled baking dish. Sauté the onion, celery, and garlic in the oil in a saucepan. Add the mushrooms and brown. Add the remaining ingredients except for the sauce and stir for 1 minute. Divide this mixture among the fillets and roll up tightly. Pour the sauce over all; cover and bake for 30 minutes in a preheated 350° F. oven.

Serves 8.

Zucchini Sauce

½ cup carrot juice
½ cup skim milk
1 teaspoon lecithin
1 tablespoon brown-rice flour
1 tablespoon soybean powder
⅓ cup shredded zucchini
   with skin

¼ teaspoon sea salt
¼ teaspoon garlic powder
¼ teaspoon Brownies
   Vege-C-Salt (see page 40)
¼ teaspoon Italian Seasoning
   (see page 41)

Combine the first 5 ingredients and mix until smooth in a saucepan. Stir constantly on a low fire until thickened. Add the remaining ingredients and stir for 1 minute.

SOLE CUCUMBER SQUARES

1 cup coarsely cut-up sole
1 cup Cucumber PUFA Sauce
   (see page 104)
2 eggs
½ cup alfalfa sprouts
¼ cup tomato puree
2 cloves garlic, minced
2 tablespoons brown-rice flour
2 tablespoons lecithin

2 teaspoons Sesame Salt
   (see page 40)
¼ teaspoon sea salt
1 teaspoon Brownies
   Vege-C-Salt (see page 40)
1 teaspoon Italian Seasoning
   (see page 41)
Few grindings of pepper
¼ cup sliced toasted almonds

Blend all the ingredients except for the almonds in the blender for 1 minute at high speed. Pour into a lightly oiled square baking pan. Top with almonds and bake in a preheated 350° F. oven for 30 minutes. Cut into 6 portions.
   Serves 6.

SOLE MOUSSE IN RED-PEPPER SHELLS

3 large sweet red peppers
1 cup coarsely cut-up sole
2 eggs
½ cup diced zucchini with skin
½ cup diced Spanish onion
¼ cup sliced celery
¼ cup fresh parsley
2 tablespoons fresh dill
¼ cup millet meal
1 tablespoon Krisp
1 tablespoon snipped fresh chives
½ teaspoon sea salt
½ teaspoon Brownies Vege-C-Salt (see page 40)
½ teaspoon garlic powder
½ teaspoon Italian Seasoning (see page 41)
¼ cup sliced filberts

Cut peppers in half, remove seeds and membranes, and wash. Place in a lightly oiled baking pan and set aside. Combine the next 8 ingredients in the blender for 1 minute at high speed. Pour into a bowl and add the remaining ingredients except for the filberts, mixing thoroughly. Divide mixture among the 6 pepper halves. Top with sliced filberts and bake in a preheated 375° F. oven for 40 minutes.

Serves 6.

SOLE SESAME CROQUETTES

1 cup ground sole
2 tablespoons diced Spanish onion
2 tablespoons diced pitted black olives
2 tablespoons diced canned water chestnuts
2 tablespoons minced fresh parsley
1 tablespoon minced fresh dill
¾ cup skim milk
2 tablespoons powdered nonfat dry milk
2 tablespoons soybean powder
2 tablespoons brown-rice flour
1 tablespoon millet meal
1 tablespoon sesame meal
1 egg
¼ cup toasted wheat germ
½ teaspoon sea salt
½ teaspoon garlic powder
¼ teaspoon Italian Seasoning (see page 41)
1 teaspoon Krisp
1 tablespoon vegetable-broth powder
¼ teaspoon celery seed
1 cup sesame seeds
Safflower oil

Combine the first 6 ingredients, mix thoroughly, and set aside. In a saucepan on a low fire mix the next 6 ingredients and stir until thick. Combine with fish mixture. Add the next 8 ingredients and stir thoroughly. Refrigerate for 30 minutes. Form into 12 croquettes, roll in sesame seeds, and brown in ½-inch-deep safflower oil on moderate heat.

Serves 6.

SOLE RICE BALLS

1 cup flaked cooked sole
1 cup Basic Brown Rice
  (see page 150)
2 eggs
¼ cup sliced toasted almonds
2 teaspoons snipped fresh
  chives
¼ cup Fearn Whole-Wheat
  Soy-O Mix

2 tablespoons lecithin
4 teaspoons *tamari* sauce
½ teaspoon garlic powder
½ teaspoon oregano
½ teaspoon basil
½ teaspoon nutmeg
Safflower oil

Combine all the ingredients but last and mix thoroughly. Form into small balls and brown in ½-inch-deep safflower oil on moderate heat.

Serves 6.

SOLE SCROD PUFF

½ cup coarsely cut-up sole
½ cup coarsely cut-up scrod
½ cup sliced carrots
⅓ cup diced Spanish onion
¼ cup sliced celery
½ cup water
¼ cup sesame oil
½ cup brown-rice flour
2 eggs
1 tablespoon snipped fresh
chives
¼ cup diced pimiento
¼ cup sliced pitted black
olives
½ teaspoon sea salt
½ teaspoon Brownies
Vege-C-Salt (see page 40)
½ teaspoon thyme
½ teaspoon Italian Seasoning
(see page 41)
¼ teaspoon garlic powder
¼ teaspoon celery seed
Paprika

Put the first 5 ingredients through a grinder and set aside.
Combine the water and oil in a saucepan until boiling, then
quickly add the brown-rice flour and stir until the dough forms
a ball and leaves the sides of the pan. Remove from heat, cool
to lukewarm, and beat in the eggs 1 at a time, beating thoroughly
after each addition. Blend with the fish mixture and mix very
well. Add the next 9 ingredients and stir thoroughly. Place in
a lightly oiled baking pan. Sprinkle with paprika and bake for
45 minutes in a preheated 400° F. oven.
Serves 6.

FLOUNDER IN A ROBE

2 1-pound whole flounders,
cleaned
¼ teaspoon Brownies
Vege-C-Salt (see page 40)
¼ teaspoon oregano
½ cup water
¼ cup safflower oil
¼ cup brown-rice flour
¼ cup Fearn Whole-Wheat
Soy-O Mix
¼ cup shredded Cheddar
cheese
2 eggs
½ teaspoon garlic powder
½ teaspoon Italian Seasoning
(see page 41)
¼ teaspoon sea salt
2 teaspoons snipped fresh
chives
1 tablespoon poppy seeds

Arrange the flounders in a lightly oiled baking dish. Sprinkle with the Vege-C-Salt and oregano and set aside. Bring the water and oil to a boil in a saucepan. Add the next 2 ingredients all at once and stir quickly until the dough forms a ball and leaves the sides of the pan. Remove from the heat and add the cheese, stirring constantly. Add the eggs 1 at a time, stirring thoroughly after each addition. Add the next 4 ingredients and mix well. Divide the mixture between the 2 flounders, covering each one completely except for the tail. Sprinkle with poppy seeds and bake for 30 minutes in a preheated 400° F. oven.

Serves 4.

TURBOT AVOCADO LOAF

2 1-pound turbot fillets	1 teaspoon sea salt
½ cup cubed avocado	½ teaspoon oregano
⅓ cup sliced bananas	½ teaspoon nutmeg
1 egg	½ teaspoon garlic powder
2 tablespoons *tahini*	¼ teaspoon celery seed
¼ cup cut-up celery	¼ teaspoon basil
2 tablespoons diced scallions	¼ cup diced pimiento
1 clove garlic	1 tablespoon snipped fresh
2 tablespoons brown-rice flour	chives
1 tablespoon lecithin	Paprika
1 tablespoon soybean powder	Toasted sesame seeds

Place 1 turbot fillet in the bottom of a lightly oiled loaf pan, fitting snugly. Combine the next 18 ingredients in the blender at medium speed for 1 minute. Pour on top of the turbot, spreading it smooth. Top with the other fillet and sprinkle with paprika and sesame seeds. Bake for 45 minutes in a preheated 375° F. oven.

Serves 6.

TAHITIAN BLUEFISH

6 8-ounce portions bluefish
fillets
1 cup orange juice
1 tablespoon brown-rice flour
1 tablespoon millet meal
2 tablespoons orange-blossom
honey
2 tablespoons *tahini*
1 clove garlic, minced
½ teaspoon sea salt
½ teaspoon Brownies
Vege-C-Salt (see page 40)

¼ teaspoon nutmeg
¼ teaspoon cumin
½ cup green peas
½ cup sliced bananas
⅓ cup canned unsweetened
pineapple chunks *
¼ cup diced pimiento
4 preserved kumquats, sliced
2 tablespoons diced scallions
Parsley Brown Rice
(see page 153) (optional)

Arrange the fillets in a baking dish and set aside. Combine the next 3 ingredients in a saucepan and stir until thickened. Add the remaining ingredients except for the rice and stir gently for 1 minute. Pour over the fish fillets and bake in a preheated 375° F. oven for 30 minutes. Nice to serve with Parsley Brown Rice.

Serves 6.

ORIENTAL CODFISH

2 pounds cod fillets
2 tablespoons Sesame Salt
(see page 40)
Boiling water
1¼ cups canned unsweetened
pineapple juice
1 tablespoon brown-rice flour
1 tablespoon millet meal
1 tablespoon sesame meal
2 tablespoons clover honey
1 tablespoon fresh lime juice
1 teaspoon *tamari* sauce

½ teaspoon sea salt
½ teaspoon garlic powder
¼ teaspoon powdered ginger
1 garlic clove, minced
½ cup orange chunks
⅓ cup canned unsweetened
pineapple chunks
½ cup snow peas
⅓ cup diced green pepper
¼ cup diced scallions
Basic Brown Rice
(see page 150) (optional)

Sprinkle the fillets with 1 tablespoon of the Sesame Salt and steam over the boiling water. Combine the remaining Sesame Salt with next 11 ingredients in a saucepan on a low fire and stir until thickened. Add the remaining ingredients except for the rice and cook for 10 minutes, stirring occasionally. Pour over steamed fish and serve, or if desired, place steamed fish on a bed of cooked brown rice and pour sauce over all.

Serves 4.

BAKED SCROD NEAPOLITAN

1 tablespoon snipped fresh chives
¼ teaspoon nutmeg
½ teaspoon paprika
6 8-ounce portions thick scrod fillets
1 cup diced red onion
½ cup diced celery
1 cup coarsely chopped tomatoes
2 cups diced eggplant
½ cup diced green pepper
1 cup diced red new potatoes with skin
½ cup diced carrots
½ cup sliced mushrooms
1 cup lima beans
¼ cup chopped fresh parsley
½ cup tomato juice
¼ cup safflower oil
1 teaspoon sea salt
1 teaspoon Sesame Salt (see page 40)
½ teaspoon garlic powder
½ teaspoon Italian Seasoning (see page 41)
¼ teaspoon Brownies Vege-C-Salt (see page 40)
¼ teaspoon celery seed

Sprinkle the chives, nutmeg, and paprika over the fish fillets and set aside. Combine all the remaining ingredients and mix thoroughly. Place in a large baking pan and arrange the fish fillets over the vegetable mixture. Cover pan tightly and bake in a preheated 375° F. oven for 45 minutes. Remove cover, baste with some of the liquid, and return to oven without covering for 30 minutes at 350° F.

Serves 6.

SCROD FILBERT FISH PIE

1 cup coarsely cut-up scrod
4 eggs
⅔ cup buttermilk
½ cup sliced carrots
¼ cup diced Spanish onion
⅓ cup whole filberts
2 tablespoons millet meal
2 tablespoons soybean powder
¼ cup diced pimiento
⅓ cup sliced pitted black
  olives

2 tablespoons minced fresh
  parsley
1 tablespoon Sesame Salt (see
  page 40)
2 teaspoons *tamari* sauce
½ teaspoon sea salt
½ teaspoon garlic powder
1 teaspoon basil
½ teaspoon Italian Seasoning
  (see page 41)
¼ teaspoon nutmeg
¼ teaspoon mace

Combine the first 8 ingredients in a blender and blend for 1 minute at high speed. Pour into a bowl and mix with the remaining ingredients, stirring lightly. Place in a lightly oiled deep pie pan and bake in a preheated 375° F. oven for 45 minutes.
  Serves 6.

PLANKED LAKE TROUT

2 pounds lake trout, cut in 4
  portions
6 tablespoons Brownies Fish
  Dressing (see page 42)
1 teaspoon paprika
1 medium avocado, peeled,
  pitted, and sliced
1 pimiento, cut in fine strips
1 cup canned button
  mushrooms

½ teaspoon Brownies
  Vege-C-Salt (see page 40)
4 cups Hawaiian Yam Pie
  filling (see page 200)
¼ cup toasted pignolias
2 teaspoons minced fresh
  parsley
1 lemon, quartered

Season fish with 3 tablespoons of the dressing, sprinkle with paprika, and place under preheated broiler for 10 minutes. Season avocado, pimiento, and mushrooms with the Vege-C-Salt and a little of the dressing. Put in a baking dish and broil for 5 minutes.

Pipe yam-pie filling around edges of 4 6-inch-wide planks or suitable dishes. Place broiled trout in center. Garnish with broiled vegetables and pour remaining dressing over fish and vegetables. Top with pignolias and parsley. Reheat if necessary and serve each portion with lemon quarter.

Serves 4.

PLANKED BASS

2 pounds striped bass, cut in 4 portions
6 tablespoons Brownies Fish Dressing (see page 42)
1 teaspoon paprika
2 green peppers, cut in strips
2 tomatoes, cut in 6 sections
12 canned artichoke hearts
4 cups Koos-Koos (see page 151)
¼ cup toasted sunflower seeds
2 teaspoons minced fresh parsley
1 lemon, quartered

Season fish with 3 tablespoons of the dressing, sprinkle with paprika, and place under preheated broiler for 10 minutes. Season peppers, tomatoes, and artichoke hearts with a little of the dressing and place in a baking dish under broiler for 5 minutes. Arrange Koos-Koos around edges of 4 6-inch-wide planks or suitable dishes. Place broiled bass in center. Garnish with broiled vegetables and pour remaining dressing over all. Top with sunflower seeds and parsley. Reheat if necessary and serve each portion with lemon quarter.

Serves 4.

STRIPED BASS IN MARINE MUSHROOM SAUCE

4 8-ounce portions striped-bass fillets
½ cup skim milk
1 egg
½ cup sliced mushrooms
¼ cup diced scallions
½ cup diced sweet red pepper
2 tablespoons minced fresh *cilantro* (or fresh parsley)
2 tablespoons sesame oil

2 tablespoons powdered nonfat dry milk
2 tablespoons soybean powder
2 tablespoons sesame-sunflower meal
1 tablespoon lecithin
½ teaspoon sea salt
½ teaspoon garlic powder
½ teaspoon oregano
¼ teaspoon cumin
¼ teaspoon mace
¼ cup diced pimiento

Arrange the bass fillets in a baking dish. Combine the remaining ingredients except for the pimiento in the blender and blend for 1 minute at high speed. Pour over the fillets and top with the pimiento. Cover and bake in a preheated 350° F. oven for 30 minutes.

Serves 4.

SPINACH-TOPPED RED SNAPPER

4 8-ounce portions red-snapper fillets

½ recipe Spinach Cheese Stuffed Salmon filling (see page 103)
¼ cup sunflower seeds

Arrange the red-snapper fillets in a baking dish. Divide the spinach-cheese mixture on top of the fillets. Top with the sunflower seeds. Bake for 30 minutes in a preheated 375° F. oven.

Serves 4.

POMPANO AMANDINE

1 2-pound pompano
Boiling water
3 tablespoons Brownies Fish
  Dressing (see page 42)
¼ teaspoon paprika

2 tablespoons toasted sliced
  almonds
1 teaspoon minced fresh
  parsley

Steam pompano over boiling water for 10 minutes. Place in a
baking dish and baste with the dressing. Sprinkle with paprika;
broil in a preheated broiler for 3 minutes. Top with toasted
almonds and garnish with parsley.
  Serves 2.

SPINACH CHEESE STUFFED SALMON

4 thick salmon steaks
1 cup finely chopped spinach
¼ cup finely diced canned
  water chestnuts
¼ cup diced scallions
¼ cup minced fresh parsley
2 tablespoons minced fresh dill
⅔ cup shredded Cheddar
  cheese
3 tablespoons sesame meal

¼ cup carrot juice
½ teaspoon Brownies
  Vege-C-Salt (see page 40)
¼ teaspoon sea salt
¼ teaspoon garlic powder
¼ teaspoon nutmeg
½ teaspoon tarragon
2 teaspoons Krisp
Fresh lime juice (optional)

Slice each salmon steak in half lengthwise and set aside. Combine the remaining ingredients except for the lime juice and mix
thoroughly. Divide the mixture among 4 salmon-steak halves.
Top with remaining 4 salmon-steak halves and arrange in a
baking dish. Squeeze a little fresh lime juice on top of fish if
desired. Cover and bake for 30 minutes in a preheated 375° F.
oven.
  Serves 4.

DOUBLE SALMON TOPPER

4 8-ounce portions salmon
  steaks
1 cup coarsely cut-up salmon
½ cup carrot juice
2 eggs
2 tablespoons diced scallions
2 tablespoons diced Spanish
  onion

1 teaspoon sea salt
¼ teaspoon nutmeg
¼ teaspoon allspice
½ teaspoon oregano
2 tablespoons toasted sesame
  seeds .

Arrange the salmon steaks in a lightly oiled baking dish. Combine the remaining ingredients except for the sesame seeds in a blender at medium speed until smooth. Divide the mixture among the salmon steaks, covering them completely. Sprinkle with sesame seeds and bake for 30 minutes in a preheated 350° F. oven.

Serves 4.

SAUCY CUCUMBER SALMON

4 8-ounce portions salmon
  steaks
Cucumber PUFA Sauce

2 teaspoons snipped fresh
  chives

Place the salmon in a baking dish. Pour the sauce over the salmon and sprinkle with the chives. Cover and bake in a preheated 350° F. oven for 30 minutes.

Serves 4.

Cucumber PUFA Sauce

¼ cup Brownies PUFA
  Dressing (see page 42)
1 egg
½ cup diced cucumber with
  skin

2 tablespoons diced scallions
1 garlic clove
⅛ teaspoon turmeric
⅛ teaspoon mace

Combine all ingredients in blender at high speed for 1 minute.

SALMON EGGPLANT TOWERS

4 baby eggplants
½ cup diced Spanish onion
¼ cup diced scallions
2 garlic cloves, minced
¼ cup sesame oil
½ cup sliced mushrooms
⅓ cup diced sweet red
  pepper
⅓ cup diced canned water
  chestnuts
¼ cup minced fresh parsley
2 tablespoons minced fresh dill
⅓ cup tomato puree
1 tablespoon snipped fresh
  chives

1 cup drained canned salmon
⅓ cup toasted pignolias
¼ cup toasted wheat germ
¼ cup pecan meal
½ teaspoon sea salt
½ teaspoon Brownies
  Vege-C-Salt (see page 40)
½ teaspoon Italian Seasoning
  (see page 41)
½ teaspoon basil
¼ teaspoon cumin
2 teaspoons *tamari* sauce
2 tablespoons toasted sesame
  seeds

Cut each eggplant in half. Scoop out flesh, cut in small dice, and set both shells and diced flesh aside. Sauté the onion, scallions, and garlic in the oil in a deep saucepan. Add the mushrooms and pepper and stir for 5 minutes. Add the reserved diced eggplant and the next 5 ingredients and cook for 10 minutes on a low fire. Add the remaining ingredients except for the sesame seeds and stir well. Stuff each eggplant shell, mounding high. Sprinkle with sesame seeds. Place in a baking dish and bake in a preheated 375° F. oven for 30 minutes.

Serves 4.

TERRIFIC TUNA LOAF

1 7-ounce can water-packed
  salt-free tuna, drained
½ cup cut-up string beans
¼ cup diced Spanish onion
¼ cup sliced celery
¼ cup diced green pepper
1 garlic clove
2 eggs
⅓ cup creamed cottage
  cheese
¼ cup diced pimiento

¼ cup diced canned water
  chestnuts
2 tablespoons soybean powder
2 tablespoons millet meal
½ teaspoon sea salt
½ teaspoon Italian Seasoning
  (see page 41)
½ teaspoon basil
¼ teaspoon mace
¼ teaspoon garlic powder
⅓ cup shredded Cheddar
  cheese

Put the first 6 ingredients through a grinder. Combine with
the remaining ingredients except for the cheese and blend thoroughly. Place in a lightly oiled loaf pan and top with the cheese.
Bake in a preheated 375° F. oven for 45 minutes.
    Serves 6.

AN ENTRÉE TO VEGETARIANISM
(Vegetable Main Dishes)

Since Adam and Eve there have been many celebrated vege-
tarians, as various as Mahatma Gandhi, George Bernard Shaw,
the poet Percy Shelley, actress Gloria Swanson, and the Beatles.
Lately, with the return-to-the-land movement that is one of the
by-products of the Age of Ecology, their ranks have been swell-
ing dramatically. The young, particularly, seem to be turned on

by meatless diets, certifying them not only as nutritionally superior but also as in tune with the cosmos.

Religious influences aside, there have always been those who reasoned that if the animals man eats get all *their* nourishment from vegetables, wouldn't it be more logical for man to go directly to the same source? For aesthetic and humane considerations, legions have put down the killing and eating of animals as barbaric. Countless millions of others have been too poor to afford to eat meat. And there are those who have had dietary restrictions imposed by illness or body malfunction.

All these factors spark the current fervor for vegetarian meals, but there is also a growing conviction that meat-eating exacts a far heavier toll than that which we pay the butcher. For the cruelty and death we inflict on our four-legged friends, the new truth holds, we who eat their flesh can expect to be poisoned—not just because of the poisons they've taken in their food but also because of what is in their systems just before they're slaughtered.

We personally do not abstain entirely from eating meat, but Brownies began as a fruit-juice bar and evolved as a vegetarian restaurant. If we tried now to introduce meat or poultry dishes on our menus, there would probably be a howl of protest which could be heard in every health-foods store, commune, and ashram clear around the world.

Depending on who is defining it, vegetarianism can signify everything from a diet of legumes, fruits, and nuts to one including the whole spectrum of foods exclusive of meat and poultry. We ourselves incline toward the latter definition.

Is a vegetarian diet safe? Can it provide all the nutrients necessary for good health? Absolutely. If it contains fish, milk, eggs, or soybeans, you need have no fear of protein deficiency. These foods all contain "perfect" proteins. The vegetable kingdom also provides us with all the vitamins and minerals essential to the human diet. Our only caution would be against the narrower concepts of vegetarianism such as the macrobiotic diets, which are long on seaweed and brown rice but skimpy on protein.

Actually, every recipe in this book is vegetarian (according to the definition we accept). Here, however, we present some special main dishes that we have developed over the years and have featured on Brownies menus.

BEAN BEEF BAKE

1 15-ounce can soybeans in tomato sauce
1 14-ounce can Beef-Style Soyameat, diced
½ cup sautéed onions
2 eggs
¼ cup diced green pepper
¼ cup powdered nonfat dry milk
1 cup Brownies Tomato Sauce (see page 46)
½ teaspoon Italian Seasoning (see page 41)
¼ teaspoon dill
6 tablespoons grated cheese
½ cup toasted wheat germ
1 tablespoon sesame seeds

Combine first 9 ingredients and ¼ cup of the cheese in a large bowl, mixing thoroughly. Combine well reserved 2 tablespoons cheese with the remaining ingredients to make topping. Pour bean mixture into lightly oiled baking pan, sprinkle with topping, and bake in a preheated 350° F. oven about 30 minutes.
Serves 6.

SOY-NUT MEATBALLS

1 16-ounce can soybeans in tomato sauce
1 13½-ounce can VegeBurger, mashed
2 eggs
¼ cup soybean granules
2 tablespoons rice polishings
3 tablespoons *tamari* sauce
2 tablespoons safflower oil
½ cup finely diced onion
¼ cup finely diced green pepper
¼ teaspoon tarragon
¼ teaspoon savory
Toasted Soy Nuts
Soybean granules
Nutty Sauce (see page 47)

Put soybeans in blender and blend until smooth. Pour into mixing bowl and add VegeBurger, eggs, soybean granules, rice polishings, and *tamari* sauce. Mix thoroughly. Sauté in the 2 tablespoons oil the onion and green pepper. Add to first mixture, along with tarragon and savory. Mix thoroughly. Form into 24 balls, enclosing 3 or 4 toasted Soy Nuts in the center of each ball. Sprinkle each ball with soybean granules and let dry about 10 minutes. Brown each ball in safflower oil. Serve with Nutty Sauce. Serves 10–12.

PIQUANT CHICKEN-STYLE SOYAMEAT IN LEMON SAUCE

2 13-ounce cans Chicken-Style Soyameat
2 eggs
⅓ cup grated Monterey jack cheese
¼ cup grated Cheddar cheese
¼ cup toasted sesame seeds
¼ cup chopped black olives
¼ cup toasted wheat germ
¼ teaspoon sea salt
¼ teaspoon garlic powder
¼ teaspoon Italian Seasoning (see page 41)
Dash of freshly ground pepper
Lemon Sauce

Open the cans of Soyameat and separate the slices. Beat eggs lightly, add both cheeses, and blend thoroughly. Stir in remaining ingredients and mix well. Make sandwiches by dividing cheese mixture among half the Soyameat slices; cover with remaining slices. Put in baking pan and cover with Lemon Sauce. Bake in a preheated 375° F. oven for 20 minutes.
    Serves 8.

Lemon Sauce

2 eggs
2 tablespoons fresh lemon juice
1 cup Brownies Consommé (see page 53)
¼ teaspoon oregano
¼ teaspoon Spike
¼ cup chopped pimiento

Beat eggs until frothy, then add remaining ingredients and mix well.

CRUSTY SKALLOP CHEESE PIE

1½ cups cottage cheese
2 eggs
½ cup California tomato juice
½ cup soybean granules
2 tablespoons grated Cheddar cheese
½ teaspoon Italian Seasoning (see page 41)
¼ teaspoon sea salt

¼ teaspoon dill
¼ teaspoon garlic powder
Few grindings of pepper
Cornmeal Crust (see page 169)
1 20-ounce can Vegetable Skallops, drained
6 cherry tomatoes, halved
¼ teaspoon sesame oil

Combine in mixing bowl first 10 ingredients and mix thoroughly. Spread thin layer of this mixture in bottom of Cornmeal Crust in a 10-inch pie pan. Cut Skallops in small chunks and put on top of cheese mixture. Cover with remaining cheese mixture, spreading it evenly and smoothly. Arrange the cherry tomatoes on the outer edge of the pie, putting one in the center. Lightly brush each tomato half with oil. Bake in a preheated 350° F. oven about 45 minutes or until center of pie is firm to the touch.
Serves 6–8.

BROWNIES BLINTZES

6 eggs
9 tablespoons raw sugar
1 teaspoon sea salt
1 cup milk
1 cup unbleached white–and–wheat-germ flour

1½ pounds farmer cheese
3 ounces cream cheese
1 teaspoon vanilla extract
Sour cream

Whip 4 of the eggs, 1 tablespoon of the sugar, the salt, and the milk thoroughly in a bowl. Continue whipping and add the flour gradually until mixture is smooth. Let rest for 15 minutes. Lightly oil an 8-inch frying pan and heat on a low fire. Spread 3 tablespoons batter in the pan to form a crepe, and when underside is lightly browned, flip over and lightly brown the other side. Continue until all the batter is used, stacking crepes on top of one another. Set aside. Combine the reserved eggs and sugar with both cheeses and the vanilla extract in an electric mixer at medium speed and mix for 5 minutes. Place ¼ cup of the cheese filling on each crepe. Fold in the sides of the crepe and roll up loosely. Brown lightly on both sides in a lightly oiled skillet on a low fire. Serve warm with sour cream on the side.

Serves 6.

BAKED CHEESE FLUFF

2 pounds farmer cheese
½ cup shredded Cheddar
  cheese
3 eggs

1 teaspoon Brownies
  Vege-C-Salt (see page 40)
1 cup Viobin Wheat Germ
Cheddar-Cheese Sauce

Combine all the ingredients except for ½ cup of the wheat germ in an electric mixer at medium speed for 5 minutes. Form into patties, using ½ cup of the mixture for each fluff, and roll in the remaining wheat germ. Bake for 15 minutes in a preheated 350° F. oven. Serve with Cheddar-Cheese Sauce.

Serves 12.

Cheddar-Cheese Sauce

2 cups milk
1 cup shredded Cheddar
  cheese
1 cup carrot juice

1½ teaspoons Brownies
  Vege-C-Salt (see page 40)
½ cup unbleached white–and–
  wheat-germ flour

Scald the milk in a saucepan. Add the cheese and stir on a low fire until melted. Combine the remaining ingredients until smooth and add slowly, stirring constantly, to the milk-cheese mixture until thickened.

CHEESE MEDLEY IN MILLET CRUST

1 cup cottage cheese
1 egg
1 cup Basic Lentils (see page 133)
½ cup shredded carrots
½ teaspoon sea salt
¼ teaspoon thyme

⅛ teaspoon celery seed
⅛ teaspoon Italian Seasoning (see page 41)
⅛ teaspoon garlic powder
Millet Crust (see page 169)
2 tablespoons soybean granules

In mixing bowl mix cottage cheese with egg until smooth. Add the lentils and carrots and mix well. Stir in the next 5 ingredients and blend thoroughly. Pour into Millet Crust in a 9-inch pie pan and sprinkle with the soybean granules. Bake in a preheated 375° F. oven about 45 minutes.

Serves 6–8.

VEGETABLE CHOW MEIN

¼ cup soybean oil
2 cups Brownies Consommé (see page 53)
½ cup diced tomatoes
1 cup sliced mushrooms
4 cups diced Spanish onion
4 cups diagonally thinly sliced celery
3 cups thinly sliced cabbage
1 cup shredded carrots

2 cups mung-bean sprouts
1 13-ounce can Chicken-Style Soyameat, sliced thin
1 tablespoon Brownies Vege-C-Salt (see page 40)
1 tablespoon Bakon Yeast
2 tablespoons *tamari* sauce
2 tablespoons brown-rice flour
Basic Brown Rice (see page 150)

In a large skillet combine the first 6 ingredients on high heat, stirring occasionally for approximately 8 minutes or until celery is crisply tender. Add the cabbage and carrots and cook for 4 minutes. Stir in the next 4 ingredients and cook until simmering. Combine the *tamari* sauce and brown-rice flour and add to the simmering ingredients, stirring until thickened. Serve with brown rice.

Serves 6–8.

VEGETABLE CUTLETS

1 20-ounce can Tastee Cuts, drained
2 eggs
¼ cup water
½ teaspoon sea salt
¼ teaspoon paprika
¼ teaspoon Italian Seasoning (see page 41)
⅛ teaspoon garlic powder
1½ cups Brownies Breading Mix (see page 169)
¼ cup soybean powder
1 cup soybean oil
Brownies Tomato Sauce (see page 46) (optional)

Separate the Tastee Cuts. Combine the next 6 ingredients. Put the breading mix and soybean powder on large flat plates. Heat the oil in a large skillet on a moderate fire. Dip each Tastee Cut in the soybean powder, then dip in the egg wash, and last, coat with the breading mix. Let them dry about 5 minutes and then brown on both sides in the oil. Serve with Brownies Tomato Sauce if desired.

Serves 4–6.

EGGPLANT STEAK

1 large eggplant
2 eggs
¼ cup water
½ teaspoon sea salt
¼ teaspoon paprika
¼ teaspoon Italian Seasoning (see page 41)
⅛ teaspoon garlic powder
¼ cup soybean powder
1½ cups Brownies Breading Mix (see page 169)
1 cup soybean oil
Brownies Tomato Sauce (see page 46) (optional)

Peel and slice eggplant lengthwise about ½-inch thick. Combine the next 6 ingredients in a small shallow mixing bowl. Put the soybean powder and the breading mix each on large flat plates. Pour the oil into a large skillet and heat on a moderate fire. Dip each eggplant slice in powder, then immerse in the egg wash, and last, coat each side with the breading mix. Let dry about 5 minutes, then brown on both sides in oil. Serve with Brownies Tomato Sauce if desired.

Serves 4–6.

STUFFED ELEGANT EGGPLANT

1 large eggplant
½ cup soybean oil
½ cup finely diced celery
4 scallions, diced
1 large tomato, diced
½ teaspoon paprika
2 tablespoons chopped fresh
  cilantro (or fresh parsley)
1 14-ounce can Beef-Style
  Soyameat, diced

1 cup Basic Lentils (see page
  133)
⅓ cup soybean granules
¼ teaspoon Italian Seasoning
  (see page 41)
¼ teaspoon Spike
¼ teaspoon oregano
⅛ teaspoon garlic powder
2 tablespoons grated Cheddar
  cheese
Paprika

Cut eggplant in half lengthwise. Leaving a ½-inch border, scoop out flesh, dice into small cubes, and set aside. In a large frying pan sauté in the oil the celery, scallions, and tomato. Stir in cubed eggplant and cook about 10 minutes. Remove from fire, add next 9 ingredients, and mix thoroughly. Divide mixture between the two eggplant shells. Sprinkle cheese on top of each one. Lightly sprinkle paprika over cheese. Bake 1 hour in a preheated 375° F. oven.

Serves 4–6.

SCRUMPTIOUS EGGPLANT BAKE

¾ cup safflower oil
4 cups cubed eggplant (approximately 1 large eggplant)
¾ cup diced onion
2 garlic cloves, minced
½ cup diced celery
½ cup diced green pepper
¾ cup diced pimiento
1 15-ounce can Boston-baked–
  style soybeans

½ cup ground pecans
½ cup sesame-sunflower meal
1 egg
2 tablespoons minced fresh
  parsley
1 tablespoon minced fresh dill
1 teaspoon Spike
½ teaspoon basil
¼ teaspoon grated lemon peel
½ cup pumpkin seeds

In a large skillet stir ½ cup of the oil and the eggplant for several minutes. Cover and cook for 10 minutes. In another skillet heat the remaining oil and sauté the onion, garlic, celery, green pepper, and ½ cup of the pimiento. Combine ingredients from both skillets in a large mixing bowl and blend thoroughly. Add the remaining ingredients except for the pumpkin seeds and reserved pimiento and mix lightly. Pat into a lightly oiled 10-inch pie pan and top with the pumpkin seeds and pimiento. Bake in a preheated 350° F. oven for 1 hour.

Serves 6.

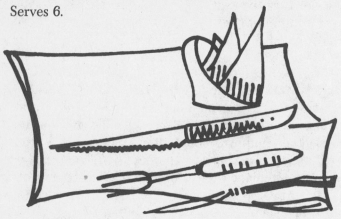

WHAM EGGPLANT STACKS

8 large slices Eggplant Steak (see page 114)
1 package Wham
½ cup drained cooked spinach

8 slices Cheddar cheese
Brownies Tomato Sauce (see page 46)

Cut each eggplant slice in half. Top each half with 1 slice Wham. Cover with 1 tablespoon spinach. Top with 1 slice cheese and cover with the other eggplant-slice half. When all the eggplant stacks are assembled, place in a lightly oiled baking pan and bake in a preheated 350° F. oven for 15 minutes. Serve with Brownies Tomato Sauce.

Serves 8.

STUFFED PEPPERS

6 large green peppers
Boiling water
4 cups Basic Brown Rice (see page 150)
1 13½-ounce can VegeBurger
1 cup sautéed diced onions
1 cup sunflower meal
2 teaspoons Brownies Vege-C-Salt (see page 40)
1 tablespoon Bakon Yeast
4 cups Brownies Tomato Sauce (see page 46)

Cut the peppers in half, wash, and remove seeds and membranes. Blanch for 5 minutes in boiling water and set aside. Combine the next 6 ingredients in a bowl and mix thoroughly. Divide between the pepper halves and place them in a lightly oiled baking pan. Cover with the tomato sauce and bake for 30 minutes in a preheated 350° F. oven.
Serves 12.

STUFFED PEPPERS IN MARENGO SAUCE

4 large green peppers
1 14-ounce can Vegelona, diced small
1 cup Basic Brown Rice (see page 150)
2 eggs
2 tablespoons chopped fresh parsley
½ cup diced onion
¼ cup diced celery
2 tablespoons soybean oil
½ teaspoon sea salt
¼ teaspoon oregano
¼ teaspoon Italian Seasoning (see page 41)
¼ teaspoon basil
¼ cup soybean granules
Marengo Sauce

Cut peppers in half, wash, remove seeds and membranes, and set aside. Combine in a mixing bowl the Vegelona, rice, and eggs, mix thoroughly, and blend in the parsley. Sauté the onion and celery in the oil and add to first mixture. Add the next 4 ingredients and mix well. Divide mixture among the pepper halves, sprinkling some soybean granules on top of each one. Place peppers in a lightly oiled baking pan and bake in a preheated 375° F. oven for 45 minutes. Serve with Marengo Sauce.
Serves 8.

Marengo Sauce

2 scallions, diced fine
1 garlic clove, minced
½ cup sliced mushrooms
2 tablespoons soybean oil
2 tablespoons minced fresh
  parsley
½ cup Brownies Tomato Sauce
  (see page 46)

½ cup sliced pitted black
  olives
1 teaspoon Stripple Zips
¼ teaspoon Spike
1 tablespoon green-banana
  flour
1 tablespoon Bakon Yeast
½ cup liquid from olives

Sauté the scallions, garlic, and mushrooms in the oil. Add the parsley, tomato sauce, olives, Stripple Zips, and Spike, stirring constantly. Combine the banana flour, Bakon Yeast, and olive liquid and slowly add to the hot sauce, stirring until thick.

NUTTY MUSHROOM SQUARES

½ cup diced onion
⅓ cup soybean oil
4 cups finely diced mushrooms
1 cup chopped spinach
¾ cup sunflower meal
¾ cup toasted wheat germ
¾ cup toasted ground
  walnuts

1 egg
1 teaspoon sea salt
1 teaspoon vegetable-broth
  powder
¼ teaspoon Italian Seasoning
  (see page 41)
¼ teaspoon oregano

Sauté the onion in the oil for 5 minutes. Add mushrooms and sauté for 10 minutes, stirring occasionally. Add spinach and cook several minutes. Remove from fire and transfer to a mixing bowl. Add ½ cup of the sunflower meal, ¼ cup of the wheat germ, and remaining 6 ingredients and blend together. Put into a lightly oiled large square baking pan. Combine reserved wheat germ and sunflower meal and sprinkle on top. Bake in a preheated 350° F. oven for 30 minutes.
    Serves 4–6.

MUSHROOM PATTIES

½ cup diced Spanish onion
1 cup sliced mushrooms
¼ cup soybean oil
1 13½-ounce can VegeBurger
2 cups Basic Brown Rice (see page 150)
2 eggs

2 tablespoons Stripple Zips
¾ teaspoon sea salt
¼ teaspoon Italian Seasoning (see page 41)
¼ teaspoon garlic powder
2 tablespoons minced fresh dill
½ cup toasted sesame seeds

Sauté the onion and mushrooms in the oil. In a mixing bowl combine this mixture with the remaining ingredients except for the sesame seeds. Shape into 12 patties and dip each patty in sesame seeds. Place in a lightly oiled baking pan and bake for 30 minutes in a preheated 350° F. oven.

Serves 6.

STUFFED CABBAGE

1 medium cabbage
Boiling water
4 cups Koos-Koos (see page 151)
1 13-ounce can Chicken-Style Soyameat, diced
1 cup sautéed onions

1 cup sunflower meal
2 teaspoons *tamari* sauce
1 teaspoon Sesame Salt (see page 40)
1 tablespoon Bakon Yeast
4 cups Brownies Tomato Sauce (see page 46)

Cut out the core of the cabbage and discard along with any tough outer leaves. In a large kettle of boiling water cook cabbage until the leaves separate easily. Drain and separate the leaves. Cut out hard veins, if any, and set aside. Combine the next 7 ingredients in a bowl and blend thoroughly. Place ½ cup of the filling on each cabbage leaf and roll up tightly, enclosing filling completely. Continue until filling is used up. Place rolls seam side down in a lightly oiled baking pan. Cover with the tomato sauce and bake for 30 minutes in a preheated 300° F. oven.

Serves 12.

HUBBARD-SQUASH TOWERS

1 Hubbard squash (about 2½ pounds) or 2 large acorn squashes
Soybean oil
⅓ cup finely diced scallions
¼ cup soybean oil
½ cup Koos-Koos (see page 151)
1 egg

1 14-ounce can Proteena, mashed
2 tablespoons toasted sesame seeds
½ teaspoon Krisp
½ teaspoon basil
Few grindings of pepper
Sunflower seeds

Cut squash in half and remove seeds. Scoop out the insides of the squash, leaving a 1-inch border, and dice flesh fine. Lightly rub oil over the outside of each shell. Place in a preheated 350° F. oven cut side down on foil and bake for 45 minutes. Remove from oven, turn upside down, and cool. Sauté the scallions in the oil, add the diced squash, and stir for 5 minutes. Remove from fire and put into a large mixing bowl. Add the next 7 ingredients and mix thoroughly. Divide between squash halves, mounding mixture high, and covering it with sunflower seeds. Lightly oil cut edge of squash, place in baking dish, and bake in a preheated 350° F. oven for 45 minutes.
Serves 6–8.

CARROT ASPARAGUS SPOKES

½ cup diced onion
¼ cup soybean oil
4 cups shredded carrots
¼ cup finely chopped fresh cilantro (or fresh parsley)
3 eggs
¼ cup toasted sesame seeds
¼ cup grated cheese
¼ cup soybean granules
½ teaspoon rosemary

¼ teaspoon Salad Herbs (see page 41)
¼ teaspoon grated orange peel
1 teaspoon sea salt
12 cooked asparagus spears
¼ cup pecan meal
¼ cup sesame-sunflower meal
3 tablespoons toasted sesame seeds
2 tablespoons shredded carrots

Sauté onion in the oil and add to the carrots. Stir in *cilantro* and eggs and mix well. Add next 7 ingredients and mix lightly. Arrange half of the carrot mixture in a lightly oiled pie pan. Arrange the asparagus spears in spoke fashion on top. Cover with remaining carrot mixture. Combine remaining ingredients and sprinkle on top. Bake for 45 minutes in a preheated 350° F. oven.
Serves 6–8.

STRING-BEAN SENSATION

1 cup diced Spanish onion
3 scallions, diced fine
¼ cup safflower oil
1½ cups finely cut-up string beans
3 cups Basic Brown Rice (see page 150)
½ cup shredded carrots
1 egg
⅓ cup pecan meal
⅓ cup sesame-sunflower meal
¼ cup minced fresh parsley

1 teaspoon Spike
½ teaspoon Italian Seasoning (see page 41)
½ teaspoon sea salt
¼ teaspoon rosemary
⅛ teaspoon garlic powder
Few grindings of pepper
¼ cup toasted sesame seeds
2 tablespoons toasted wheat germ
2 tablespoons sesame-sunflower meal

Sauté the onion and scallions in the oil until light brown. Add string beans and stir for several minutes. Remove from fire and put into a mixing bowl. Add the next 12 ingredients and mix thoroughly. Put into a lightly oiled large loaf pan. Combine remaining ingredients and sprinkle on top of loaf. Bake in a preheated 375° F. oven for 45 minutes.
Serves 6–8.

SAUERKRAUT CUPS

1 19-ounce can VegeBurger
½ cup drained chopped
    sauerkraut
2 eggs
¼ cup toasted wheat germ
½ cup Brownies Tomato Sauce
    (see page 46)

¼ cup sautéed onions
⅛ teaspoon garlic powder
¼ teaspoon basil
2 tablespoons chopped fresh
    parsley

Combine all ingredients thoroughly, then divide among 12 muffin cups that have been lightly oiled or lined with paper liners. Bake until brown—about 30 minutes—in a preheated 375° F. oven.
Serves 6–8.

COCONUT KALE SQUARES

3 scallions, diced fine
½ cup finely diced
    mushrooms
¼ cup safflower oil
¼ cup minced fresh
    cilantro (or fresh parsley)
2 cups cooked kale
2 eggs
¼ cup soybean granules
¼ cup toasted wheat germ
½ cup Basic Mung Beans
    (see page 131)

1 teaspoon sea salt
½ teaspoon Bakon Yeast
¼ teaspoon dill
¼ teaspoon Spike
⅛ teaspoon garlic powder
½ cup skim milk
⅓ cup shredded unsweetened
    coconut
¼ cup toasted wheat germ
¼ cup shredded unsweetened
    coconut

Sauté the scallions and mushrooms in the oil. Add *cilantro* and kale and mix thoroughly. Put in a large mixing bowl and add the next 9 ingredients. Scald the milk, remove from fire, and add coconut. Let stand for a few minutes and incorporate into kale mixture. Put into a lightly oiled large square baking pan. Top with combined wheat germ and coconut. Bake in a preheated 350° F. oven for 45 minutes.
Serves 6.

APPLE MOUNDS

1 19-ounce can VegeChee
1 cup Basic Brown Rice
(see page 150)
1 egg
⅔ cup toasted sliced filberts

1½ teaspoons vegetable-broth
powder
¼ teaspoon rosemary
¾ teaspoon grated orange peel
4 McIntosh apples
1½ cups apple juice

In mixing bowl mash the VegeChee smooth. Add the rice, egg, filberts, ½ teaspoon of the vegetable-broth powder, rosemary, and ½ teaspoon of the orange peel and mix thoroughly. Cut each apple in half and remove core. Place in a deep baking pan and mound about ⅓ cup of filling on top of each apple half. Combine reserved vegetable-broth powder and orange peel with the apple juice and pour over the apples. Bake for 1 hour in a preheated 350° F. oven, basting apples with pan juices several times. Serves 8.

VEGETARIAN LASAGNA

1 pound ricotta cheese
2 eggs
1 teaspoon sea salt
1 teaspoon Italian Seasoning
 (see page 41)
½ teaspoon garlic powder
½ cup minced fresh parsley
Dash of pepper
3 cups Brownies Tomato
 Sauce (see page 46)

1½ cups Choplet Burger,
 mashed
1 tablespoon Krisp
1 tablespoon Bakon Yeast
1 1-pound package lasagna
 noodles, cooked, drained,
 and covered with cold water
½ cup shredded Cheddar
 cheese

In a mixing bowl combine ricotta cheese, eggs, salt, Italian Seasoning, ¼ teaspoon of the garlic powder, parsley, and pepper, mixing well. In another bowl combine tomato sauce, Choplet Burger, Krisp, Bakon Yeast, and remaining garlic powder. Oil a large, deep baking pan lightly and lay 3 or 4 lasagna noodles in bottom of pan. Alternate cheese mixture and tomato mixture with layers of noodles, ending with tomato mixture. Sprinkle the Cheddar on top of tomato mixture and bake in a preheated 300° F. oven for 45 minutes.
  Serves 12.

RAVIOLI ROLL

2 pounds ricotta cheese
1 cup drained cooked spinach
¼ cup minced fresh parsley
4 eggs
2 teaspoons sea salt
½ cup toasted wheat germ
½ teaspoon garlic powder

1 teaspoon oregano
2 tablespoons Krisp
1 1-pound package lasagna
 noodles, cooked, drained,
 and covered with cold water
4 cups Brownies Tomato
 Sauce (see page 46)

Combine first 9 ingredients in a large mixing bowl and mix thoroughly. Remove noodles from the water, spread each one with about ½ cup of cheese mixture, and roll up loosely. Place seam side down in a lightly oiled baking pan. Cover with tomato sauce. Bake in a preheated 300° F. oven for 30 minutes.
  Serves 12.

COUSCOUS BROCCOLI NUT WEDGE

2 cups Koos-Koos
(see page 151)
¼ cup soybean oil
½ cup diced onion
2 cups chopped broccoli
1 egg
⅓ cup toasted ground
chickpeas
⅓ cup toasted ground
cashews

½ teaspoon sea salt
½ teaspoon Spike
¼ teaspoon cumin
⅛ teaspoon garlic powder
1 teaspoon Krisp
2 teaspoons toasted sesame
seeds
3 tablespoons toasted wheat
germ

Put Koos-Koos in mixing bowl and set aside. In the oil sauté the onion and broccoli for about 10 minutes, covering pan. Add to Koos-Koos and blend thoroughly. Beat in the egg, ground chickpeas, and ground cashews. Stir in the next 5 ingredients and mix well. Spread mixture in a lightly oiled 10-inch pie pan. Combine the sesame seeds and wheat germ and sprinkle on top. Bake in a preheated 350° F. oven for about 30 minutes.
Serves 6–8.

MIXED-UP MILLET LOAF

2 cups Basic Millet
(see page 152)
2 eggs
2 cups shredded carrots
1 15½-ounce can green
soybeans
6 tablespoons grated cheese

⅓ cup toasted cashew meal
¼ cup toasted sesame seeds
1 teaspoon Spike
½ teaspoon vegetable-broth
powder
½ teaspoon basil
¼ teaspoon grated orange peel

Combine in a mixing bowl the millet and eggs, stirring thoroughly. Add carrots and soybeans and mix well. Lightly stir in ¼ cup of the cheese and the remaining ingredients and mix completely. Put into a lightly oiled loaf pan and top with the remaining cheese. Bake in a preheated 375° F. oven for 1 hour.
Serves 6–8.

SOY, GARBANZO, 'N' MILLET PIE

1 15-ounce can green
soybeans with their liquid
1 15-ounce can garbanzo
beans with their liquid
2 eggs
⅓ cup soybean powder
2 tablespoons rice polishings
½ cup diced onion
¼ cup diced green pepper
2 tablespoons safflower oil

¼ cup diced pimiento
1 tablespoon vegetable-broth
powder
¼ teaspoon dill
⅛ teaspoon garlic powder
¼ teaspoon tarragon
Millet Crust (see page 169)
⅓ cup unsalted toasted
Soy Nuts

Put the soybeans, and garbanzo beans, and their liquid in
blender and blend until smooth. Add eggs, soybean powder, and
rice polishings and blend 1 minute. Pour into a large mixing bowl
and set aside. Sauté the onion and pepper in the oil. Add to bean
mixture. Add pimiento, vegetable-broth powder, dill, garlic powder, and tarragon. Mix well. Pour into Millet Crust in a 9-inch
pie pan, top with Soy Nuts, and bake in a preheated 350° F.
oven for 1 hour.
    Serves 6–8.

LENTIL MILLET LOAF

1½ cups Basic Lentils
(see page 133)
1 cup Basic Millet
(see page 152)
2 eggs
1 Delicious apple with
skin, shredded
½ cup finely chopped
cooked spinach
2 tablespoons sesame oil

½ cup soybean granules
1 teaspoon sea salt
1 teaspoon Krisp
¼ teaspoon savory
¼ teaspoon Salad Herbs
(see page 41)
½ teaspoon Spike
2 tablespoons toasted sesame
seeds

Combine all ingredients but last in order given and mix thoroughly. Pour mixture into a lightly oiled loaf pan and sprinkle with the sesame seeds. Bake for 45 minutes in a preheated 375° F. oven.

Serves 6–8.

CHILI NO CARNE

1 cup diced Spanish onion
1 cup diced celery
⅓ cup soybean oil
2 cups Basic Red Kidney
  Beans (see page 131)

1½ cups Brownies Tomato
  Sauce (see page 46)
1 13½-ounce can
  VegeBurger, mashed
½ teaspoon chili powder
½ teaspoon garlic powder

Sauté the onion and celery in the oil until transparent. Combine in a large saucepan with the remaining ingredients and heat through.

Serves 4–6.

THE MIRACULOUS SOYA—
AND OTHER MEMBERS OF THE CLAN

(Beans)

The soybean has been a staple of the Chinese diet—in fact, virtually the sole source of protein—for centuries. This extraordinary legume, however, did not reach the Western Hemisphere until early in the nineteenth century, and only within the last few decades has it begun to make its power felt here. In the American cuisine, with nutritional sophistication accelerating headily, we have a hunch that the fame and the acclaim of the "wonder bean" is at hand.

For good and abundant reason soybeans have been called the meat that grows on vines. Along with meat, milk, fish, and eggs, they rank as one of the five great sources of protein and are the number-one source in the vegetable kingdom. Not only is the quality of the protein high, but also the quantity exceeds that of all other protein-potent foods; they contain approximately twice as much as does lean beef, for example, when calorically equal amounts are compared. Nearly as complete a food as cow's milk, soybeans have many times the calcium content of an equal amount of milk and much more iron than an equal amount of spinach. They are rich in vitamins (including vitamin U, the antiulcer vitamin) and low in starch. They also contain lecithin, a fat-soluble agent that makes war on cholesterol deposits, and they are rated as a strong nerve and brain food. Not the least virtue of the "king of the beans" is that it comes cheap: With a few cents' worth of dried beans, you can feed 4 or 6 people as richly as if you had put outsized servings of meat or fish on their plates. We personally think there is no praise too extravagant for the glorious soybean.

Soybeans have many guises. You can use them dried, whole, cracked, powdered, granulated, or sprouted. Their versatility is enormous. Their most obvious role is as a cooked vegetable, but they can also become a meatlike entrée; the foundation of a salad; ersatz coffee, milk, cheese, nuts; oil; and the secret weapon in an inexhaustible range of breads, cereals, cakes, pastries, and confections.

And they even taste good too! Perhaps "nutlike" is the adjective that best describes their flavor.

At Brownies we feature soybeans on the relish tray, on the salad menu, and as a meat substitute. We use soybean flour in almost everything that comes out of our ovens. For all home cooks except the extremely budget-bound, we advise buying the canned cooked beans because the dried beans must be cooked for many hours. If you do use the dried soybeans, they (and all dried beans, incidentally) should be picked over and rinsed off before cooking.

In the following recipes, along with paying proper deference to the sovereign, we take at least a passing look at a few other members of the wonderful kingdom of beans: mung, red kidney, pinto, black turtle, marrow, lima, garbanzo, lentil, red lentil, and *cannelli*.

BASIC SOYBEANS

1 cup dried soybeans   1 teaspoon sea salt
4 quarts water

Combine ingredients in a very large kettle, cover, and cook for 5 hours or until tender, adding more water as needed.
Serves 4.

BASIC MUNG BEANS

1 cup dried green mung   1½ quarts water
 beans   1 teaspoon sea salt

Wash the mung beans under cold running water. Combine with the water and salt in a saucepan and cook for about 45 minutes on medium fire or until tender.
Serves 4.

BASIC RED KIDNEY BEANS

1 cup dried red kidney beans   1 teaspoon sea salt
2 quarts water

Combine ingredients in kettle and bring to boil, then cook on medium fire for 1 hour and 15 minutes.
Serves 4.

BASIC PINTO BEANS

1 cup dried pinto beans   1 teaspoon sea salt
2 quarts water

Combine ingredients in a saucepan and bring to a boil, then cook on medium heat for 1 hour or until tender.
Serves 4.

BASIC BLACK TURTLE BEANS

1 cup dried black turtle   4 quarts water
  beans   1 teaspoon sea salt

Combine all ingredients in a large kettle and cook until tender —about 1 hour and 15 minutes.
Serves 4.

BASIC MARROW BEANS

1 cup dried marrow beans   1 teaspoon sea salt
2 quarts water

Combine ingredients in a saucepan and bring to a boil, then cook on medium flame for 1 hour and 30 minutes or until tender.
Serves 4.

BASIC LIMA BEANS

1 cup dried lima beans   1 teaspoon sea salt
2 quarts water

Combine ingredients in a saucepan and bring to a boil, then cook on medium flame for 1 hour and 30 minutes or until tender.
Serves 4.

BASIC GARBANZO BEANS

1 cup dried garbanzo beans   1 teaspoon sea salt
4 quarts water

Combine all ingredients in a large kettle, bring to a boil, lower to a medium flame, and cook until tender—about 2 hours.
Serves 4.

BASIC LENTILS

1 cup dried brown lentils   1 teaspoon sea salt
1½ quarts water

Wash the lentils under cold running water, combine with the water and salt in a saucepan, and cook for 30 minutes on medium fire or until tender.
Serves 4.

BASIC RED LENTILS

½ cup red lentils   2 cups water
1 tablespoon soybean oil   ¼ teaspoon sea salt

Sauté the lentils in the oil until light brown. Add water and salt, cover, and cook about 30 minutes.
Serves 2.

ZIPPY SOYBEAN SALAD

2 cups Basic Soybeans
(see page 131)
1 cup diced cucumber with
skin
1 cup diced tomato
½ cup mung-bean sprouts
½ cup chopped watercress
¼ cup minced fresh parsley

2 tablespoons snipped fresh
chives
1 teaspoon sea salt
½ teaspoon garlic powder
½ teaspoon Italian Seasoning
(see page 41)
2 tablespoons *tamari* sauce
Brownies PUFA Dressing
(see page 42)

Combine cooled soybeans with remaining ingredients in a salad bowl and mix thoroughly. Serve with Brownies PUFA Dressing.
Serves 4.

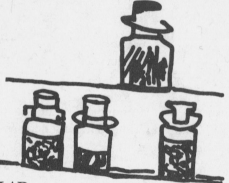

MINTY SOYBEAN SALAD

2 cups Basic Soybeans
(see page 131)
1 cup diced zucchini with
skin
1 Delicious apple with skin,
diced
⅓ cup sliced radishes
¼ cup diced red onion

1 tablespoon minced fresh
mint
½ teaspoon sea salt
2 teaspoons fresh lemon juice
½ cup Brownies PUFA
Dressing (see page 42)
¼ cup Brownies Lo-Cal
Dressing (see page 41)

Combine all ingredients in a salad bowl and mix thoroughly.
Serves 4.

SOYBEAN RATATOUILLE

½ cup diced scallions
⅓ cup diced celery
½ cup sliced mushrooms
2 garlic cloves, minced
¼ cup safflower oil
2 cups peeled and cubed
  eggplant
1 cup cubed zucchini with
  skin

¾ cup cubed tomatoes
1 cup California tomato juice
¼ cup tomato puree
1 cup canned green soybeans
1½ teaspoons sea salt
½ teaspoon oregano
½ teaspoon basil
Few grindings of pepper
½ teaspoon rosemary

In a large saucepan sauté the scallions, celery, mushrooms, and garlic in oil until light brown. Add the eggplant and zucchini and stir for several minutes. Add the tomatoes, tomato juice, and tomato puree. Cover and cook on low fire for 20 minutes. Add soybeans and seasonings and cook 5 minutes more, stirring thoroughly.

Serves 4.

SCRUMPTIOUS SOY PUDDING

1 15-ounce can green
  soybeans
1 cup diced avocado
⅓ cup buttermilk
2 eggs
½ cup cottage cheese
½ cup diced Spanish onion
¼ cup toasted seasame seeds
2 tablespoons soybean
  powder

1 tablespoon rice polishings
½ teaspoon sea salt
1 tablespoon *tamari* sauce
½ teaspoon marjoram
¼ teaspoon garlic powder
¼ teaspoon celery seed
2 tablespoons toasted sesame
  seeds

Combine all but the last ingredient in a blender at low speed for 1 minute, then at high speed for 1 minute. Pour into a lightly oiled baking pan, top with the 2 tablespoons toasted sesame seeds, and bake in a preheated 350° F. oven for 45 minutes.

Serves 4–6.

SOY WALNUT LOAF

2 cups canned green
  soybeans
2 eggs
½ cup soybean granules
2 tablespoons soybean
  powder
1 tablespoon rice polishings
3 pieces roasted dried
  seaweed, chopped
⅓ cup chopped toasted
  walnuts

½ cup goat-milk yogurt
½ cup buttermilk
2 tablespoons soybean oil
¼ cup diced pimiento
½ teaspoon sea salt
½ teaspoon Brownies
  Vege-C-Salt (see page 40)
½ teaspoon Italian Seasoning
  (see page 41)
¼ teaspoon nutmeg
¼ cup chopped walnuts

Combine all ingredients but last in a large mixing bowl and mix thoroughly. Pour into a lightly oiled loaf pan, sprinkle with walnuts, and bake for 45 minutes in a preheated 350° F. oven. Serves 6–8.

PROTEIN CASSEROLE

¼ cup diced scallions
¼ cup safflower oil
1 cup sliced mushrooms
½ cup diced celery
1 15-ounce can green
  soybeans with their liquid
1 14-ounce can Beef-Style
  Soyameat, diced, with its
  liquid

¼ cup minced fresh parsley
2 eggs
⅓ cup soybean granules
1 tablespoon vegetable-broth
  powder
½ teaspoon sea salt
½ teaspoon Italian Seasoning
  (see page 41)
¼ teaspoon garlic powder

Sauté the scallions in the oil in a saucepan. Add the mushrooms and celery and stir for 5 minutes. Combine with the remaining ingredients in a bowl and mix thoroughly. Pour into a lightly oiled baking pan and bake for 45 minutes in a preheated 350° F. oven. Serves 4–6.

MUNG-BEAN MEDLEY

1 cup Basic Mung Beans
(see page 131)
½ cup Basic Marrow Beans
(see page 132)
1 13½-ounce can VegeBurger,
mashed
⅓ cup diced Spanish onion
½ cup shredded Cheddar
cheese

½ cup shredded carrots
3 eggs
1 cup buttermilk
1 teaspoon sea salt
½ teaspoon basil
½ teaspoon marjoram
¼ teaspoon garlic powder

Combine all ingredients in a large mixing bowl and mix together thoroughly. Pour into a lightly oiled baking pan and bake for 30 minutes in a preheated 375° F. oven.
Serves 4–6.

KIDNEY TUNA FIESTA

2 cups Basic Red Kidney
Beans (see page 131)
1 cup cold cooked whole wax
beans
1 cup tuna-fish chunks
½ cup diced cucumber with
skin
½ cup diced celery

¼ cup diced scallions
¼ cup minced fresh parsley
½ cup chopped watercress
¼ cup toasted pine nuts
1 tablespoon Krisp
Brownies Lo-Cal Dressing
(see page 41)

Combine cooled red kidney beans with remaining ingredients except for dressing in a salad bowl and mix thoroughly. Serve cold with the dressing.
Serves 4–6.

PINTO-BEAN PATTIES

1½ cups Basic Pinto Beans
  (see page 132)
¼ cup tomato puree
1 egg
½ cup cottage cheese
¼ cup diced Spanish onion
¼ cup diced celery
2 tablespoons safflower oil
½ cup shredded carrots
2 teaspoons Krisp

¼ cup soybean granules
2 tablespoons toasted wheat
  germ
½ teaspoon sea salt
¼ teaspoon garlic powder
¼ teaspoon thyme
¼ teaspoon basil
½ cup Brownies Breading
  (Mix (see page 169)
Safflower oil

Combine the first 4 ingredients in a blender for 1 minute. Pour into mixing bowl. Sauté the onion and celery in the 2 tablespoons safflower oil until light brown. Add to first mixture. Add the remaining ingredients except for the last 2 and mix thoroughly. Form into 8 patties and dip each patty in the breading mix. Brown in ½-inch-deep safflower oil over moderate heat on both sides.
  Serves 4.

FLAMENCO TURTLE BEANS

2 cups Basic Black Turtle
  Beans (see page 132)
½ cup Basic Red Lentils
  (see page 133)
1 cup cubed avocado
⅓ cup diced cucumber with
  skin
¼ cup diced scallions
¼ cup diced pimiento
1 tablespoon snipped fresh
  chives

1 tablespoon fresh lemon
  juice
2 tablespoons rice-wine
  vinegar
¼ cup seasame oil
1½ teaspoons sea salt
½ teaspoon garlic powder
½ teaspoon basil
¼ teaspoon oregano

Combine cooled turtle beans and cooled lentils with remaining ingredients in a large salad bowl and toss lightly. Serve cold.
  Serves 4.

LUSCIOUS LIMAS

½ cup diced Spanish onion
½ cup diced green pepper
¼ cup safflower oil
1 cup diced tomatoes
½ cup tomato puree
2 cups Basic Lima Beans (see
page 132)

1 cup Basic Mung Beans (see
page 131)
1 teaspoon sea salt
¼ teaspoon garlic powder
Few grindings of pepper

Sauté the onion and green pepper in the oil until light brown.
Add the tomatoes and tomato puree and cook for 5 minutes. Add
the 2 beans and seasonings and cook 5 minutes more.
Serves 4–6.

CHEESY GARBANZO BEANS

2 cups Basic Garbanzo Beans
(see page 133)
2 eggs, beaten
1½ cups skim milk
⅓ cup toasted cashew meal
2 tablespoons soybean powder
2 tablespoons soybean
granules
2 tablespoons diced scallions

¼ cup diced pimiento
½ cup grated Cheddar cheese
1 teaspoon sea salt
1 teaspoon Brownies
Vege-C-Salt (see page 40)
¼ teaspoon nutmeg
2 tablespoons toasted sesame
seeds

Combine all ingredients except sesame seeds in a large bowl
and mix thoroughly. Pour into a lightly oiled baking dish and
sprinkle the sesame seeds on top. Bake in a preheated 350° F.
oven for 30 minutes.
Serves 4–6.

ORIENTAL LENTILS

¼ cup sesame oil
½ cup diced Spanish onion
½ cup diced celery
1 cup sliced mushrooms
2 cups Basic Lentils
(see page 133)
1 cup cooked cooled *cannelli* beans

½ cup mung-bean sprouts
½ cup sliced canned water chestnuts
2 teaspoons *tamari* sauce
1 teaspoon sea salt
½ teaspoon marjoram
¼ teaspoon nutmeg
¼ teaspoon garlic powder

Heat the oil in a saucepan and sauté the onion, celery, and mushrooms until brown. Add the remaining ingredients and cook, stirring, for 5 minutes.
Serves 4.

PROVENÇALE LENTILS

1½ cups Basic Lentils
(see page 133)
1½ cups Basic Mung Beans
(see page 131)
2 cups shredded Chinese cabbage
½ cup shredded carrots
2 hard-cooked eggs, diced
½ cup halved and pitted black olives
¼ cup diced celery
¼ cup diced red onion
¼ cup sliced radishes
¼ cup diced green pepper

Cucumber Dressing:
½ cup goat-milk yogurt
½ cup sour cream
¼ cup buttermilk
¼ cup cottage cheese
¼ cup tomato puree
½ cup diced cucumber with skin
1 teaspoon sea salt
½ teaspoon Brownies Vege-C-Salt (see page 40)
½ teaspoon Italian Seasoning (see page 41)
¼ teaspoon basil
¼ teaspoon garlic powder

Combine cooled lentils and cooled mung beans with next 8 ingredients in a salad bowl, mixing thoroughly. To make dressing, combine remaining ingredients in blender for 1 minute at low speed, then for 1 minute at high speed. Refrigerate lentil mixture and dressing separately, combining just before serving.
Serves 4–6.

LENTIL SOY CASSEROLE

1 cup Basic Lentils
(see page 133)

1 cup canned soybeans with
their liquid

1 cup shredded zucchini
with skin

1 cup sour cream

2 eggs

½ cup pecan meal

⅓ cup millet meal

¼ cup toasted wheat germ

¼ cup diced Spanish onion

1 teaspoon sea salt

½ teaspoon dill

¼ teaspoon nutmeg

¼ teaspoon garlic powder

Combine all ingredients in a bowl and mix thoroughly. Pour into a lightly oiled casserole and bake for 35 minutes in a preheated 375° F. oven.

Serves 4.

TRICOLOR BEAN SALAD

1 cup Basic Soybeans
(see page 131)

1 cup Basic Marrow Beans
(see page 132)

1 cup Basic Red Kidney
Beans (see page 131)

1 cup finely cut spinach

¼ cup thinly sliced scallions

½ cup shredded carrots

4 pieces roasted dried
seaweed, chopped

½ cup toasted salted
Soy Nuts

Brownies Lo-Cal Dressing
(see page 41)

Combine cooled soy, marrow, and kidney beans with next 5 ingredients in a salad bowl and mix thoroughly. Serve accompanied by dressing.

Serves 4.

BAVARIAN BEAN SALAD

1 cup canned green soybeans
1 cup cooked cooled *cannelli* beans
½ cup Basic Red Lentils (see page 133)
1 cup cold cooked wax-bean pieces

2 garlic cloves, minced
2 tablespoons snipped fresh chives
½ cup chopped macadamia nuts
Brownies Lo-Cal Dressing (see page 41)

Combine soybeans, cooled *cannelli* beans and lentils, and next 4 ingredients in a salad bowl. Mix thoroughly. Serve with the dressing.
Serves 4–6.

EXOTIC BEAN SALAD

1 cup Basic Pinto Beans (see page 132)
1 cup Basic Soybeans (see page 131)
2 cups finely cut Chinese cabbage
½ cup canned sliced water chestnuts
½ cup alfalfa sprouts
¼ cup diced red onion
½ cup diced pineapple

1 tablespoon minced candied ginger
1 cup Brownies PUFA Dressing (see page 42)
½ cup goat-milk yogurt
2 tablespoons canned unsweetened pineapple juice
½ teaspoon sea salt
¼ teaspoon nutmeg
⅛ teaspoon powdered ginger

Combine the cooled pinto beans, cooled soybeans, and the next 6 ingredients in a salad bowl. Mix the remaining ingredients together in a small bowl to make dressing. Pour the dressing over the bean mixture and mix thoroughly.
Serves 4–6.

SAM'S FAVORITE BEANS

2 cups Basic Red Kidney
Beans (see page 131)
1½ cups Basic Garbanzo
Beans (see page 133)
1½ cups cold cooked
green peas
½ cup alfalfa sprouts
¼ cup diced scallions
½ cup toasted chickpeas

½ cup lemon-juice
mayonnaise
½ cup goat-milk yogurt
½ cup diced avocado
½ teaspoon Brownies
Vege-C-Salt (see page 40)
¼ teaspoon celery seed
¼ teaspoon garlic powder
¼ teaspoon marjoram

Combine cooled kidney and garbanzo beans with next 4 ingredients; mix lightly. Combine remaining ingredients in blender
at low speed for 30 seconds and then at high speed for 1 minute
to make dressing. Mix together thoroughly bean mixture and
dressing and refrigerate.
Serves 6–8.

NEAPOLITAN BEAN SALAD

2 cups Basic Garbanzo Beans
(see page 133)
1 cup Basic Soybeans (see
page 131)
½ cup slivered Swiss cheese
1 cup halved cherry
tomatoes
½ cup diced red onion
¼ cup diced celery
¼ cup diced pimiento
¼ cup sliced pitted black
olives

¼ cup sliced pitted ripe green
olives
½ teaspoon sea salt
½ teaspoon Sesame Salt
(see page 40)
2 teaspoons poppy seeds
¼ teaspoon oregano
¼ teaspoon garlic powder
Brownies PUFA Dressing
(see page 42)

Combine cooled garbanzo beans, cooled soybeans, and next
12 ingredients in a salad bowl, mixing thoroughly. Serve with
the dressing.
Serves 4–6.

PEPPY BEAN PUREE

½ cup Basic Mung Beans
  (see page 131)
½ cup Basic Lentils
  (see page 133)
½ cup Basic Soybeans
  (see page 131)
1 cup cooked carrots
1 egg
¼ cup goat-milk yogurt

2 tablespoons safflower oil
½ teaspoon sea salt
½ teaspoon dill
¼ teaspoon celery seed
¼ teaspoon nutmeg
¼ teaspoon garlic powder
2 tablespoons toasted sesame
  seeds

Combine all ingredients but last for 1 minute in blender at medium speed. Pile into a lightly oiled baking dish. Sprinkle with sesame seeds and bake for 15 minutes in a preheated 375° F. oven.

Serves 4.

BOUNTIFUL BEAN PUREE

2 cups Basic Red Kidney
  Beans (see page 131)
2 cups Basic Garbanzo Beans
  (see page 133)
½ cup cubed avocado
2 eggs
¼ cup diced red onion
1 garlic clove, minced
½ teaspoon sea salt

½ teaspoon Brownies
  Vege-C-Salt (see page 40)
½ teaspoon thyme
½ teaspoon savory
½ cup shredded Cheddar
  cheese
2 tablespoons toasted
  sunflower seeds

Combine the first 10 ingredients in a blender for 2 minutes at medium speed. Spread in a lightly oiled baking dish and sprinkle the cheese and sunflower seeds on top. Bake for 15 minutes in a preheated 375° F. oven.

Serves 6–8.

TRIPLE BEAN BAKE

2 cups Basic Marrow Beans
(see page 132)
½ cup Basic Black Turtle
Beans (see page 132)
½ cup Basic Garbanzo Beans
(see page 133)
½ cup Barbados molasses
½ cup tomato puree

½ cup water
1 tablespoon raw sugar
¼ cup diced Spanish onion
1 teaspoon sea salt
¼ teaspoon garlic powder
½ teaspoon turmeric
Few grindings of pepper

Combine all ingredients and mix thoroughly. Pour into a baking dish and bake in a preheated 350° F. oven for 1 hour, stirring occasionally.

Serves 6–8.

ANY-NIGHT BEANS

2 cups Basic Soybeans (see
page 131)
¾ cup Basic Red Lentils (see
page 133)
½ cup California tomato juice
½ cup diced Spanish onion
½ cup diced green pepper
2 cups sliced mushrooms
¼ cup safflower oil
½ cup cubed Edam cheese

2 tablespoons powdered nonfat
dry milk
2 tablespoons Barbados
molasses
½ teaspoon sea salt
½ teaspoon vegetable-broth
powder
½ teaspoon Italian Seasoning
(see page 41)
¼ teaspoon thyme

Combine soybeans, lentils, and tomato juice in a large mixing bowl and set aside. Sauté the onion, pepper, and mushrooms in the oil until light brown. Add to bean mixture and mix thoroughly. Add the remaining ingredients and mix well. Pour into a lightly oiled baking dish and bake in a preheated 350° F. oven for 30 minutes.

Serves 4.

RAINBOW BEANS

½ cup diced Spanish onion
1 cup sliced mushrooms
¼ cup soybean oil
1 cup Basic Black Turtle Beans
(see page 132)
1 cup cooked julienne of string
beans
1 cup cooked carrot rounds

½ cup Basic Pinto Beans (see
page 132)
½ cup cooked baby lima beans
2 tablespoons Krisp
1 teaspoon sea salt
½ teaspoon oregano
¼ teaspoon garlic powder
¼ teaspoon dill

Sauté the onion and mushrooms in the oil in a saucepan until light brown. Add the remaining ingredients to the saucepan, combine, and serve hot.

Serves 4–6.

GOING WITH THE GRAIN...WHOLLY
(Whole Grains)

Our ancestors never had to ask, "Just what are whole grains?" For them whole grains often constituted the whole table, and they ate a lot richer than we—of *necessity*.

In recent times we have been warned ad infinitum about the poisons in and on our food. We have become aware of how heavily our diets are weighted with "junk" foods like carbonated soft drinks, candy bars, and potato chips, but we are just beginning to grasp the extent to which our staple foods have become "unfoods." At last we can recognize that "enriched" claim on packaged flours, breads, and cereals for the phony it is.

Time was when whole-grain bread symbolized the simple life and the good countryside. The wheat was ground between millstones that crushed the grain without removing any part of it. Bread rated its billing as the staff of life. Came the Industrial Revolution and the staff was broken. Machines were invented that could separate the various components of the grain. The first casualty was the outer 3 layers, called bran, where much of the grain's protein and minerals is concentrated. Discarded also was the germ, containing considerable protein, wheat oil, the B vitamins, and vitamin E. What was left was mostly starch. The bran was used to feed farm animals—so they could eat a lot higher off the grain than their two-legged friends!—and the wheat germ ultimately ended up in health-foods stores.

As for flour, rich and poor alike became convinced that "white is beautiful." Enter the bleaches. But say this for devitalized white flour: Insects won't touch it. Human beings should be so shrewd. In a widely publicized recent experiment rats on an exclusive diet of white bread died of malnutrition!

The chemicalization of bread came with the growth of big commercial bakeries. Now bread had to stand the test of time on grocery shelves. A whole laboratory of chemicals was drafted into service: emulsifiers, softeners, whiteners, fresheners, preservatives, and mold-and-fungus inhibitors. The mass-produced loaf became a chemical-ridden, tasteless thing, nearly as innocent of nourishment as a cloud of cotton candy.

The milling company that labels its flour "enriched" is like a thief on the street who steals a man's wallet and thoughtfully gives his victim enough change to get home on the bus. The refining process removes some 20 nutrients, of which maybe 3 are partially restored; so much for "enrichment."

Grains other than wheat are also stripped down, pulverized, and destroyed. All those charmingly boxed breakfast foods are, for the most part, castrated cereals that have properly been exposed as "empty calories," yielding high profits and low food values. Again, polishing throws the best of the rice into the discard pile.

The happy news is that not all grains await this fate. More and more are escaping the milling and cereal predators. Increasingly they are available to those of us who find them desirable in their wholeness.

The family of whole grains includes brown rice, corn, millet, wheat, oats, rye, barley, and buckwheat. With a minimum of handling they reach us, straight from God's green acres. Precisely because they have not been folded, mutilated, or spindled, they are superior both in flavor and in healthfulness to their refined siblings.

Whole grains are precious chiefly for their B vitamins, vitamin E, and protein. Of them all, millet has the most protein. For pancakes buckwheat soars universes above white-flour mixes. Old-fashioned oatmeal made from steel-cut oats is richer nutritionally than oatmeal made from rolled oats. The potency of all cereals can be increased by the addition of such enrichers as soybean granules (cracked soybeans), rice polishings, powdered milk, and wheat germ. Wheat germ is a powerful cereal all by itself. For many people, however, the taste takes a bit of getting used to, and gentle infiltration—by adding a little bit and then a little bit more—into cooked or cold cereals may be the conscientious cook's solution.

Here we show you how you can make the delicious grains–nuts–dried fruits cereal that was created by the Swiss and now even reposes on many of our supermarket shelves. We also have a recipe for our own version of Granola, the new whole-grain breakfast food that has beat a pathway to the palates of Americans—especially those of the young.

We have taken whole grains far beyond their application to the breakfast table, however. In later chapters we will feature whole-grain flours as the essence of bread- and pastry-baking. In the following recipes we have couscous, buckwheat groats, brown rice, cracked wheat, millet, steel-cut oats, and barley showing up in croquettes, casseroles, vegetable dishes, meatless loaves, and puddings.

Remember—whole grains are better than hollow ones!

BASIC BROWN RICE

1 cup brown rice
2 tablespoons sesame oil

4 cups water
1 teaspoon sea salt

Stir the rice with the oil for about 5 minutes on low heat until the rice is popping and light brown. Slowly add the water, stir in the salt, and bring to a boil. Cover the pot. Cook about 45 minutes on a low fire or until all the water is absorbed.

Serves 4–6.

BASIC WILD RICE

¾ cup wild rice
3 cups water

1 teaspoon sea salt

Combine the wild rice, water, and salt in a large saucepan and bring to a boil. Cover and simmer for 45 minutes or until tender. Drain.

Serves 6–8.

BASIC CRACKED WHEAT

1 quart water
½ teaspoon sea salt

1 cup cracked wheat

Bring the water and salt to a boil. Gradually add the cracked wheat, stirring until well mixed. Cook on a low fire until thick— about 30 minutes—stirring occasionally.

Serves 4.

KOOS-KOOS

¼ cup soybean oil   1 quart water
1 cup medium-grade couscous   1 teaspoon sea salt

Heat the oil in a saucepan. Add the couscous and stir until light brown. Add the water and salt. Bring to a boil, then cover and cook on a low fire for 20 minutes or until all the water is absorbed.
Serves 4.

BASIC WHOLE BUCKWHEAT GROATS

1 cup whole buckwheat groats   1 quart water
1 egg   1 teaspoon sea salt
1 tablespoon soybean oil

Combine the buckwheat groats with the egg and mix thoroughly. Heat the oil in a saucepan, add the groats, and keep stirring on a medium fire until all the groats are separate. Add the water and salt. Bring to a boil, cover, and cook on a low fire for about 20 minutes or until all the water is absorbed.
Serves 4.

POLENTA

3 cups cold water   1 cup yellow cornmeal
1 teaspoon sea salt

Bring 2 cups of the water and the salt to a boil. Combine the cornmeal and the remaining water to make a smooth mixture. Add slowly to the boiling water, stirring constantly. Cover and cook on a low fire for 20 minutes, stirring occasionally. This can be used as a cereal.
Serves 4.

BASIC STEEL-CUT OATS

3 cups water   1 cup steel-cut oats
1 teaspoon sea salt

Bring the water and salt to a boil. Slowly add the oats, stirring constantly. Cook on a low fire for 30 minutes, stirring occasionally. This can be used as a cereal.
  Serves 4.

BASIC WHOLE UNPEARLED BARLEY

½ cup whole unpearled barley   3 cups water

Put barley and water in a saucepan. Bring to a boil, cover, and cook for 1 hour.
  Serves 4.

BASIC MILLET

4 cups water   1 cup millet
1 teaspoon sea salt

Bring the water and salt to a boil in a saucepan. Gradually add the millet, stirring constantly. Cook on a low fire for 30 minutes or until all the water is absorbed.
  Serves 4.

SAFFRON BROWN RICE

½ cup diced Spanish onion   1 cup brown rice
¼ cup soybean oil   ½ teaspoon Spanish saffron
3 cups Brownies Consommé   threads
  (see page 53)   ¼ teaspoon garlic powder

Sauté the onion in the oil and add to the hot consommé and the remaining ingredients, mixing thoroughly. Pour into a baking dish and cover. Bake in a preheated 350° F. oven for 45 minutes or until the consommé is fully absorbed.
  Serves 6.

PARSLEY BROWN RICE

4 cups Basic Brown Rice (see
page 150)
½ cup sautéed onions
½ cup minced fresh parsley

¼ cup diced pimiento
2 tablespoons soybean oil
1 tablespoon Brownies
Vege-C-Salt (see page 40)

Combine all ingredients and mix thoroughly. Place in a baking dish and heat in a preheated 350° F. oven for 20 minutes.
Serves 6.

SPANISH BROWN RICE

1 cup diced Spanish onion
½ cup diced green pepper
⅓ cup soybean oil
2 cups Brownies Tomato Sauce
(see page 46)

½ teaspoon garlic powder
1 teaspoon Bakon Yeast
4 cups Basic Brown Rice (see
page 150)

Sauté the onion and pepper in the oil and combine with the remaining ingredients. Mix thoroughly and heat through well.
Serves 6.

ORIENTAL RICE

1 cup diced Spanish onion
¼ cup soybean oil
4 cups Basic Brown Rice (see
page 150)
2 tablespoons *tamari* sauce

1 teaspoon Sesame Salt (see
page 40)
2 eggs
½ cup diced scallions

Sauté the onion in the oil and add to the next 3 ingredients, stirring thoroughly. Make an omelet from the eggs and cut into shreds. Stir lightly into the rice mixture. Place in a baking dish and bake in a preheated 350° F. oven for 15 minutes. Top with the diced scallions before serving.
Serves 6.

BROWN RICE WITH MUSHROOMS

½ cup diced Spanish onion
⅓ cup diced celery
⅓ cup diced green pepper
¼ cup soybean oil
1½ cups sliced mushrooms
½ teaspoon paprika
1 14-ounce can Beef-Style Soyameat with gravy

1 cup Basic Brown Rice (see page 150)
¼ teaspoon garlic powder
1 tablespoon snipped fresh chives
¼ teaspoon celery seed
½ cup shredded Swiss cheese
Paprika

Sauté the onion, celery, and green pepper in the oil in a saucepan until golden. Add the mushrooms and stir until light brown. Add the paprika and Soyameat slices and stir for a couple of minutes. Place in a bowl and add all the remaining ingredients except the cheese and paprika. Spread in a baking dish, top with the cheese, and sprinkle with paprika. Bake in a preheated 375° F. oven for 15 minutes.

Serves 4–6.

BROWN RICE WITH SNOW PEAS

¼ cup diced scallions
1 cup diced celery
1 cup sliced mushrooms
¼ cup soybean oil
1 teaspoon fresh diced ginger root
1½ cups fresh snow peas
2 cups Basic Brown Rice (see page 150)

1 tablespoon *tamari* sauce
½ teaspoon sea salt
1 teaspoon Sesame Salt (see page 40)
¼ teaspoon garlic powder
⅛ teaspoon powdered ginger
¼ cup toasted walnut pieces

Sauté the scallions, celery, and mushrooms in the oil until light brown. Add the ginger root and snow peas and stir together. Cover and cook for 5 minutes. Add the remaining ingredients, mix lightly, and cook until heated through.

Serves 4–6.

BROWN RICE WITH SQUASH SAUCE

¼ cup safflower oil
½ cup diced scallions
½ cup diced celery
1 cup sliced mushrooms
2 cups diced yellow or green
  squash with skin
¾ cup California tomato juice
½ cup skim milk
2 tablespoons soybean powder

¼ teaspoon minced fresh
  ginger root
½ teaspoon paprika
½ teaspoon sea salt
½ teaspoon marjoram
¼ teaspoon garlic powder
Few grindings of pepper
4 cups Basic Brown Rice (see
  page 150)

Heat the oil in a saucepan and sauté the scallions and celery. Add the mushrooms and stir until light brown. Add the squash, ½ cup of the tomato juice, and skim milk. Cover and cook on a low flame for 15 minutes. Make a smooth paste of the remaining tomato juice and soybean powder. Add to squash mixture and stir for 5 minutes. Add next 6 ingredients and mix well. Serve over hot brown rice.
    Serves 6–8.

RICE CARROT FLIP

2 cups Basic Brown Rice (see
  page 150)
1 cup shredded carrots
2 eggs
½ cup shredded Monterey
  jack cheese
¼ cup toasted sesame seeds
¼ cup minced fresh parsley

¼ cup sour cream
2 tablespoons toasted wheat
  germ
1 teaspoon sea salt
½ teaspoon Italian Seasoning
  (see page 41)
¼ teaspoon garlic powder
¼ teaspoon marjoram

Combine all ingredients in a bowl and mix very well. Place in a lightly oiled baking pan and bake for 45 minutes in a preheated 375° F. oven.
    Serves 6–8.

SAUCY TWO-GRAIN CHEESE BALLS

1 cup Basic Brown Rice (see page 150)
½ cup Basic Millet (see page 152)
1 egg
¼ cup toasted sesame seeds
2 tablespoons *tahini*
½ cup shredded Cheddar cheese

1 teaspoon Sesame Salt (see page 40)
¼ teaspoon sea salt
¼ teaspoon garlic powder
½ teaspoon marjoram
Soybean oil
Cheesy Tomato Sauce

Combine all ingredients but last 2 in a bowl and mix thoroughly. Form into about 24 small balls and brown on all sides in ½-inch-deep soybean oil on moderate heat. Serve with Cheesy Tomato Sauce.
Serves 4–6.

Cheesy Tomato Sauce

1 cup skim milk
½ cup tomato puree
2 tablespoons soybean powder
½ cup shredded Cheddar cheese

½ teaspoon paprika
¼ teaspoon sea salt
¼ teaspoon garlic powder
¼ teaspoon oregano
½ teaspoon basil

Combine all ingredients in a saucepan on a low fire and stir until cheese melts.

BROWNIES OWN RICE PUDDING
(Gayle's Favorite)

1½ cups Basic Brown Rice (see
  page 150)
⅓ cup Monukka raisins
2 cups milk
2 tablespoons soybean powder

¼ cup raw sugar
2 eggs
2 tablespoons tupelo honey
1 teaspoon vanilla extract
½ teaspoon cinnamon

In a deep square baking pan spread the rice in an even layer.
Sprinkle the raisins over the rice and set aside. Combine the milk,
soybean powder, and sugar in a saucepan and heat until the sugar
dissolves. In a bowl beat the eggs together with the honey and
vanilla. Slowly pour the milk mixture into the eggs, beating con-
stanty. Pour over the rice and raisins, sprinkle with cinnamon,
and bake for 1 hour in a preheated 300° F. oven. Serve warm or
cold.
  Serves 6–8.

COLORFUL RICE PUDDING

¼ cup diced scallions
2 tablespoons sesame oil
½ cup quartered pitted prunes
1 cup canned unsweetened
  crushed pineapple with its
  juice
2 cups Basic Brown Rice (see
  page 150)
2 eggs

⅓ cup honey strawberry
  preserves
⅓ cup raw sugar
⅓ cup sliced filberts
1 teaspoon vanilla extract
½ teaspoon cinnamon
¼ teaspoon sea salt
¼ cup toasted wheat germ

Sauté the scallions in the sesame oil. Add the prunes and pineapple and stir for 2 minutes. Combine with the remaining ingredients and mix thoroughly. Pour into a lightly oiled baking dish
and bake for 45 minutes in a preheated 350° F. oven. Serve hot
or cold.
  Serves 6–8.

MILLET RICE PUDDING

1½ cups Basic Brown Rice (see page 150)
1 cup Basic Millet (see page 152)
2 eggs
½ cup raw sugar
½ cup goat-milk yogurt

¼ cup Papaya Syrup Concentrate
½ cup sliced dates
1 teaspoon vanilla extract
1 teaspoon orange extract
¼ cup unsweetened shredded coconut

Mix all ingredients except the coconut thoroughly in a bowl. Pour into a lightly oiled baking dish and sprinkle the coconut on top. Bake for 45 minutes in a preheated 375° F. oven.
    Serves 6–8.

WILD RICE WITH MUSHROOMS AND PIGNOLIAS

Basic Wild Rice (see page 150)   Mushroom Sauté

Combine hot wild rice with the Mushroom Sauté. Place in a baking dish and cover. Bake in a preheated 350° F. oven for 20 minutes.
    Serves 8–10.

Mushroom Sauté

½ cup diced Spanish onion
¼ cup diced celery
2 garlic cloves, minced
2 tablespoons safflower oil
1 cup sliced mushrooms
2 teaspoons Krisp

1½ teaspoons Brownies Vege-C-Salt (see page 40)
⅛ teaspoon garlic powder
Few grindings of pepper
¼ cup toasted pignolias

Sauté the first 3 ingredients in the oil. Add the mushrooms and stir until brown. Add the remaining ingredients and mix.

EVERYBODY'S FAVORITE CRACKED-WHEAT PUDDING

2 cups Basic Cracked Wheat
  (see page 150)
⅓ cup granulated maple sugar
2 tablespoons clover honey
⅓ cup fresh-ground peanut
  butter
⅔ cup toasted wheat germ

2 eggs
¼ cup toasted sesame seeds
2 tablespoons dried currants
⅓ cup chopped dates
¼ teaspoon sea salt
½ teaspoon cinnamon
1 teaspoon vanilla extract

Combine all the ingredients and mix thoroughly. Pour into a lightly oiled baking pan and bake for about 45 minutes in a preheated 350° F. oven or until brown on top.

Serves 4–6.

PEACHY GRAIN MOLASSES PUDDING

1 cup Basic Cracked Wheat
  (see page 150)
½ cup Basic Brown Rice (see
  page 150)
¼ cup toasted sesame seeds
½ cup unsweetened shredded
  coconut
¼ cup maple syrup
¼ cup Barbados molasses

1 egg
¼ teaspoon sea salt
1 teaspoon cinnamon
1 teaspoon vanilla extract
½ cup buttermilk
1 cup diced peaches
Unsweetened shredded coconut
Toasted sesame seeds

Combine all ingredients except for last 2 thoroughly in a bowl, mixing well. Pour into a lightly oiled baking dish. Sprinkle some coconut and sesame seeds on top of pudding. Bake for 1 hour in a preheated 375° F. oven.

Serves 4–6.

SUNFLOWER COUSCOUS

½ cup toasted sunflower seeds
2 cups Koos-Koos (see page 151)
2 tablespoons safflower oil
2 tablespoons diced red onion
¼ cup sliced canned water chestnuts

½ cup alfalfa sprouts
¼ cup diced pimiento
½ teaspoon sea salt
2 teaspoons *tamari* sauce
¼ teaspoon garlic powder

Reserving ¼ cup of the sunflower seeds, combine remaining ingredients in a bowl and mix lightly. Put in a baking dish, sprinkle the reserved sunflower seeds on top, and bake in a preheated 375° F. oven for 15 minutes.
Serves 4–6.

SERENDIPITY COUSCOUS PATTIES

1 cup Koos-Koos (see page 151)
½ cup toasted sesame seeds
1 egg
2 tablespoons millet meal
2 tablespoons brown-rice flour
1 scallion, diced

1 tablespoon snipped fresh chives
1 tablespoon minced fresh dill
½ teaspoon sea salt
¼ teaspoon garlic
¼ teaspoon Italian Seasoning (see page 41)
Soybean oil

Combine all ingredients but last in a bowl and mix thoroughly. Form into 8 patties and brown on both sides in ½-inch-deep soybean oil on moderate heat.
Serves 4.

STUFFED CHINESE CABBAGE

12 leaves Chinese cabbage
Boiling water
2 cups Couscous Appetizer (see page 16)
1 13-ounce can Chicken-Style Soyameat, drained and diced

2 eggs
2 tablespoons Monukka raisins
2 cups Brownies Tomato Sauce (see page 46)

Wash the cabbage leaves thoroughly and cut off their hard bottom cores. Blanch in boiling water for 5 minutes. Combine the Couscous Appetizer, Soyameat, and eggs and mix very well. Place 2 tablespoons of this mixture on each cabbage leaf and roll up tightly, making sure that all the filling is enclosed. Place seam side down in a baking pan. Add the raisins to the tomato sauce and pour over the stuffed cabbage. Cover tightly and bake in a preheated 350° F. oven for 1 hour.

Serves 6–8.

KASHA WITH MUSHROOMS

1½ cups Basic Whole Buck-wheat Groats (see page 151)
1 cup VegeBurger
¼ cup diced canned water chestnuts

½ teaspoon sea salt
¼ teaspoon garlic powder
1 cup diced red onion
⅓ cup safflower oil
1½ cups sliced mushrooms

Combine the first 5 ingredients in a bowl and mix well. Sauté the onion in the safflower oil until light brown, then add the mushrooms and brown. Add to the first mixture and mix thoroughly. Place in a baking pan and bake for 15 minutes in a preheated 375° F. oven.

Serves 4–6.

BUCKWHEAT SENSATION

3 cups Basic Whole Buckwheat
  Groats (see page 151)
½ cup Basic Cracked Wheat
  (see page 150)
½ cup diced red onion
⅓ cup diced celery
¼ cup diced green pepper

¼ cup safflower oil
1 cup sliced mushrooms
1 cup diced tomatoes
⅓ cup pumpkin seeds
1 teaspoon sea salt
¼ teaspoon garlic powder
½ teaspoon rosemary

Combine the buckwheat groats and cracked wheat in a bowl and set aside. Sauté the onion, celery, and green pepper in the oil until light brown. Add the mushrooms and brown. Stir in the tomatoes and mix thoroughly for 2 minutes. Add to the buckwheat mixture and mix well. Add the remaining ingredients and mix thoroughly. Put into a lightly oiled baking dish and bake for 30 minutes in a preheated 375° F. oven.

Serves 6–8.

SPRINGTIME BUCKWHEAT BALLS

1½ cups Basic Whole Buck-
  wheat Groats (see page 151)
1 cup shredded peeled
  eggplant
¼ cup diced scallions
¼ cup diced green pepper
¼ cup diced pimiento
2 eggs

2 tablespoons brown-rice flour
1 teaspoon sea salt
½ teaspoon basil
½ teaspoon oregano
¼ teaspoon garlic powder
Cheesy Tomato Sauce (see page
  156) (optional)

Combine all ingredients but last in a bowl and mix thoroughly. Form into 12 balls and place in an oiled baking pan. Bake for 30 minutes in a preheated 375° F. oven, then put under the broiler for several minutes to brown. If desired, serve with Cheesy Tomato Sauce.

Serves 4–6.

MEATLESS BUCK-OAT WEDGE

1 14-ounce can Nuteena, mashed

½ cup Basic Steel-Cut Oats (see page 152)

½ cup Basic Whole Buckwheat Groats (see page 151)

2 eggs

½ cup diced scallions

½ cup diced celery

¼ cup sesame oil

½ cup sliced mushrooms

⅓ cup diced canned water chestnuts

¼ cup diced pimiento

¼ cup minced fresh parsley

2 tablespoons minced fresh dill

½ cup goat-milk yogurt

½ teaspoon sea salt

½ teaspoon garlic powder

¼ teaspoon nutmeg

½ teaspoon Italian Seasoning (see page 41)

2 tablespoons sunflower seeds

Combine the first 4 ingredients, mix well in a bowl, and set aside. Sauté the scallions and celery in the oil. Add the mushrooms and brown. Add the next 4 ingredients, mix well, and add to first mixture. Add all the remaining ingredients but the last and mix thoroughly. Place in one large or two small pie pans. Sprinkle with sunflower seeds and bake for 45 minutes in a preheated 375° F. oven.

Serves 6–8.

POLENTA WITH EGGPLANT SAUCE

1 recipe Polenta (see page 151)

½ cup cottage cheese

2 teaspoons Sesame Salt (see page 40)

¼ teaspoon garlic powder

Few grindings of pepper

Paprika

Eggplant Sauce

Add to the hot polenta the next 4 ingredients, stirring thoroughly. Pour into a lightly oiled baking dish, sprinkle with paprika, and bake in a preheated 375° F. oven for 30 minutes. Serve with the Eggplant Sauce.

Serves 4–6.

Eggplant Sauce

½ cup diced red onion
⅓ cup diced celery
¼ cup safflower oil
½ cup sliced mushrooms
1⅓ cups tomato puree
1¼ cups tomato juice
4 cups peeled and cubed
  eggplant
1 cup water
¼ cup diced pimiento

1 tablespoon raw sugar
¼ cup minced fresh parsley
¼ cup toasted pignolias
1 teaspoon sea salt
½ teaspoon garlic powder
½ teaspoon celery seed
½ teaspoon basil
1 tablespoon snipped fresh
  chives

Sauté the onion and celery in the oil in a saucepan. Add the mushrooms and brown lightly. Add the next 6 ingredients, cover, and cook on a low fire for 45 minutes or until eggplant is tender. Add the remaining ingredients and stir thoroughly.

POLENTA WITH RAINBOW CHEESE SAUCE

3 cups Polenta (see page 151)
½ cup shredded Cheddar
  cheese
1 egg
2 tablespoons safflower oil
2 tablespoons Sesame Salt
  (see page 40)

¼ teaspoon sea salt
¼ teaspoon garlic powder
Few grindings of pepper
Paprika
Rainbow Cheese Sauce

Combine all ingredients except paprika and sauce in a bowl and mix thoroughly. Pour into a lightly oiled baking dish and sprinkle with paprika. Bake for 20 minutes in a preheated 375° F. oven. Serve sauce with baked polenta.

Serves 6–8.

Rainbow Cheese Sauce

2 cups skim milk
½ cup soybean powder
3 tablespoons brown-rice flour
1½ cups shredded Cheddar
 cheese
2 teaspoons paprika

⅓ cup sliced pitted black
 olives
¼ cup diced pimiento
⅓ cup minced fresh parsley
¼ teaspoon sea salt
¼ teaspoon nutmeg
¼ teaspoon garlic powder

Combine all ingredients in a saucepan and stir constantly on a low fire until smooth and thick.

OAT HONEY CHERRY PUDDING

2 cups Basic Steel-Cut Oats
 (see page 152)
¼ cup almond oil
⅓ cup orange-blossom honey
½ cup soybean granules
¼ cup toasted wheat germ
⅓ cup toasted sesame seeds
2 tablespoons soybean powder
2 eggs
½ teaspoon sea salt

½ cup Papaya Syrup
 Concentrate
⅓ cup honey black-cherry
 preserves
2 slices canned unsweetened
 pineapple, slivered
1 teaspoon vanilla extract
1 teaspoon orange extract
½ cup walnut pieces

Combine all the ingredients but the walnuts and mix thoroughly. Pour into a lightly oiled baking pan and top with walnuts. Bake for 1 hour in a preheated 350° F. oven or until brown.
 Serves 8.

WHOLE BARLEY WITH WALNUTS

½ cup diced red onion
¼ cup diced celery
¼ cup safflower oil
1 cup sliced mushrooms
½ cup walnut pieces
¼ cup halved pitted black
   olives
¼ cup diced pimiento

2 cups Basic Whole
   Unpearled Barley
   (see page 152)
¾ teaspoon sea salt
½ teaspoon marjoram
¼ teaspoon oregano
¼ teaspoon garlic powder
1 teaspoon Sesame Salt
   (see page 40)

In a saucepan sauté the onion and celery in the oil until light brown. Add the mushrooms and stir until brown. Add the walnuts, olives, and pimiento and stir for 2 minutes. Add the remaining ingredients and mix thoroughly. Heat through in a covered baking dish in a preheated 350° F. oven.

Serves 4–6.

FRUITED BARLEY

¼ cup diced scallions
¼ cup diced celery
2 tablespoons safflower oil
2 cups Basic Whole
   Unpearled Barley
   (see page 152)
¼ cup Monukka raisins
¼ cup diced dates
⅓ cup sliced dried apricots

⅓ cup canned unsweetened
   crushed pineapple with its
   juice
2 tablespoons *tahini*
½ teaspoon sea salt
1 tablespoon Sesame Salt
   (see page 40)
1 teaspoon orange extract

Sauté the scallions and celery in the oil. Add to the barley. Combine with the remaining ingredients and mix thoroughly. Place in a baking dish and bake for 15 minutes in a preheated 375° F. oven.

Serves 4–6.

MILLET CHEESE CROQUETTES

2 cups Basic Millet
(see page 152)
½ cup soybean granules
2 eggs
1 cup shredded Cheddar
cheese
¼ cup shredded Spanish
onion

2 teaspoons vegetable-broth
powder
½ teaspoon sea salt
1 teaspoon thyme
¼ teaspoon garlic powder
Safflower oil
Eggplant Sauce (see page 164)
(optional)

Combine all ingredients except oil and Eggplant Sauce and mix thoroughly. Form into croquettes and brown in ½-inch-deep oil on moderate heat. If desired, serve with Eggplant Sauce.
Serves 4–6.

MILLET CORNMEAL LOAF

2 cups Basic Millet
(see page 152)
1 cup Polenta (see page 151)
1 cup VegeBurger
2 eggs
½ cup cottage cheese
½ cup ground walnuts
¼ cup Sesame Salt
(see page 40)

2 tablespoons diced red onion
¼ cup minced fresh parsley
½ teaspoon sea salt
½ teaspoon garlic powder
¼ teaspoon celery seed
1 teaspoon basil
Cheesy Tomato Sauce
(see page 156) (optional)

Combine all ingredients except sauce in a bowl and mix thoroughly. Pour into a lightly oiled loaf pan and bake for 1 hour in a preheated 375° F. oven. Serve with Cheesy Tomato Sauce if desired.
Serves 6–8.

BROWNOLA PLUS

3 cups rolled oats
½ cup unsweetened shredded
   coconut
½ cup sesame seeds
½ cup sliced almonds
¼ cup safflower oil
¼ cup clover honey
¼ cup powdered nonfat
   dry milk

1 cup toasted wheat germ
¼ cup rice polishings
¼ cup lecithin
1 cup dried currants
½ cup date chips
1 teaspoon cinnamon
1 teaspoon vanilla extract

Combine the first 6 ingredients and mix lightly. Place on a baking sheet in a preheated 325° F. oven for about 30 minutes or until all is toasted. Cool and then blend with the remaining ingredients. Store refrigerated in closed containers or bags. Use as a cold cereal, served with milk.

Yield: about 8 cups.

BROWNILIA

2 cups rolled oats
2 tablespoons soybean oil
1 cup toasted wheat germ
½ cup date sugar
½ cup toasted sunflower
   seeds
¼ cup toasted pumpkin seeds
¼ cup powdered nonfat
   dry milk

¼ cup lecithin
¼ cup soybean powder
2 tablespoons brewer's yeast
1 cup diced honey-dipped
   dried apples
1 cup Monukka raisins
1 teaspoon orange extract
1 teaspoon almond extract

Combine the oatmeal flakes and oil and place on a baking sheet in a preheated 325° F. oven for about 20 minutes or until light brown. Add the remaining ingredients and mix thoroughly. Keep in refrigerator in closed containers or bags. Use as a cold cereal, served with milk.

Yield: about 8 cups.

BROWNIES BREADING MIX

1 cup soybean or
  whole-wheat bread crumbs
1 cup stone-ground yellow
  cornmeal

½ cup toasted wheat germ
½ cup sesame seeds
½ teaspoon basil

Mix all ingredients thoroughly. This will keep indefinitely if refrigerated in a closed container.
    Yield: 3½ cups.

MILLET CRUST

2 cups Basic Millet
  (see page 152)
1 teaspoon soybean oil

1 tablespoon grated Cheddar
  cheese
¼ teaspoon Spike

Combine hot millet and remaining ingredients thoroughly and cool until lukewarm. Spread in a lightly oiled 9- or 10-inch pie pan to form a crust.
    Yield: 1 pie crust.

CORNMEAL CRUST

½ cup yellow cornmeal
¾ cup cold water
¾ cup boiling water
½ teaspoon sea salt

2 tablespoons ground walnuts
⅛ teaspoon Spike
1 tablespoon sesame oil

Mix cornmeal with cold water until smooth. Add to boiling water slowly along with salt, stirring constantly. Cook until thick. Remove from fire and add remaining ingredients. Stir well and cool to lukewarm. Spread in a lightly oiled 9- or 10-inch pie pan to form crust.
    Yield: 1 pie crust.

VEGETABLE FRITTERS

Any of the following vegetables: cubed eggplant, string beans, snow peas, sliced tomatoes, drained canned corn kernels, etc.

Vegetable Fritter Batter   Soybean oil

Dip each piece of vegetable in the batter (when using corn, add ¾ cup kernels to 1 cup batter and mix). Brown vegetable pieces or tablespoonfuls of corn-batter mixture on all sides in ½-inch-deep oil on moderate heat.

Vegetable Fritter Batter

2 eggs
¼ cup soybean oil
¼ cup toasted wheat germ
⅓ cup poppy seeds
½ teaspoon Brownies
  Vege-C-Salt (see page 40)

½ teaspoon Bakon Yeast
¼ teaspoon garlic powder
1 cup skim milk
1¾ cups Fearn Whole-Wheat
  Soy-O Mix

Beat the eggs and mix with the next 7 ingredients until smooth. Add the Soy-O Mix gradually, blending until smooth.
    Yield: 3 cups.

FRUIT FRITTERS

Any of the following fruits: sliced apples, halved plums, sliced peaches, halved apricots, pitted prunes stuffed with walnuts, pitted dates stuffed with pecans.

Fruit Fritter Batter   Soybean oil

Dip each piece of fruit in the batter. Brown on all sides in ½-inch-deep oil on moderate heat.

Fruit Fritter Batter

2 eggs	1 cup skim milk
¼ cup soybean oil	1 teaspoon vanilla extract
¼ cup toasted wheat germ	½ teaspoon cinnamon
½ cup toasted sesame seeds	1¾ cups Fearn Soy-O Mix

Beat the eggs and mix until smooth with the next 6 ingredients. Gradually add the Soy-O Mix, blending until smooth.

Yield: 3 cups.

11

OODLES OF NOODLES
(Pasta and Pancakes)

We have Italy to thank for a disproportionate number of the world's most enduring art treasures. The Italians have also given us something else just as likely to inspire passionate gratitude: To them we are indebted for the wonderful world of pastas! You might as well tell the great American public to turn its back on hamburgers, hot dogs, and ice cream as expect it to give up macaroni, spaghetti, and noodles. Warnings about starchiness and calories just won't register. Pastas *will* prevail.

We say, "Up with pastas!" By "up" we mean let's boost their nutritional quotient. Instead of pastas made from "enriched" white flour, why not try soybean noodles or whole-grain spaghetti and macaroni shells? They have more protein and less starch. The good-foodiness can be hiked some more with the addition of spinach and artichoke powders to the pasta. These richer pastas can get still another beefing up with the addition of wheat germ, brewer's yeast, rice polish, and powdered nonfat dry milk. They are a nice substitute for potatoes—and infinitely more potent.

To us pastas are a vehicle of great versatility. Mix them with cheese, meats, eggs, or fish and almost limitless combinations of vegetables and seasonings, and you have a one-dish meal that can be as original as it is kind to the budget.

Pastas as *salad?* Certainly. Consult our Artichoke Elbows Salad, as an example, where said elbows rub elbows with tuna chunks, cubed Swiss cheese, fresh string beans, scallions, peppers, pimientos, et cetera, et cetera.

Desserts? Absolutely. How about our Oodles of Noodles Pudding or our Carrot Honey Noodle Pudding?

The national craze for pancakes—witness the proliferation of pancake houses from coast to coast—is a phenomenon to make any nutritionist edgy: more tons and tons of valueless calories being consumed daily! But pancakes can be nourishing too. Those made with buckwheat flour are a big improvement over the empty white-flour cakes. We have gone further afield to come up with Soy Wheat Noodle Pancakes and Noodle Poppy Pancakes, just as a beginning. Let your own imagination take it from there!

PASTA

SAVORY SOY SPAGHETTI

½ cup diced green pepper
1 cup sliced mushrooms
¼ cup safflower oil
1 cup diced Proteena
2 cups Brownies Tomato
    Sauce (see page 46)

1 tablespoon Krisp
½ teaspoon celery seed
½ teaspoon dill
¼ teaspoon garlic powder
1 pound soybean spaghetti,
    cooked and kept hot

Sauté the green pepper and mushrooms in the oil until light brown. Add the remaining ingredients except for the spaghetti and mix thoroughly. Stir until very hot. Pour over hot spaghetti. Serves 6–8.

SOY SPAGHETTI WITH SAUCY FRANKS

4 cups cooked soybean
    spaghetti
½ cup safflower oil
4 Big Franks, sliced
4 pieces roasted dried
    seaweed, crumbled
½ cup diced Spanish onion
⅓ cup diced celery
1 garlic clove, minced
⅓ cup diced green pepper
½ cup sliced mushrooms
1 cup California tomato juice

½ cup tomato puree
⅓ cup shredded Cheddar
    cheese
2 tablespoons brown-rice flour
2 tablespoons soybean powder
½ teaspoon sea salt
½ teaspoon Brownies
    Vege-C-Salt (see page 40)
½ teaspoon Italian Seasoning
    (see page 41)
½ cup shredded Cheddar
    cheese

Combine the spaghetti, ¼ cup of the safflower oil, Big Franks, and seaweed and set aside. In a saucepan sauté the onion, celery, and garlic in the remaining ¼ cup oil. Add the green pepper and mushrooms and brown lightly. Add all the remaining ingredients but the last and stir until the cheese is melted. Pour over spaghetti mixture and stir well. Place in a baking dish and sprinkle with the ½ cup Cheddar. Bake for 15 minutes in a preheated 375° F. oven, then put under the broiler until the cheese browns. Serves 4–6.

·CORNY SOY SPAGHETTI

3 cups cooked soybean
  spaghetti
2 tablespoons safflower oil
¼ cup diced pimiento
4 Big Franks, sliced
2 eggs
1 cup canned corn kernels
½ cup skim milk
2 tablespoons powdered
  nonfat dry milk

2 tablespoons rice polishings
2 tablespoons lecithin
1 tablespoon Sesame Salt
  (see page 40)
1 teaspoon sea salt
½ teaspoon thyme
½ teaspoon basil
¼ teaspoon garlic powder

Combine the first 4 ingredients and set aside. In a blender combine the remaining ingredients and blend for 1 minute at high speed. Pour over spaghetti combination and stir well. Place in a lightly oiled baking dish and bake for 45 minutes in a preheated 375° F. oven.
  Serves 4–6.

SPAGHETTI PROTEIN CASSEROLE

3 cups cooked soybean
  spaghetti
1 tablespoon snipped fresh
  chives
1 cup canned green soybeans,
  cooked
½ cup chopped Proteena
½ cup Brownies Tomato
  Sauce (see page 46)
2 eggs
½ cup skim milk
1 tablespoon millet meal

1 tablespoon lecithin
1 tablespoon *tamari* sauce
¼ teaspoon sea salt
¼ teaspoon Brownies
  Vege-C-Salt (see page 40)
½ teaspoon garlic powder
¼ teaspoon basil
¼ teaspoon Italian Seasoning
  (see page 41)
½ cup shredded Cheddar
  cheese

Mix the spaghetti and chives together and set aside. Combine the remaining ingredients except for the cheese in a blender at medium speed for 2 minutes. Pour over the spaghetti and mix thoroughly. Place in a lightly oiled baking dish. Sprinkle with cheese and bake for 45 minutes in a preheated 375° F. oven. Place under broiler for several minutes to brown cheese.

Serves 6.

SOY ELBOWS IN PARSLEY MUSHROOM SAUCE

4 cups hot cooked soybean
  elbow macaroni
¼ cup soybean oil
½ cup minced fresh parsley
1 cup diced Spanish onion
½ cup diced celery
½ cup diced green pepper
⅓ cup soybean oil

2 cups sliced mushrooms
2 teaspoons paprika
1½ cups skim milk
2 tablespoons brown-rice flour
1 teaspoon sea salt
½ teaspoon garlic powder
½ teaspoon marjoram
½ teaspoon basil

Combine the first 3 ingredients in a bowl, mixing well. Set aside and keep warm. Sauté the onion, celery, and green pepper in the ⅓ cup oil. Add the mushrooms and paprika and stir until the mushrooms are brown. Add the remaining ingredients and stir until sauce is thickened. Pour over elbows and mix thoroughly.

Serves 4–6.

ORIENTAL ELBOWS

5 cups hot cooked soybean
  elbow macaroni
6 tablespoons safflower oil
½ cup diced scallions
½ cup diced celery
1 cup julienne of string beans
2 cups water
2 tablespoons vegetable-broth
  powder
3 tablespoons brown-rice flour
2 tablespoons
  sesame-sunflower meal

1 tablespoon soybean powder
½ cup mung-bean sprouts
⅓ cup sliced canned
  water chestnuts
2 tablespoons *tamari* sauce
½ teaspoon sea salt
¼ teaspoon allspice
½ teaspoon garlic powder
½ teaspoon rosemary
¼ cup diced pimiento

Combine elbows and ¼ cup of the safflower oil. Keep warm. In the remaining 2 tablespoons of oil sauté the scallions and celery. Add the string beans, 1½ cups of the water, and the vegetable-broth powder. Cover and cook for 5 minutes. Make a smooth mixture of the brown-rice flour, sesame-sunflower meal, soybean powder, and remaining ½ cup water. Add to saucepan and stir until thickened. Add remaining ingredients and mix thoroughly. Pour over the elbows and mix together.

Serves 6–8.

SAM'S FAVORITE MACARONI

2 cups cooked soybean macaroni
½ cup diced green pepper
1 tablespoon Krisp
⅔ cup carrot juice
½ cup cottage cheese
¼ cup goat-milk yogurt
1 egg
¼ cup diced Spanish onion
2 tablespoons chopped fresh parsley
¼ cup toasted wheat germ
2 tablespoons millet meal
1 tablespoon soybean powder
1 tablespoon lecithin
½ teaspoon sea salt
¼ teaspoon Brownies Vege-C-Salt (see page 40)
½ teaspoon Bakon Yeast
¼ teaspoon garlic powder
¼ teaspoon basil

Combine first 3 ingredients and set aside. At medium speed in a blender, combine the remaining ingredients and blend for 1 minute. Pour over the macaroni combination and mix thoroughly. Place in a lightly oiled baking dish and bake for 30 minutes in a preheated 375° F. oven.

Serves 4.

ARTICHOKE ELBOWS WITH WALNUT PESTO

2 cups cooked artichoke
  elbow macaroni
⅔ cup toasted sunflower
  seeds
1 cup skim milk
½ cup walnuts
½ cup chopped fresh parsley
¼ cup toasted wheat germ
⅓ cup diced Cheddar cheese
⅓ cup almond oil

2 tablespoons diced scallions
2 tablespoons vegetable-broth
  powder
1 tablespoon lecithin
1 tablespoon rice polishings
½ teaspoon sea salt
½ teaspoon Italian Seasoning
  (see page 41)
¼ teaspoon garlic powder

Combine the macaroni and sunflower seeds. In a blender combine the remaining ingredients at medium speed for 1 minute. Combine with the macaroni mixture and stir thoroughly. Place in a lightly oiled baking pan and bake for 30 minutes in a preheated 375° F. oven.

Serves 4.

ARTICHOKE-ELBOWS SALAD

3 cups cold cooked artichoke
  elbow macaroni
1 cup water-packed tuna
  chunks
¾ cup safflower oil
½ cup cubed Swiss cheese
1 cup cold cooked cut-up
  string beans
¼ cup diced pimiento
¼ cup diced green pepper
¼ cup sliced radishes

2 tablespoons rice-wine vinegar
2 tablespoons fresh lime juice
¼ cup diced scallions
1 tablespoon snipped fresh
  chives
1 tablespoon lecithin
1 tablespoon rice polishings
¾ teaspoon sea salt
½ teaspoon garlic powder
¼ teaspoon celery seed
½ teaspoon basil

Combine all ingredients in a salad bowl and mix lightly. Refrigerate.

Serves 6.

ARTICHOKE-SHELL SALAD

3 cups cooked artichoke shells
1 cup shredded spinach
2 hard-cooked eggs, diced
¼ cup diced celery
¼ cup sliced mushrooms
½ cup diced avocado
2 tablespoons diced scallions
2 tablespoons sliced pitted
  black olives
2 tablespoons toasted
  pignolias

½ cup Brownies PUFA
  Dressing (see page 42)
¼ cup Brownies Lo-Cal
  Dressing (see page 41)
2 tablespoons diced pimiento
1 tablespoon lecithin
1 tablespoon rice polishings
¼ teaspoon sea salt
¼ teaspoon Brownies
  Vege-C-Salt (see page 40)
¼ teaspoon garlic powder

Combine the first 9 ingredients and mix lightly. Combine the remaining ingredients, stir well, pour over first combination, and mix thoroughly.
Serves 4–6.

ARTICHOKE SHELLS WITH VEGE-CHEESE SAUCE

6 cups hot cooked artichoke
  shells
2 eggs
2 cups skim milk
1 cup ricotta cheese
½ cup shredded Cheddar
  cheese
2 tablespoons brown-rice flour
2 tablespoons millet meal
2 tablespoons soybean powder
2 tablespoons Sesame Salt
  (see page 40)
1 teaspoon sea salt
½ teaspoon garlic powder

½ teaspoon Brownies
  Vege-C-Salt (see page 40)
¼ teaspoon nutmeg
½ teaspoon Italian Seasoning
  (see page 41)
2 tablespoons minced fresh
  parsley
1 tablespoon snipped fresh
  chives
⅓ cup diced Spanish onion
1 garlic clove, minced
½ cup sliced mushrooms
2 tablespoons safflower oil
⅓ cup finely diced carrots
1 cup green peas

Keep artichoke shells hot and set aside. Combine the next 15 ingredients and mix very well in a saucepan on a low fire, stirring until thickened. Sauté the onion, garlic, and mushrooms in the oil until brown. Add the carrots and peas, cover, and cook for 5 minutes. Add to the cheese sauce and mix thoroughly. Serve hot over hot artichoke shells.

Serves 8–10.

ARTICHOKE SHELLS IN ZUCCHINI SAUCE

8 ounces artichoke shells, cooked and kept hot
¼ cup safflower oil
½ cup diced red onion
½ cup diced celery
⅓ cup safflower oil
2 cups diced zucchini with skin
1 cup California tomato juice
½ cup tomato puree
2 diced ripe tomatoes

1 cup VegeBurger
½ cup shredded Muenster cheese
1 tablespoon rice polishings
1 tablespoon lecithin
1 tablespoon snipped fresh chives
1 teaspoon sea salt
½ teaspoon garlic powder
½ teaspoon marjoram
¼ teaspoon celery seed

Combine the artichoke shells and ¼ cup safflower oil in a bowl; set aside and keep warm. Sauté the onion and celery in ⅓ cup safflower oil. Add the next 4 ingredients, cover, and cook on a low fire for 15 minutes. Add the remaining ingredients and mix until the cheese melts. Pour over the artichoke shells and mix well.

Serves 4–6.

SALMON NOODLE BAKE

4 cups cooked soybean
noodles
1 cup salmon chunks,
canned or fresh
½ cup cubed avocado
½ cup diced zucchini with
skin
⅓ cup diced Spanish onion
3 eggs
½ cup sour cream

½ cup buttermilk
¼ cup soybean oil
1 tablespoon snipped fresh
chives
1 teaspoon sea salt
½ teaspoon Brownies
Vege-C-Salt (see page 40)
½ teaspoon basil
½ teaspoon rosemary
¼ teaspoon garlic powder

Combine the first 5 ingredients and mix lightly. In another bowl combine the remaining ingredients and mix thoroughly. Pour over noodle mixture and stir together. Place in a lightly oiled baking dish and bake for 45 minutes in a preheated 350° F. oven.
Serves 6.

TUNA NOODLE SQUARES

4 cups cooked soybean
noodles
½ cup diced Spanish onion
¼ cup soybean oil
1 cup water-packed tuna
¼ cup diced pimiento
1½ cups skim milk
3 tablespoons soybean powder
½ cup powdered nonfat
dry milk

2 tablespoons brown-rice flour
1 tablespoon lecithin
1 teaspoon sea salt
¼ teaspoon garlic powder
¼ teaspoon Italian Seasoning
(see page 41)
¼ teaspoon celery seed
1½ cups shredded Cheddar
cheese

Spread ⅓ of the noodles in a lightly oiled square baking dish. Sauté the onion in the oil until golden and combine with the tuna and pimiento. Combine the remaining ingredients except for ½ cup of the cheese in a saucepan on a low fire, stirring until the sauce is thickened. Sprinkle half of the tuna mixture over the noodles, pour half the sauce over the tuna, and top with ⅓ of the noodles. Repeat the process, ending with noodles. Sprinkle the reserved ½ cup cheese over the noodles and bake for 45 minutes in a preheated 375° F. oven.

Serves 6–8.

STUPENDOUS SOY SPINACH BAKE

4 cups cooked soybean
  noodles
¼ cup safflower oil
2 cups ricotta cheese
3 eggs   .
1 cup cooked minced spinach
¼ cup diced scallions
¼ cup diced pimiento
½ cup unsalted toasted
  Soy Nuts
2 tablespoons
  sesame-sunflower meal

2 tablespoons soybean powder
1 tablespoon lecithin
1 tablespoon snipped fresh
  chives
1 tablespoon vegetable-broth
  powder
½ teaspoon garlic powder
½ teaspoon marjoram
1 teaspoon sea salt
Paprika
Sesame seeds

Combine noodles and oil and set aside. In a large bowl combine all but last 2 ingredients and mix thoroughly. Lightly oil a baking dish. Place half of the noodles on bottom. Cover with the cheese mixture and top with the remaining noodles. Sprinkle with paprika and some sesame seeds. Bake for 45 minutes in a preheated 375° F. oven.

Serves 8.

SESAME FILBERT NOODLES

3 cups cooked soybean
noodles
2 tablespoons sesame oil
2 eggs
1 cup goat-milk yogurt
½ cup sour cream
⅓ cup toasted sesame seeds

⅓ cup toasted sliced filberts
¼ cup diced pimiento
2 tablespoons Sesame Salt
(see page 40)
1 teaspoon raw sugar
½ teaspoon sea salt
¼ teaspoon nutmeg

Combine the noodles and oil in a bowl and set aside. Combine the remaining ingredients and mix thoroughly. Pour over the noodles and mix well. Place in a baking dish and bake for 30 minutes in a preheated 375° F. oven.
Serves 4.

WHOLE-WHEAT WHEAT-GERM NOODLES

⅔ cup diced Spanish onion
⅓ cup soybean oil
4 cups cooked whole-wheat
noodles

¼ cup toasted wheat germ
2 teaspoons Brownies
Vege-C-Salt (see page 40)
1 teaspoon Bakon Yeast

Sauté the onion in the oil and add to the remaining ingredients, stirring lightly. Place in a baking dish and bake for 30 minutes in a preheated 350° F. oven.
Serves 4.

BUCKWHEAT NOODLES ORIENTAL

¼ cup chopped Spanish onion
¼ cup chopped scallions
2 tablespoons sesame oil
8 ounces Japanese buckwheat
noodles, cooked and kept hot

2 tablespoons toasted sesame
seeds
1 tablespoon *tamari* sauce
½ teaspoon sea salt
¼ teaspoon garlic powder

Sauté onion and scallions in oil until onion is transparent and add to noodles. Add remaining ingredients and mix thoroughly.
Serves 4.

VERSATILE SPINACH NOODLES

2 cups cooked spinach
noodles
2 tablespoons sesame oil
½ cup shredded carrots
1 ripe tomato, diced
½ cup ricotta cheese
2 eggs
⅓ cup sour cream

½ cup Brownies Tomato
Sauce (see page 46)
2 tablespoons diced red onion
½ teaspoon sea salt
½ teaspoon Brownies
Vege-C-Salt (see page 40)
¼ teaspoon garlic powder
¼ teaspoon marjoram
¼ teaspoon oregano

Combine the first 4 ingredients and mix well. In another bowl combine the remaining ingredients and mix thoroughly. Pour over the noodle combination and mix lightly. Place in a lightly oiled baking dish and bake for 30 minutes in a preheated 375° F. oven.

Serves 4.

CARAWAY CELERY SPINACH NOODLES

3 cups cooked spinach
noodles
1 tablespoon snipped fresh
chives
1 tablespoon Krisp
1 cup skim milk
1 cup diced celery
2 eggs
2 tablespoons soybean oil
¼ cup diced pimiento

3 tablespoons
sesame-sunflower meal
2 tablespoons soybean powder
1 tablespoon lecithin
2 tablespoons Sesame Salt
(see page 40)
½ teaspoon sea salt
½ teaspoon garlic powder
¼ teaspoon celery seed
1 tablespoon caraway seeds

Combine the noodles, chives, and Krisp and set aside. In a blender at medium speed combine the remaining ingredients except for the caraway seeds for 1 minute. Pour over the noodle combination and mix lightly. Place in a lightly oiled baking pan and sprinkle with caraway seeds. Bake for 30 minutes in a preheated 375° F. oven.

Serves 4–6.

GREEN AND YELLOW NOODLE QUICHE

2 eggs
½ cup Brownies Tomato
  Sauce (see page 46)
½ cup skim milk
2 tablespoons soybean powder
⅓ cup sliced almonds
½ cup shredded Cheddar
  cheese
¼ teaspoon sea salt

⅛ teaspoon garlic powder
¼ teaspoon nutmeg
1½ cups cooked spinach
  noodles
1½ cups cooked soybean-
  wheat noodles
¼ cup safflower oil
½ cup shredded Swiss cheese

Combine the first 9 ingredients and mix thoroughly. Combine
the two kinds of noodles and the oil. Spread them in a 9-inch
pie pan. Sprinkle the Swiss cheese over the noodles, then pour
the first mixture on top of the cheese. Bake for 30 minutes in a
preheated 375° F. oven.
    Serves 6–8.

SORBA 'N' SEAWEED

8 ounces Japanese green
  noodles (*sorba*)
2½ quarts water
1 teaspoon sea salt
½ cup *hijiki*
½ cup chopped Spanish onion

2 tablespoons sesame oil
½ cup slivered bean curd
1 tablespoon Sesame Salt
  (see page 40)
1 tablespoon *tamari* sauce
1 tablespoon poppy seeds

Add noodles to 2 quarts of the water, boiling, to which ½
teaspoon of the salt has been added. Cook approximately 8 minutes or until tender. Drain and set aside, keeping hot. Soak *hijiki*
in the remaining 2 cups water for ½ hour. Pour off water and
squeeze *hijiki* dry. Sauté onion in oil until transparent. Add
hijiki and bean curd to oil and mix thoroughly. Add mixture
to noodles and season with remaining ingredients, mixing thoroughly.
    Serves 4.

TWO-TONE NOODLE PUDDING

3 cups cooked soybean
  noodles
2 tablespoons safflower oil
½ cup diced preserved
  kumquats
⅓ cup diced dates
¼ cup walnut pieces
1 cup cooked sliced carrots
2 eggs
2 tablespoons Papaya Syrup
  Concentrate

2 tablespoons tupelo honey
1 tablespoon Barbados
  molasses
1 teaspoon vanilla extract
1 teaspoon cinnamon
½ cup sour cream
½ cup honey strawberry
  preserves
2 tablespoons soybean powder
1 teaspoon orange extract
Walnut pieces

Combine the first 5 ingredients and set aside. Combine the carrots, eggs, Papaya Syrup Concentrate, honey, molasses, vanilla, and ½ teaspoon of the cinnamon in a blender for 1 minute at medium speed. Combine thoroughly with the noodle mixture. Place in a lightly oiled baking dish and bake for 25 minutes in a preheated 375° F. oven. Meanwhile combine remaining ½ teaspoon cinnamon, sour cream, preserves, soybean powder, and orange extract to make topping, mixing until smooth. Remove pudding from oven, spread with topping, and sprinkle with walnut pieces. Return to oven and continue baking for about 20 minutes or until topping is firm to the touch.

Serves 4–6.

OODLES-OF-NOODLES PUDDING

3 eggs
1 cup cottage cheese
1 cup sour cream
1 whole orange with skin, cut
  in small pieces and seeded
½ cup maple syrup
2 tablespoons soybean powder
1 tablespoon rice polishings

½ teaspoon sea salt
1 teaspoon vanilla extract
½ teaspoon cinnamon
6 cups cooked soybean
  noodles
⅓ cup sesame-sunflower meal
1 cup Monukka raisins
Cinnamon

In a blender at medium speed combine the first 10 ingredients for 2 minutes. Pour over the noodles and mix thoroughly. Add the next 2 ingredients and mix well. Pour into a lightly oiled deep baking pan, heart-shaped if available. Sprinkle with cinnamon and bake for 1 hour in a preheated 375° F. oven.
Serves 8–10.

CAROB NOODLE PUDDING

3 cups cooked soybean noodles
2 tablespoons safflower oil
⅓ cup diced dried pineapple
¼ cup diced dried bananas
¼ cup pecan pieces
2 eggs
½ cup buttermilk
½ cup sour cream
⅓ cup carob powder

⅓ cup date sugar
¼ cup clover honey
2 tablespoons Barbados molasses
2 tablespoons soybean powder
2 tablespoons lecithin
1 teaspoon vanilla extract
1 teaspoon cinnamon
¼ teaspoon sea salt
Sliced almonds

Combine the first 5 ingredients and mix well. In a blender combine the remaining ingredients except for the almonds for 1 minute at medium speed. Add to the noodle combination and mix thoroughly. Place in a lightly oiled baking dish and top with sliced almonds. Bake for 45 minutes in a preheated 375° F. oven.
Serves 6.

CARROT HONEY NOODLE PUDDING

2 cups cooked soybean-wheat
  noodles
2 eggs
½ cup carrot juice
½ cup canned crushed
  unsweetened pineapple
¼ cup tupelo honey
3 tablespoons granulated
  maple sugar

2 tablespoons safflower oil
2 tablespoons millet meal
2 tablespoons soybean powder
1 teaspoon orange extract
½ cup Monukka raisins
¼ teaspoon sea salt
½ teaspoon cinnamon

Combine all the ingredients and mix thoroughly. Place in a
lightly oiled baking pan and bake for 45 minutes in a preheated
375° F. oven.
  Serves 4–6.

CHERRY APPLE NOODLE PUDDING

3 cups cooked soybean-wheat
  noodles
1 cup canned water-packed
  sour red cherries
2 eggs
½ cup cottage cheese
½ cup sour cream
¼ cup canned unsweetened
  pineapple juice
2 tablespoons tupelo honey
1 cup diced McIntosh apple
  with skin

½ cup raw sugar
1 tablespoon Sesame Salt
  (see page 40)
1 tablespoon lecithin
1 teaspoon vanilla extract
1 teaspoon cinnamon
½ cup toasted wheat germ
2 tablespoons safflower oil
½ cup sliced almonds
2 tablespoons
  sesame-sunflower meal

Combine the noodles and cherries and set aside. In a blender
combine the next 10 ingredients and ½ teaspoon of the cinnamon
at high speed for 1 minute. Pour over the noodle mixture and
stir thoroughly. Place in a lightly oiled baking pan. Combine
reserved ½ teaspoon cinnamon with the remaining ingredients
and sprinkle on top of the noodles to make topping. Bake for
45 minutes in a preheated 375° F. oven.
  Serves 6.

PANCAKES

SOY-WHEAT NOODLE PANCAKES

2 cups cooked soybean-wheat
   noodles
2 eggs
¼ cup goat-milk yogurt
¼ cup minced fresh parsley
½ cup pumpkin seeds
2 tablespoons sesame oil
2 tablespoons diced Spanish
   onion

2 tablespoons millet meal
2 tablespoons brown-rice flour
½ teaspoon sea salt
¼ teaspoon Brownies
   Vege-C-Salt (see page 40)
¼ teaspoon garlic powder
¼ teaspoon cumin
Sesame oil

Cut the noodles in small pieces and combine in a bowl with the remaining ingredients except for the sesame oil. Over a moderate flame heat sesame oil in a large skillet to a depth of ½ inch and drop batter by tablespoonfuls, browning on both sides.

    Yield: about 24.

NOODLE POPPY PANCAKES

2 cups cooked soybean-wheat
   noodles
1 cup ricotta cheese
2 eggs
¼ cup sour cream
¼ cup diced scallions
¼ cup diced pimiento
2 tablespoons poppy seeds
1 tablespoon snipped fresh
   chives

½ cup toasted wheat germ
½ cup millet meal
½ teaspoon sea salt
¼ teaspoon Brownies
   Vege-C-Salt (see page 40)
¼ teaspoon garlic powder
¼ teaspoon mace
Sesame oil

Cut the noodles in small pieces and set aside. Combine the remaining ingredients except for the last and mix thoroughly. Add the cut noodles and stir well. On a moderate flame heat sesame oil to a depth of ½ inch in a large skillet and drop batter by tablespoonfuls, browning on both sides.

    Yield: about 24.

RICOTTA PANCAKES

1 pound part-skim ricotta
cheese
3 eggs
¼ cup diced scallions
¼ cup diced pimiento
⅔ cup Fearn Whole Wheat
Soy-O Mix
⅓ cup toasted wheat germ

¼ cup toasted sesame seeds
½ teaspoon Brownies
Vege-C-Salt (see page 40)
¼ teaspoon garlic powder
¼ teaspoon Bakon Yeast
½ teaspoon Italian Seasoning
(see page 41)
Soybean oil

Combine all the ingredients except the soybean oil and mix thoroughly. Drop batter by tablespoonfuls into ½-inch-deep soybean oil and brown on both sides on moderate heat.

Yield: about 24.

WHOLE-WHEAT WHAMMIES

2 eggs
¼ cup soybean oil
1½ cups buttermilk
1 cup stone-ground whole-
wheat flour
½ cup toasted wheat germ
¼ cup toasted sesame seeds
2 tablespoons soybean powder
2 tablespoons lecithin

2 tablespoons powdered
nonfat dry milk
2 tablespoons raw sugar
1½ teaspoons tartrate baking
powder
½ teaspoon sea salt
Strawberry Blueberry Sauce
(see page 47)

Beat the first 3 ingredients until smooth. Blend the remaining ingredients except for the sauce separately and add all at once to the egg mixture; mix until smooth. Drop batter from a spoon onto a hot oiled griddle and brown on both sides. Serve with Strawberry Blueberry Sauce.

Yield: about 24.

BUCKWHEAT BUSTERS

2 eggs
1 cup goat-milk yogurt
1 cup buttermilk
¼ cup safflower oil
2 tablespoons clover honey
¾ cup Fearn Whole Wheat
    Soy-O Mix

¾ cup buckwheat flour
¼ cup toasted wheat germ
¼ cup sesame meal
Raspberry Maple Sauce (see
    page 47)

Combine the first 5 ingredients and beat until smooth. Blend the remaining ingredients except for the sauce, add all at once to the egg mixture, and mix until smooth. Drop batter from a spoon onto a hot oiled griddle and brown on both sides. Serve with Raspberry Maple Sauce.

Yield: about 24.

CORNMEAL FLAPS

2 eggs
¼ cup safflower oil
1½ cups buttermilk
2 tablespoons clover honey
1 cup Fearn Soy-O Mix
½ cup yellow cornmeal

¼ cup toasted wheat germ
¼ cup unsweetened shredded
    coconut
2 tablespoons lecithin
Sour-Cream Date Sauce (see
    page 49)

Combine the first 4 ingredients and whip until smooth. Blend the remaining ingredients except for the sauce and add all at once to the egg mixture, mixing until smooth. Drop batter from a spoon onto a hot oiled griddle and brown on both sides. Serve with Sour-Cream Date Sauce.

Yield: about 18.

OATMEAL FLIPS

2 eggs
¼ cup carrot juice
1 cup buttermilk
¼ cup soybean oil
2 tablespoons Barbados
    molasses
1½ cups stone-ground whole-
    wheat flour

1 cup rolled oats
2 tablespoons lecithin
2 tablespoons soybean powder
1½ teaspoons baking powder
½ teaspoon sea salt
Lemon Cranberry Sauce (see
    page 48)

Whip the first 5 ingredients until smooth. Blend the remaining ingredients except for the sauce and add all at once to the egg mixture, mixing until smooth. Drop batter from a spoon onto a hot oiled griddle and brown on both sides. Serve with Lemon Cranberry Sauce.

Yield: about 24.

RICE-POLISH RINGERS

2 eggs
¼ cup sesame oil
½ cup goat-milk yogurt
½ cup canned unsweetened
    pineapple juice
1 cup buttermilk
¾ cup Fearn Whole Wheat
    Soy-O Mix

½ cup rice polishings
¼ cup brown-rice flour
¼ cup sesame-sunflower meal
2 tablespoons lecithin
2 tablespoons raw sugar
Carrot Currant Sauce (see page
    48)

Beat the first 5 ingredients until smooth. Blend the remaining ingredients except for the sauce, add all at once to the egg mixture, and mix until smooth. Drop batter from a spoon onto a hot oiled griddle and brown on both sides. Serve with Carrot Currant Sauce.

Yield: about 24.

CHICKPEA PLANTERS

2 eggs
¼ cup safflower oil
½ cup sour cream
1½ cups buttermilk
1 cup unbleached white–and–
  wheat-germ flour
½ cup chickpea flour
2 tablespoons soybean powder

2 tablespoons green-banana
  flour
2 tablespoons raw sugar
1½ teaspoons baking powder
½ teaspoon sea salt
⅔ cup unsalted Soy Nuts
Cherry Pineapple Sauce (see
  page 48)

Combine the first 4 ingredients and beat smooth. Blend the remaining ingredients except for the sauce, add all at once to the egg mixture, and mix until smooth. Drop from a spoon onto a hot oiled griddle and brown on both sides. Serve with Cherry Pineapple Sauce.

Yield: about 24.

THE VITAL COMPLEMENT

(Vegetables)

The vegetable has become the neglected foster child of the American table. The troubles of the luckless legume begin at birth. Seeds are sown in impoverished soil. During its growth the plant is doused with poisonous sprays. Careless handling between garden and market is the usual fate of produce. What little life is left is often extinguished before the vegetable reaches the dinner plate—by soaking, peeling, boiling, and the passage of time itself.

Mostly the vegetable dies because we do not love it enough.

But a corner has been turned. Today more and more barren ground is being reclaimed. The growth of organic gardening means the return to the soil of the trace minerals that were lost through negligence and the use of chemical fertilizers. Now we know about "internal pollution" and the danger of insecticide residues in our bodies. We have also learned that the best foods are those that ripen naturally on plants and trees, exposed to sun and rain—not in hothouses.

Gradually we are rediscovering the delights of fresh vegetables, low in calories and loaded with vitamins and minerals. True, Americans have long been devoted to at least two vegetables: French-fried potatoes and corn on the cob. Even French-fries addicts, though, would hardly argue that they are hooked on something healthful. Corn on the cob rates its popularity, but how many of us are fortunate enough to eat it as it should be eaten—straight off the stalk, immediately shucked and cooked?

Cooking vegetables—and cooking them right—is an act of caring. Our own feeling is that nothing so distinguishes the home chef as a mastery of the alphabet of vegetable cookery from artichokes to zucchini.

Vegetables are wondrously various, offering almost limitless opportunities for improvisation. And what a feast they can be for the eye! A plate composed of vegetables of contrasting colors is as visually seductive as a Japanese flower arrangement. Just close your eyes, as a test, and evoke the image of kelly-green broccoli, the magenta of red cabbage, sun-colored kernels of corn, scarlet wedges of tomato, and the dusky orange of yams . . . all of them clustered around a snowy hillock of cauliflower.

As we've said before, we recommend using organic vegetables whenever they are available. They are superior in flavor, as well as in nutrients. Fresh vegetables are always preferable to frozen ones. With quick, cautious freezing, the nutrients of frozen vegetables can mostly be saved, but the taste will never measure up to that of fresh ones. In terms of desirability, dried vegetables come next; at the bottom of the pecking order is the canned product.

The faster a vegetable moves from picking to pot, the better. Blessed are those with a home garden, who can pick their beans or squash or peas just before cooking time. The rest of us should try to shop for produce when it arrives at the market—and eat it as soon afterward as possible.

Brevity is the soul of vegetable cookery. To maintain flavor, nutrients, color, and texture cook just long enough for tenderness. You will save time, taste, and trouble—not to mention food value —if you can get out of the peeling habit. The best of the vegetable lies close to the skin and is lost in peeling. Peel only when the skin is too tough or bitter or so irregular that it can't be cleaned carefully.

Vegetables are largely water, so they need very little added for cooking. Total immersion can wash away all the nutrients—and all the edibility. The one absolute cookery imperative is: *Do not boil.* Boiling practically guarantees tasteless, valueless, water-logged vegetables.

As every devotee of the superlative Chinese cuisine knows, the Chinese have an admirable way with vegetables: stir-frying in a small amount of vegetable oil—and no water at all—quickly enough so that vegetables always keep their character and bite.

In our experience, however, the supremely desirable way to cook vegetables is to steam them. This relatively waterless method also assures maximum crispness, flavor, and nutrient retention. Steaming can be done in the top of a double boiler, in a pressure cooker, or best of all, in a steamer especially designed for the preparation of vegetables. Since the steam above boiling water is the same temperature as the water, the vegetables cook as quickly as they would if you boiled them.

A steamed vegetable dressed with just a little oil will always be enticing, but the vegetable buff has a whole kingdom to explore and can bring together some of the most astonishingly diverse elements. Some of the recipes here you will never find on Brownies' menu. In our own kitchen we let ourselves go a bit and began fantasizing. . . . If you think a baked potato is a baked potato is a baked potato—well, you are oversimplifying. *Our* baked potato has *ingredients:* mashed carrots, spinach, cottage cheese, and goat-milk yogurt! Nor is it true the British buried Brussels sprouts forevermore—in a sea of boiling water. Here those same sprouts surface in a surprise resurrection, mixing companionably with wax beans, water chestnuts, hunks of orange, and seedless green grapes.

To vegetables! Steam on!

VEGETABLE MÉLANGE

½ cup diced Spanish onion
2 garlic cloves, minced
½ cup sliced mushrooms
¼ cup sesame oil
3 cups peeled cubed eggplant
⅓ cup tomato puree
1½ cups California tomato juice
2 tablespoons soybean powder
½ cup diced new potatoes with skin
½ cup canned artichoke hearts

½ cup green peas
1 cup cut-up wax beans
½ cup diced tomato
½ cup cubed Swiss cheese
2 tablespoons snipped fresh chives
1 teaspoon sea salt
¼ teaspoon garlic powder
1 teaspoon Italian Seasoning (see page 41)
1 teaspoon dill

Sauté the onion, garlic, and mushrooms in the sesame oil. Add the eggplant, tomato puree, and tomato juice. Cover and cook for 10 minutes. Add remaining ingredients and mix thoroughly. Pour into a baking dish and bake for 1 hour in a preheated 375° F. oven.

Serves 6–8.

POTATOES O'BROWNIE

½ cup diced Spanish onion
⅓ cup soybean oil
4 cups cold cooked sliced Idaho potatoes
½ teaspoon sea salt

½ teaspoon kelp
¼ teaspoon garlic powder
Few grindings of pepper
½ teaspoon paprika

Sauté the onion in the oil and mix together with the next 5 ingredients. Place in a lightly oiled baking dish and sprinkle with the paprika. Bake in a preheated 350° F. oven for 45 minutes.
Serves 6–8.

BAKED-POTATO TRIO

3 baked potatoes
1 cup steamed sliced carrots, mashed
½ cup drained steamed spinach, chopped
¼ cup cottage cheese
⅓ cup goat-milk yogurt

2 teaspoons Sesame Salt (see page 40)
½ teaspoon sea salt
¼ teaspoon garlic powder
¼ teaspoon nutmeg
Paprika

Halve the potatoes, scoop out insides, and mash in a bowl. Add the remaining ingredients except for the paprika and mix thoroughly. Refill each potato shell with the mixture. Sprinkle paprika on top of each and broil until light brown.
Serves 6.

POTATO PANCAKES
(Gayle's Favorite)

4 cups peeled and cut-up Idaho potatoes
½ cup diced Spanish onion
¼ cup soybean oil
2 eggs

¼ cup toasted wheat germ
1 teaspoon Brownies Vege-C-Salt (see page 40)
Soybean oil

Grind the potatoes in a grinder and set aside in a bowl. Sauté the onion in the oil and add with the next 3 ingredients to the ground potatoes, mixing thoroughly. Put soybean oil in a large skillet to a depth of ½ inch, then place over moderate flame and brown 2 tablespoons of potato mixture for each pancake.
Serves 8.

HAWAIIAN YAM PIE

1 pound cooked yams, peeled
and mashed
1 egg
2 tablespoons raw sugar
1 tablespoon orange-blossom
honey
¼ cup orange juice

½ cup canned crushed
unsweetened pineapple
2 tablespoons safflower oil
1 tablespoon fresh lemon juice
¼ cup toasted unsweetened
shredded coconut
¼ cup toasted sesame seeds

In a bowl, using an electric mixer at medium speed, combine the first 8 ingredients and mix for 5 minutes. Combine the remaining 2 ingredients and place half in the bottom of a pie pan. Spread the yam mixture on top and sprinkle the remaining coconut-sesame mixture over the yam mixture. Bake for 20 minutes in a preheated 350° F. oven.
Serves 6.

GOLDEN YAM DELIGHT

¼ cup maple syrup
2 tablespoons orange-blossom
honey
⅓ cup orange juice
2 tablespoons safflower oil
¼ teaspoon Sesame Salt (see
page 40)

2 medium yams, cooked,
peeled, and sliced
1 Delicious apple with skin,
sliced
1 large carrot, cooked and
sliced
2 tablespoons Monukka raisins

Combine the first 5 ingredients and mix thoroughly. In a baking pan make alternating layers of the yam, apple, and carrot slices, pouring some of the liquid mixture over each layer. Top with the raisins. Cover and bake in a preheated 375° F. oven for 35 minutes. Uncover and bake for 10 minutes more.
Serves 4–6.

AMBROSIA YAMS

6 medium yams
1½ quarts water
12 canned unsweetened
   pineapple slices
½ cup canned unsweetened
   pineapple juice

½ cup orange juice
⅔ cup maple syrup
¼ cup safflower oil
1 teaspoon orange extract
½ teaspoon lemon extract
¼ teaspoon cinnamon

Simmer the yams in the water in a saucepan until tender. Drain yams, discarding water, peel, and cut in half lengthwise. Arrange the pineapple slices in a baking dish. Place a yam half, cut side down, on each slice. Combine the remaining ingredients and pour over the yams. Bake for 1 hour in a preheated 375° F. oven, basting occasionally with pan juices.
   Serves 12.

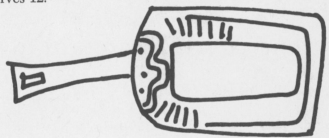

CORN COMBINE

⅓ cup diced red onion
½ cup sliced mushrooms
¼ cup safflower oil
2 cups canned corn kernels
1 cup cauliflower florets

¾ cup water
¼ cup diced pimiento
½ teaspoon Brownies
   Vege-C-Salt (see page 40)
¼ teaspoon thyme

Sauté the onion and mushrooms in the oil in a saucepan until light brown. Add the corn, cauliflower, and water. Cover and cook on a low flame for 15 minutes. Add remaining ingredients and stir thoroughly.
   Serves 4.

CONFETTI CORN PUDDING

2 cups canned corn with its liquid
½ cup shredded carrots
1 scallion, diced
1 tablespoon snipped fresh chives
3 eggs
1 cup goat-milk yogurt

¼ cup soybean granules
¼ cup toasted wheat germ
1 tablespoon rice polishings
½ teaspoon sea salt
½ teaspoon Brownies Vege-C-Salt (see page 40)
¼ teaspoon tarragon
¼ teaspoon garlic powder

In a large mixing bowl combine the first 4 ingredients. In another bowl beat the eggs briskly and combine with the remaining ingredients. Add to the corn mixture and mix thoroughly. Pour into a lightly oiled baking pan and bake for 45 minutes in a preheated 350° F. oven.
Serves 6–8.

MEDITERRANEAN VEGETABLES

2 cups green peas
1 cup cauliflower florets
½ cup water
1 cup skim milk
½ cup shredded Cheddar cheese
1 egg

¼ cup soybean powder
1 teaspoon sea salt
1 teaspoon Sesame Salt (see page 40)
¼ teaspoon garlic powder
½ teaspoon dill

Combine peas, cauliflower, and water in a covered saucepan and cook for 10 minutes on a low fire. In a mixing bowl combine the remaining ingredients. Add the drained cooked vegetables and stir lightly. Pour into a lightly oiled baking dish and bake for 30 minutes in a preheated 350° F. oven.
Serves 4–6.

PEAS AND MUSHROOMS

½ cup diced Spanish onion
¼ cup diced celery
1 garlic clove, minced
¼ cup soybean oil
1 cup sliced mushrooms
1 cup green peas
¾ cup skim milk
1 tablespoon soybean granules

2 teaspoons soybean powder
½ teaspoon sea salt
½ teaspoon Brownies
   Vege-C-Salt (see page 40)
½ teaspoon Italian Seasoning
   (see page 41)
¼ teaspoon marjoram
¼ teaspoon paprika

Sauté the onion, celery, and garlic in the oil in a saucepan. Add the mushrooms and brown lightly. Add the remaining ingredients and stir thoroughly. Cover and cook for 10 minutes on a low fire. Serves 4–6.

MUSHROOMS AND ARTICHOKE HEARTS

½ cup diced Spanish onion
⅓ cup diced celery
⅓ cup diced green pepper
¼ cup safflower oil
1 cup sliced mushrooms
1 cup frozen artichoke hearts, thawed

¼ cup diced pimiento
⅓ cup tomato puree
½ teaspoon sea salt
½ teaspoon dill
¼ teaspoon garlic powder
¼ cup goat-milk yogurt

Sauté the onion, celery, and green pepper in the oil in a saucepan. Add the mushrooms and brown lightly. Add the next 6 ingredients, cover, and cook for 10 minutes. Remove from fire and stir in the yogurt.
   Serves 4.

GRAND GREEN BEANS
(Dennis's Favorite)

¼ cup sesame oil
½ cup diced scallions
1 cup sliced mushrooms
2 cups inch-long pieces green
  beans
⅔ cup California tomato juice

1 cup sliced canned water
  chestnuts
½ teaspoon sea salt
½ teaspoon savory
⅛ teaspoon garlic powder

In a saucepan heat the oil and sauté the scallions and mushrooms until light brown. Add the green beans and tomato juice, cover, and cook for 10 minutes. Add the water chestnuts and seasonings and stir together.
    Serves 4–6.

ASPARAGUS SOY QUICHE

Crust:
½ cup toasted wheat germ
⅓ cup soybean granules
⅓ cup ground walnuts.
2 tablespoons soybean oil

Filling:
20 steamed asparagus spears
1 cup diced Spanish onion
¼ cup soybean oil
½ cup shredded Cheddar
  cheese

½ cup shredded Swiss cheese
3 eggs
1 cup skim milk
1 cup goat-milk yogurt
1 teaspoon sea salt
¼ teaspoon nutmeg
¼ teaspoon garlic powder
1 tablespoon snipped fresh
  chives
Paprika

To make crust combine wheat germ, soybean granules, walnuts, and soybean oil and mix thoroughly. Press into the bottom and up the sides of a 10-inch pie pan. Arrange the asparagus on the crust. Sauté the onion in the soybean oil until golden and put over the asparagus. Sprinkle the Cheddar and Swiss cheeses over the onions. Beat the next 6 ingredients lightly together and pour over the cheese. Sprinkle with the chives and paprika. Bake in a preheated 350° F. oven for 45 minutes.
    Serves 10–12.

CABBAGE SUPREME

¼ cup diced scallions
¼ cup soybean oil
2 cups finely cut cabbage
1 Delicious apple with skin, diced
1 cup sauerkraut with its juice

2 tablespoons Monukka raisins
¼ cup water
¼ teaspoon sea salt
¼ teaspoon celery seed
⅛ teaspoon garlic powder
1 tablespoon Krisp

Sauté the scallions in the oil in a saucepan. Add the next 5 ingredients, cover, and cook on a medium fire for 15 minutes. Add the remaining ingredients and stir thoroughly.
Serves 4–6.

APPLE RED CABBAGE

8 cups sliced red cabbage
1 Delicious apple with skin, diced
2 cups apple juice

½ cup Monukka raisins
1 tablespoon fresh lemon juice
½ teaspoon sea salt

Combine the first 4 ingredients in a large covered kettle over a low flame for about 30 minutes or until cabbage is tender. Add the lemon juice and salt and stir.
Serves 8.

CREOLE BROCCOLI

½ cup diced red onion
½ cup diced celery
½ cup diced green pepper
⅓ cup safflower oil
2 cups chopped broccoli
2 cups diced tomatoes
½ cup water
1 tablespoon snipped fresh chives

2 teaspoons Krisp
1 teaspoon Brownies Vege-C-Salt (see page 40)
¼ teaspoon garlic powder
¼ teaspoon nutmeg
¼ teaspoon marjoram
½ cup sliced pitted black olives

In a saucepan sauté the onion, celery, and green pepper in the oil for 5 minutes. Add the broccoli, tomatoes, and water. Cover and cook for 10 minutes. Add remaining ingredients and mix thoroughly.

Serves 4–6.

BRUSSELS-SPROUT SURPRISE

2 cups cold steamed Brussels sprouts, halved

1 cup cold steamed wax bean pieces

⅓ cup sliced canned water chestnuts

⅓ cup cubed orange

½ cup seedless green grapes

⅔ cup canned unsweetened pineapple juice

¼ cup almond oil

1 tablespoon fresh lemon juice

½ teaspoon sea salt

2 teaspoons orange-blossom honey

2 tablespoons Papaya Syrup Concentrate

Combine first 5 ingredients in bowl. For dressing whip together thoroughly remaining ingredients. Mix dressing and Brussels-sprout mixture together. Serve hot or cold.

Serves 6.

OUR FAVORITE SPINACH PIE

Crust:
1 large baked potato
1 egg
1 tablespoon soybean oil
1 tablespoon brown-rice flour
⅛ teaspoon sea salt
Pinch of garlic powder
Pinch of freshly ground pepper

Filling:
1 cup cottage cheese
1 egg

⅓ cup goat-milk yogurt
⅓ cup steamed chopped
  spinach
⅓ cup steamed chopped
  turnip greens
1 tablespoon brown-rice flour
½ teaspoon Italian Seasoning
  (see page 41)
¼ teaspoon garlic powder
½ teaspoon sea salt
2 tablespoons diced scallions

To make crust scoop out insides of potato, discarding skin, and mash. Combine with the egg, the oil, the brown-rice flour, the salt, the pinch of garlic powder, and the pepper. Spread in a lightly oiled 9-inch pie pan in a thin layer. For the filling combine the remaining ingredients except for the scallions in blender at medium speed for 1 minute. Add scallions and mix lightly. Pour filling into potato crust and bake in a preheated 375° F. oven for 30 minutes.
    Serves 6.

TURNIP GREENS MARTINIQUE

6 large ripe tomatoes
⅔ cup steamed chopped
  turnip greens
2 scallions, diced
2 eggs
¼ cup diced green pepper
½ cup shredded Cheddar
  cheese
¼ cup toasted wheat germ

2 tablespoons toasted sesame
  seeds
1 teaspoon sea salt
½ teaspoon oregano
⅛ teaspoon garlic powder
Few grindings of pepper
1 slice Swiss cheese
Caraway seeds

Cut each tomato in quarters, but do not cut quite to the bottom. Combine all the other ingredients except the Swiss cheese and caraway seeds and mix thoroughly. Divide among the 6 tomatoes, mounding high. Cut the Swiss cheese in 6 pieces and top each tomato with 1 piece. Sprinkle with caraway seeds and bake in a preheated 375° F. oven for 25 minutes.

Serves 6.

CRISP ZUCCHINI CIRCLES

1 cup Brownies Breading Mix
  (see page 169)
⅓ cup soybean powder
1 egg
¼ cup skim milk

⅛ teaspoon garlic powder
⅛ teaspoon paprika
3 cups thinly sliced zucchini
  with skin
Safflower oil

Arrange three small bowls. Put the breading mix in one, the soybean powder in another, and then a combination of the egg, milk, garlic powder, and paprika, beaten well, in another. Dip each zucchini circle on both sides first in the soybean powder, then the egg wash, then the breading mix. Brown them on both sides in ½-inch-deep safflower oil on moderate heat.

Serves 4.

SUMMER-SQUASH SAUTÉ

⅓ cup diced Spanish onion
¼ cup safflower oil
2 cups coarsely diced yellow
  summer squash
½ cup diced tomato
½ cup sliced carrots

⅓ cup California tomato juice
¼ cup water
1 tablespoon snipped fresh
  chives
¼ teaspoon sea salt
⅛ teaspoon garlic powder

Sauté the onion in the oil in a saucepan until golden. Add the next 5 ingredients, cover, and cook for 30 minutes on a low flame. Add the seasonings and stir thoroughly.

Serves 4–6.

SQUASH POTATO PATTIES

1½ cups shredded yellow squash with skin
1 cup shredded new potatoes with skin
2 tablespoons diced Spanish onion
2 eggs
2 teaspoons rice polishings
2 tablespoons soybean powder

2 tablespoons millet meal
1 teaspoon sea salt
3 tablespoons toasted wheat germ
½ teaspoon basil
¼ teaspoon Italian Seasoning (see page 41)
Few grindings of pepper
Safflower oil

Combine all ingredients but last in a mixing bowl and mix thoroughly. Drop by tablespoonfuls into ½-inch-deep safflower oil on moderate heat and brown on both sides.

Serves 6–8.

OKRA GUMBO

⅓ cup diced Spanish onion
¼ cup diced green pepper
2 tablespoons sesame oil
1 cup cubed tomatoes
⅓ cup tomato puree
1 cup canned corn kernels with their liquid

24 whole okra pods, steamed
½ teaspoon sea salt
½ teaspoon Italian Seasoning (see page 41)
¼ teaspoon garlic powder
¼ teaspoon savory

Sauté the onion and green pepper in the sesame oil in a saucepan. Add the tomatoes and stir for several minutes. Add remaining ingredients, mix thoroughly, and heat through.

Serves 4–6.

CARROT CELERY PUREE

2 cups steamed carrot rounds
1 cup steamed cut-up celery
1 baked potato, skin removed
1 egg
2 tablespoons sesame oil
2 tablespoons *tahini*

1 tablespoon Sesame Salt (see page 40)
½ teaspoon sea salt
¼ teaspoon nutmeg
Sesame seeds (optional)
Scooped-out orange shells (optional)

Combine all ingredients except for sesame seeds and scooped-out orange shells in blender for 30 seconds at low speed, then for 1 minute at medium speed. Pour into a lightly oiled baking dish and bake for 15 minutes in a preheated 375° F. oven. Sprinkle with sesame seeds if desired. The puree can also be baked in the same way in scooped-out orange shells.
Serves 4–6.

GINGER CARROTS

2 cups carrot rounds
¾ cup water
⅓ cup orange juice
2 tablespoons orange-blossom honey

½ teaspoon sea salt
¼ teaspoon powdered ginger
⅔ cup diced orange

Cook the carrots in the water in a covered saucepan for 15 minutes on a low fire. Remove ½ cup of the cooked carrots and mash smooth. Add the orange juice, honey, salt, and ginger and mix thoroughly. Combine with the drained carrot rounds and diced orange. Heat for 2 minutes on a low fire.
Serves 4.

EGGPLANT TAHINI

1 large eggplant
Cold water
1 cup cooked dried garbanzo beans
½ cup *tahini*
2 tablespoons fresh lemon juice

¼ cup soybean oil
1 teaspoon sea salt
½ teaspoon garlic powder
2 scallions, diced
1 tablespoon minced fresh parsley

Prick eggplant all over with a fork. Place in a preheated 400° F. oven for about 45 minutes or until eggplant feels very soft to the touch. Place in a bowl of cold water and peel off skin, leaving a soft gray pulp. Drain thoroughly of any water. Place in a blender and combine with the next 6 ingredients at medium speed until smooth. Pile into a serving dish and top with the scallions and parsley. May also be used as a cold salad or as a dip with sesame crackers.

Serves 6.

13

NATURE'S OWN CONFECTIONS
(Seeds, Nuts, and Dried Fruits)

Every living thing begins with a seed. Seeds are that first miraculous whisper of life, the harbinger of growth and ripening . . . the hope of fruitful harvests.

Nutritionally, seeds are richest in vitamins B and E, minerals, and protein. Among those most favored for cooking—or eating "neat"—are sunflower, sesame, and pumpkin seeds. Sunflower seeds are loaded with high-grade protein (more than 50 percent of their content). They give a giant booster shot to anything they touch. They can be slipped whole into almost anything, from soups to soufflés, or they can be ground or blended into a paste. In the raw or lightly toasted, they make super snacks. The small, sweetish, oily sesame seed—also a vitamin and protein block-buster—is an inspired addition to breads, pastries, confections, and salads. Pumpkin or squash seeds are as American as the American Indian, their original chief consumer.

Include nuts among the very rich in proteins, vitamins, and minerals. Compared to almonds, which are older than Chris-tianity, most nuts are Johnny-come-latelys. The American Indians tucked heavily into pignolias (pine nuts), hazelnuts, and horse chestnuts. Best of breed of native-grown nuts is the pecan, but the most popular and economical is the plebeian peanut, which purists could accurately point out is not a nut at all but a legumi-nous vegetable.

"Carbohydrate" may be a dirty 12-letter word in some circles, particularly among the diet-conscious, but carbohydrates, as we all know, *are* fun. Happily, we need a certain amount of them. They are in the best of form when they turn up as tree-ripened, sun-drenched dried fruits: apricots, apples, currants, bananas, pears, peaches, prunes, raisins, dates, persimmons, pineapples, papayas.

Put them together—any mixed bag of seeds, nuts, and dried fruits—and you have nature's most sublime confection: a dynamo of natural energy, more healthful and flavorsome by far than the candies, colas, and chips which have become the instant pick-me-ups of too many of us. Truly provident is the mother who stuffs these healthful alternatives into lunch boxes and has them ready for after-school munching. Nowadays they are also com-pressed into bars, like some tastier latter-day version of K rations.

One thing the young are almost universally gung-ho on is pea-nut butter. It is among their healthier addictions, but it can be an even healthier one if the peanut butter is the fresh-ground, stick-to-the-roof-of-the-mouth variety, sans hydrogenated oils and preservatives.

We suggest also that peanuts and other nuts be eaten raw or dry-roasted (roast them in your own oven), without the usual coating of salt, undesirable fats, and additives. The new natural taste of nuts may take a bit of getting used to, but most palates will soon prefer it to the salty, oily taste of processed nuts.

Don't judge a dried fruit by its color. The darkish hues of unsulphured bananas or apricots may not quicken the pulse of an artist, but they are organically superior to the sulphured.

In this chapter we pay due homage to the sweet tooth, possibly mankind's most prominent feature. At first glance, perhaps, the recipes seem to be basically for sweets; but look again: They also have a seedy, nutty underpinning, the better to fortify the confection.

QUADRUPLE-FRUIT COMPOTE

½ cup dried apricots
½ cup dried Calimyrna figs
½ cup Monukka raisins
⅓ cup diced dried pineapple
   slices

2½ cups water
⅔ cup carrot juice
⅔ cup bottled pomegranate
   juice
⅓ cup date sugar

Combine all ingredients in a saucepan and cook for 25 minutes. Refrigerate and serve cold.

   Yield: about 8 cups.

MIXED-FRUIT MÉLANGE

½ cup pitted prunes
½ cup dried peaches
1 cup dried apple slices
   with skin
½ cup dried Smyrna figs
⅓ cup Monukka raisins
3 cups water

1 cup orange juice
1 orange with skin, thinly
   sliced and seeded
¼ cup Papaya Syrup
   Concentrate
1 tablespoon maple syrup
1 tablespoon tupelo honey

Combine all ingredients in a saucepan and cook for 20 minutes. Refrigerate and serve cold.

   Yield: about 6 cups.

SUGARLESS FRUIT JAM

1 cup pitted prunes
1 cup pitted dates
1 cup Monukka raisins
1 cup dried apricots
1 cup dried black mission figs
1 cup dried Calimyrna figs

1 orange with skin, sliced
  and seeded
1 lemon with skin, sliced
  and seeded
2½ cups water

Combine all the ingredients in a saucepan, cover, and cook on low heat until water is fully absorbed. Set aside until cool. Put through a meat grinder into a bowl and blend thoroughly. Pack into containers with tight-fitting lids and store in refrigerator.

Yield: about 8 cups.

STUFFED DATE PILLOWS

24 pitted dates, halved
¼ cup cottage cheese
¼ cup cream cheese
2 tablespoons sour cream
2 tablespoons toasted wheat
  germ
2 tablespoons clover honey
2 tablespoons *tahini*

2 tablespoons ground walnuts
1 tablespoon lecithin
1 tablespoon rice polishings
1 teaspoon vanilla extract
½ cup toasted sunflower
  seeds
Toasted unsweetened
  shredded coconut

Line up the halved dates on a large flat dish. Combine the remaining ingredients except the coconut in a bowl and mix very well. Divide the mixture among the dates and then dip each one in the coconut. Refrigerate.

Yield: 48.

FILBERT FIGS

12 dried Calimyrna figs
⅓ cup fresh-ground cashew
  butter
¼ cup shredded Cheddar
  cheese
¼ cup shredded carrots
2 tablespoons sour cream

1 tablespoon orange-blossom
  honey
2 teaspoons lecithin
½ teaspoon vanilla extract
¼ teaspoon cinnamon
½ cup sliced toasted filberts

Cut each fig in half almost through to the bottom. Combine all the remaining ingredients except the filberts and mix thoroughly. Divide mixture among the 12 figs and dip each one in the filberts. Refrigerate.

Yield: 12.

HIGH-HAT STUFFED PRUNES

24 pitted prunes
½ recipe of Divine Date
  Drops (omit coconut)
  (see page 218)

24 toasted blanched almonds

With your thumb, form a hollow in each prune. Make 24 balls of the date mixture and put 1 in each prune hollow. Top each with an almond. Refrigerate.

Yield: 24.

COMBINATION CLUSTERS

1½ cups raw sugar
¼ cup Barbados molasses
¼ cup maple syrup
½ cup buttermilk
¼ cup carrot juice
2 tablespoons safflower oil
1 tablespoon lecithin
1 tablespoon soybean powder
¾ cup toasted sesame seeds

½ cup toasted unsweetened
    shredded coconut
⅔ cup toasted sunflower
    seeds
⅓ cup toasted pumpkin seeds
⅓ cup diced pitted prunes
½ cup diced pecans
1 teaspoon lemon extract
½ teaspoon cinnamon

Combine the first 5 ingredients in a deep saucepan on a low fire for 25 minutes, stirring occasionally. Remove from fire and add the remaining ingredients, mixing very well. Drop clusters from a tablespoon onto aluminum foil or a lightly oiled baking sheet. Put clusters, still on foil, in freezer until they harden, then remove from foil and refrigerate.

Yield: 36.

DIVINE DATE DROPS

¾ cup diced pitted dates
¾ cup canned unsweetened
    pineapple juice
½ cup fresh-ground cashew
    butter
¾ cup toasted cashew pieces
⅓ cup toasted sesame seeds
2 tablespoons clover honey

2 tablespoons Barbados
    molasses
3 tablespoons carob powder
¼ cup toasted wheat germ
1 tablespoon lecithin
1 teaspoon vanilla extract
Unsweetened shredded
    coconut

Combine the dates and pineapple juice in a saucepan and cook on a low fire until thick and smooth. Remove from fire and add the remaining ingredients except for the coconut, mixing thoroughly. Drop from a teaspoon into coconut, coating all sides. Refrigerate.

Yield: 72.

PLANTATION PEANUT CLUMPS

1½ cups raw sugar
¼ cup tupelo honey
¼ cup Barbados molasses
½ cup buttermilk
¼ cup canned unsweetened
   pineapple juice
2 tablespoons lecithin

½ cup fresh-ground peanut
   butter
½ cup toasted wheat germ
⅓ cup sesame-sunflower meal
1 teaspoon vanilla extract
1½ cups toasted peanuts
1½ cups Monukka raisins

Combine the first 5 ingredients in a deep saucepan on a low fire for 25 minutes, stirring occasionally. Add the lecithin and peanut butter and cook for 2 more minutes. Remove from fire and stir in the remaining ingredients, mixing thoroughly. Drop in clusters from a tablespoon onto aluminum foil or a lightly oiled baking sheet. Place clusters, still on foil, in freezer until they harden, then remove from foil and refrigerate.

Yield: 24.

FUDGE JUMBLES

¾ cup skim milk
3 tablespoons carob powder
2 tablespoons powdered
   nonfat dry milk
2 tablespoons soybean powder
1½ cups raw sugar
¼ cup Barbados molasses
¼ cup Papaya Syrup
   Concentrate

¼ cup fresh-ground cashew
   butter
1 teaspoon vanilla extract
½ cup Monukka raisins
½ cup toasted pignolias
⅓ cup diced dried
   Calimyrna figs
¼ cup diced dried papaya

Combine the first 7 ingredients in a saucepan and cook on a low fire, stirring occasionally until ½ teaspoon of the mixture forms a soft ball when dropped into cold water. Remove from fire and cool to lukewarm without stirring. Add the remaining ingredients and beat thoroughly until mixture is thick enough to form clusters when dropped from a tablespoon onto a lightly oiled pan. Refrigerate.

Yield: 24.

BROWNIES BOMBSHELLS

¾ cup skim milk
2 tablespoons soybean powder
2 tablespoons powdered
   nonfat dry milk
3 tablespoons carob powder
1½ cups raw sugar
½ cup clover honey

¼ cup safflower oil
1 teaspoon vanilla extract
½ cup toasted blanched
   almonds
⅓ cup toasted sunflower
   seeds
⅓ cup diced pitted dates

Combine the first 6 ingredients in a saucepan and cook on a low fire, stirring occasionally, until ½ teaspoon of the mixture forms a soft ball when dropped into cold water. Remove from fire and cool to lukewarm without stirring. Add the remaining ingredients and beat until mixture is thick enough to form clusters when dropped from a tablespoon onto a lightly oiled pan. Refrigerate.

Yield: 24.

MIXED-FRUIT BALLS

½ cup pitted prunes
½ cup dried Calimyrna figs
½ cup pitted dates
½ cup Monukka raisins
½ cup whole filberts

1 orange with skin,
   quartered and seeded
⅓ cup toasted wheat germ
½ teaspoon cinnamon
¼ cup toasted sesame seeds
¼ cup toasted sliced almonds

Put the first 6 ingredients through the medium blade of a grinder. Add the wheat germ and cinnamon and mix together thoroughly. Form into 36 balls. Roll half the balls in the sesame seeds and half in the almonds. Refrigerate.

Yield: 36.

NUTTY APRICOT SOFTBALLS

1 cup dried apricots
½ cup pitted dates
2 cups water
¾ cup raw sugar
½ cup toasted unsweetened
   shredded coconut
½ cup toasted sesame seeds

½ cup toasted wheat germ
2 tablespoons soybean powder
2 tablespoons lecithin
2 tablespoons rice polishings
1 teaspoon vanilla extract
½ cup chopped macadamia
   nuts

Combine the first 3 ingredients in a saucepan on a low fire, cover, and cook for 25 minutes. Cool to lukewarm, then put in blender and blend until thick and smooth. Pour into a bowl and add the next 8 ingredients, mixing thoroughly. Form into 18 balls and roll in macadamia nuts. Refrigerate.
   Yield: 18.

CASHEW-BUTTER BALLS

1 cup fresh-ground cashew
   butter
2 tablespoons Papaya Syrup
   Concentrate
2 tablespoons Barbados
   molasses

½ teaspoon vanilla extract
¼ teaspoon cinnamon
¼ cup toasted unsweetened
   shredded coconut
½ cup diced dried bananas
Toasted wheat germ

Combine all ingredients but last in a bowl and mix thoroughly. Form into 24 balls and roll in wheat germ.
   Yield: 24.

PEANUT-BUTTER ODDBALLS

½ cup fresh-ground peanut
   butter
2 tablespoons clover honey
2 tablespoons Papaya Syrup
   Concentrate

1 teaspoon lemon extract
¼ cup toasted wheat germ
¼ cup toasted sesame seeds
½ cup Monukka raisins
Sesame-sunflower meal

Combine all the ingredients but last and mix thoroughly. Form into 12 balls and roll in sesame-sunflower meal.
Yield: 12.

CAROB FRUIT LOG SLICES

1 cup dried apples with skin
½ cup dried apricots
½ cup dried Smyrna figs
½ cup dried peaches
½ cup Brazil nuts
2 tablespoons carob powder

2 tablespoons Papaya Syrup Concentrate
1 tablespoon maple syrup
1 tablespoon Barbados molasses
⅓ cup toasted sesame seeds
½ cup toasted pignolias

Put the first 5 ingredients through the medium blade of a grinder. Combine thoroughly with all the remaining ingredients except the pignolias. Divide mixture in half and form into 2 long rolls. Coat each roll with the pignolias. Refrigerate until serving time and then cut into thin slices.
Yield: 48.

PIGNOLIA RAISIN CHEWS

½ cup raw sugar
¼ cup date sugar
2 tablespoons Barbados molasses
2 tablespoons sesame oil

1 teaspoon orange extract
1 teaspoon lemon extract
½ cup toasted pignolias
½ cup Monukka raisins
2 tablespoons *tahini*

Combine the first 4 ingredients in a heavy skillet on a low fire and stir until melted. Immediately add the remaining ingredients and mix thoroughly. Pour into a lightly oiled shallow pan and when lukewarm mark into squares with a very sharp knife. Break apart when cold.
Yield: 16.

SUNFLOWER COCONUT BRITTLE

1½ cups raw sugar
½ cup date sugar
1 tablespoon sesame oil
1 tablespoon vanilla extract

1 cup toasted sunflower seeds
½ cup toasted unsweetened
  shredded coconut

In a heavy skillet combine the 2 sugars, stirring constantly until melted. Immediately add the remaining ingredients, stirring quickly and thoroughly. Pour into a lightly oiled shallow pan, spreading evenly. Let cool and when hard break into chunks.
Yield: ½ pound.

ALMOND PUMPKIN BRITTLE

½ cup raw sugar
¼ cup maple syrup
2 tablespoons Barbados
  molasses
2 tablespoons safflower oil

1 teaspoon orange extract
½ teaspoon cinnamon
½ cup toasted sliced almonds
½ cup toasted pumpkin seeds

Combine the first 4 ingredients in a heavy skillet and stir on a low fire until melted. Immediately add the remaining ingredients and stir thoroughly. Pour into an oiled shallow pan, spreading evenly. When lukewarm mark into squares with a very sharp knife. Break apart when cold.
Yield: 16.

APRICOT CARROT TORTE

1 cup dried apricots
½ cup shredded carrots
2 cups water
3 eggs, separated
⅓ cup raw sugar
Grated rind of 1 orange
1 teaspoon lemon extract
1 teaspoon orange extract

½ cup raw sugar
⅓ cup powdered nonfat
  dry milk
½ teaspoon fresh lemon juice
⅔ cup ice water
¾ cup toasted unsweetened
  shredded coconut

Combine the first 3 ingredients in a saucepan on a low fire, cover, and cook for 25 minutes. Cool to lukewarm, then mix in blender until thick and smooth. There should be 1 cup of puree. Put this in a bowl and add the egg yolks, sugar, grated orange rind, and lemon and orange extracts and mix thoroughly. Beat the egg whites until soft peaks form, then gradually add the sugar, beating until stiff and glossy. Fold into the apricot mixture. Whip the powdered milk, lemon juice, and ice water until stiff. Fold into apricot mixture. Sprinkle ½ cup of the coconut in a 10-inch spring-form pan, cover with apricot mixture, and top with the remaining coconut. Refrigerate or freeze as desired. Remove pan before serving.

Serves 8–10.

CAROB CASHEW MOUSSE

½ cup carob powder
¾ cup water
3 eggs, separated
¾ cup raw sugar
⅓ cup safflower oil
1 teaspoon vanilla extract

½ cup powdered nonfat dry milk
1 teaspoon fresh lemon juice
1 cup ice water
1 cup toasted cashew pieces
Toasted wheat germ

In a saucepan combine the carob powder and water. Mix until very smooth. Add the egg yolks 1 at a time, beating after each addition. Add ½ cup of the sugar and mix well. Stir on a low fire until the sugar dissolves. Remove from heat and add safflower oil and vanilla, stirring thoroughly. Set aside. Beat egg whites until soft peaks form, then gradually add remaining ¼ cup sugar, beating until stiff and glossy. Fold into the cooled carob mixture. Whip the powdered milk, lemon juice, and ice water until stiff. Fold into carob mixture with the cashews. Pour into a 10-inch spring-form pan, sprinkle with toasted wheat germ, and freeze. Remove from pan to serve.

Serves 10–12.

SPICY TOASTED NUTS

1 cup toasted peanuts
½ cup Brazil nuts
½ cup pecans
2 tablespoons almond oil
1 tablespoon vegetable-broth
  powder
1 teaspoon Sesame Salt
  (see page 40)

½ teaspoon Brownies
  Vege-C-Salt (see page 40)
¼ teaspoon garlic powder
⅛ teaspoon powdered ginger
⅛ teaspoon celery seed
¼ teaspoon Bakon Yeast
1 tablespoon Krisp

Combine the first 4 ingredients and mix well. Blend the remaining ingredients and mix together with the nut mixture. Place in a baking pan and bake for 20 minutes in a preheated 375° F. oven, stirring occasionally. Serve warm or cold.

Yield: 2 cups.

SPECIAL COMPANY NUT MIX

½ cup sunflower seeds
½ cup pumpkin seeds
½ cup unsalted Soy Nuts
½ cup pignolias
3 tablespoons *tahini*
1 tablespoon almond oil
1 tablespoon orange-blossom
  honey

1 tablespoon Sesame Salt
  (see page 40)
1 tablespoon poppy seeds
1 teaspoon vanilla extract
¼ teaspoon powdered ginger
¼ teaspoon nutmeg
½ teaspoon cinnamon

Combine the first 4 ingredients. Mix the remaining ingredients thoroughly, then mix with the nut mixture. Place in a baking pan and bake for 25 minutes in a preheated 375° F. oven, stirring occasionally. Serve warm or cold.

Yield: 2 cups.

MY WIFE LOVES TO BAKE

(Breads and Muffins)

For the last 2 chapters of this book the plural "we" must be abandoned. The star attraction of Brownies happens to be its unique bakery. Which happens to be the inspiration—and the doing—of Edith. Edith's modesty prevents her from assessing her accomplishment; the baker's husband, however, feels no such restraint about proclaiming her genius.

Most of our lunch and dinner guests seem to find our menus innovative from top to bottom. The country store adjoining our restaurant brings us thousands of customers every week—at an ever-accelerating volume, with the quickened interest in good diet and natural foods. But nothing we offer in our whole enterprise has anywhere near the drawing power of the goodies from Edith's baking pans.

In the early years we went to an outside concessionaire, who supplied an assortment of breads and pastries to Brownies. "I can do better than these," said Edith one day, taste-testing some bakery goods. It wasn't too much of a boast, and I told her to go ahead. What she came up with was nothing less than a whole new concept of baking.

That was nearly 20 years ago. Since then Edith's creations have been getting rave notices from restaurant reviewers and clientele alike. Hardly a day passes when some "hooked" customer doesn't clamor to have her recipe for Soya Blueberry Muffins or whatever. Our menus used to carry this message from me: "My wife loves to bake. So with a true dedication to the art, she converts nature's most wholesome ingredients into nutritious cakes, pies, cookies, muffins. She bakes only with high-protein flour, rich in soy, wheat germ, and skim milk." Unfortunately, Edith's recipes were conceived for restaurant use and heretofore were never broken down for domestic consumption. But now, home cooks, here they come—for the first time ever—straight from the ovens of Edith Brown!

YEAST BREADS

Where approximate measurements are given for flour in the following recipes, this means that you should initially use the specified quantity. Add more, if necessary, to make a nonsticky dough, and also use it to flour your board when kneading the dough.

All yeast breads should be removed from their pans as soon as they are taken from the oven. Cool the loaves either crosswise across their pans or on a wire rack.

FIVE-GRAIN BREAD

1½ cups (approximately) stone-ground whole-wheat flour
1½ cups whole-rye flour
1½ cups brown-rice flour
½ cup buckwheat flour
½ cup chickpea flour
½ cup soybean powder

2 tablespoons active dry yeast
1 tablespoon sea salt
2 cups skim milk
½ cup tupelo honey
2 tablespoons raw sugar
⅓ cup safflower oil
1 egg white
Celery seed

Combine the first 8 ingredients in a mixer with a bread hook and blend together at low speed (mixing can also be done by hand with a wooden spoon). Heat the next 4 ingredients in a saucepan until warm and gradually add to the flour mixture until a ball forms, adding more whole-wheat flour if needed. Remove to a floured board and knead until smooth. Place in a lightly oiled bowl, turning to coat completely. Cover and let rise in a warm place until doubled. Punch down and divide into two balls. Shape 1 into a regular loaf and the other into a round. Place the loaf in an oiled standard loaf pan and the round in an oiled 9-inch pie pan. Brush with lightly beaten egg white and sprinkle with celery seed. Cover and let rise until doubled. Bake in a preheated 400° F. oven until brown—about 45 minutes to 1 hour.

Yield: 2 loaves.

TRI-GRAIN BREAD

2 tablespoons active dry yeast
½ teaspoon tupelo honey
½ cup warm water
1 cup toasted wheat germ
1 tablespoon sea salt
¼ cup soybean oil
¼ cup tupelo honey
½ cup toasted sesame seeds

2 tablespoons Krisp
1½ cups boiling water
2 eggs
1½ cups whole-rye flour
2½ cups brown-rice flour
3 cups (approximately)
   stone-ground whole-wheat
   flour

Combine the first 3 ingredients in a small bowl without stirring. When they start to increase in volume, stir smooth and set aside. In a mixer with a bread hook (or by hand, using a wooden spoon) blend the next 7 ingredients until lukewarm. Add the yeast mixture and eggs and mix until smooth. Combine the next 3 ingredients and add gradually to form a ball. Add more whole-wheat flour if needed. Remove to a floured board and knead until smooth. Place in a lightly oiled bowl, turning to coat completely. Cover and let rise in a warm place until doubled. Punch down and divide into 2 balls. Form into 2 loaves and place in 2 lightly oiled standard loaf pans. Cover and let rise until bread comes to the tops of the pans. Bake in a preheated 400° F. oven until brown—about 45 minutes to 1 hour.

Yield: 2 loaves.

MIXED-BAG BREAD

½ cup yellow cornmeal
1 cup cold water
1½ cups warm water
1 tablespoon sea salt
¼ cup clover honey
¼ cup Barbados molasses
¼ cup safflower oil

1 tablespoon active dry yeast
3 cups (approximately)
   stone-ground whole-wheat
   flour
2 cups brown-rice flour
½ cup soybean powder

Combine the cornmeal and ¾ cup of the cold water and mix until smooth. Place the warm water and salt in a saucepan and bring to a boil. Gradually add the cornmeal mixture, stirring constantly. Lower the heat and add the next 3 ingredients, mixing until thick and smooth. Place in a mixer with a bread hook (or mix by hand, using a wooden spoon) and mix until mixture is lukewarm. Mix the yeast and reserved ¼ cup cold water together and add to warm cornmeal combination at medium speed. Blend the remaining ingredients together and add gradually until a ball forms, using more whole-wheat flour if needed. Remove and knead on a floured board until smooth. Place in a lightly oiled bowl, turning to coat completely. Cover and let rise in a warm place until doubled. Punch down and shape into 2 loaves. Place in 2 oiled standard loaf pans, cover, and let rise to the tops of the pans. Bake in a preheated 400° F. oven until brown—about 45 minutes to 1 hour.

Yield: 2 loaves.

TRIPLE SUNFLOWER BREAD

2 tablespoons active dry yeast
½ cup warm water
½ teaspoon tupelo honey
½ cup toasted wheat germ
½ cup soybean powder
¼ cup lecithin
¼ cup safflower oil
¼ cup raw sugar
1 tablespoon sea salt

1 cup toasted sunflower seeds
1½ cups boiling water
2 eggs
2 cups yellow cornmeal
1 cup sunflower meal
1 cup brown-rice flour
3 cups (approximately) stone-ground whole-wheat flour

Combine the first 3 ingredients in a small bowl without stirring. When mixture starts to increase in volume, in about 5 minutes, stir it smooth and set aside. In a mixer with a bread hook combine the next 8 ingredients at medium speed until warm (mixing can also be done by hand with a wooden spoon). Add the yeast mixture and eggs and mix until smooth. Gradually add the remaining ingredients until a ball forms and leaves the sides of the bowl. Remove to a floured board and knead until smooth, adding more whole-wheat flour if necessary. Place in a lightly oiled bowl, turning to coat completely. Cover and let stand in a warm place until doubled in volume. Punch down and divide in half. Shape into 2 loaves and place in 2 lightly oiled standard loaf pans. Cover and let rise to the tops of the pans. Bake in a preheated 400° F. oven until brown—about 45 minutes to 1 hour.

Yield: 2 loaves.

HONEY WHOLE-WHEAT BREAD

2 tablespoons active dry yeast
½ cup warm water
½ teaspoon clover honey
1 cup toasted wheat germ
2 teaspoons sea salt
¼ cup soybean oil

¼ cup clover honey
1½ cups boiling water
2 eggs
7 cups (approximately) stone-ground whole-wheat flour

Combine the first 3 ingredients in a small bowl and let stand 5 minutes without stirring. When mixture starts to increase in volume, stir it smooth and set aside. Blend the next 5 ingredients at medium speed in a mixer with a bread hook (or by hand, using a wooden spoon) until lukewarm. Add the eggs and yeast mixture and mix until smooth. Add the flour gradually until a smooth ball forms and leaves the sides of the bowl. Remove and knead until smooth on floured board, adding more flour if necessary. Place in a lightly oiled bowl, turning to coat completely. Cover and let rise in a warm place until almost doubled in volume. Punch down on a floured board and divide in half. Shape into loaves and place in 2 oiled standard loaf pans. Let rise, covered, until doubled, then bake in a preheated 400° F. oven about 45 minutes.

Yield: 2 loaves.

WHOLE-WHEAT CURRANT COTTAGE BREAD

2 tablespoons active dry yeast
½ cup warm water
½ teaspoon clover honey
1 cup toasted wheat germ
¼ cup raw sugar
¼ cup soybean oil
1 cup cottage cheese

1 cup dried currants
1 teaspoon cinnamon
1 tablespoon sea salt
1½ cups boiling water
6 cups (approximately) stone-ground whole-wheat flour

Combine the first 3 ingredients in a small bowl without stirring. When mixture starts to increase in volume—in about 5 minutes—stir smooth and set aside. In a mixer with a bread hook (or by hand, using a wooden spoon) combine the next 8 ingredients and mix until lukewarm. Add the yeast mixture and mix for 1 minute. Gradually add the flour until a ball forms. Remove to a floured board and knead until smooth, adding more flour if necessary. Place in a lightly oiled bowl, turning to coat completely. Cover and let rise in a warm place until doubled. Punch down and shape into 2 loaves. Place in 2 oiled standard loaf pans. Cover and let rise to the tops of the pans. Bake in a preheated 400° F. oven until brown—about 45 minutes to 1 hour.

Yield: 2 loaves.

PRUNE DATE WHOLE-WHEAT BREAD

2 tablespoons active dry yeast
½ cup warm water
½ teaspoon clover honey
½ cup toasted wheat germ
1 cup soybean powder
¼ cup safflower oil
¼ cup clover honey
1 tablespoon sea salt
2 teaspoons cinnamon

1 cup diced pitted prunes
½ cup date chips
1½ cups boiling water
2 eggs
4 cups (approximately) stone-ground whole-wheat flour
1½ cups brown-rice flour

Combine the first 3 ingredients in a small bowl and let stand without stirring for 5 minutes. When it starts to increase in vol-

ume, stir it smooth and set aside. In a mixer with a bread hook (or by hand, using a wooden spoon) blend the next 9 ingredients at medium speed until lukewarm. Add the eggs and yeast and mix smooth. Gradually add the two flours until a ball forms and leaves the sides of the bowl. Remove from bowl and knead until smooth on a board floured with whole-wheat flour, adding more flour if necessary. Place in a lightly oiled bowl, turning to coat completely. Cover and let stand in a warm place until doubled in volume. Punch down on a floured board. Divide in half and shape into 2 loaves. Place in 2 lightly oiled standard loaf pans. Cover and let rise to the tops of the pans, then bake in a pre-heated 400° F. oven until brown—about 45 minutes to 1 hour.
     Yield: 2 loaves.

COTTAGE-CHEESE SPIRAL WHOLE-WHEAT ROLLS

1 tablespoon active dry yeast
¼ teaspoon clover honey
¼ cup warm water
½ cup toasted wheat germ
1 teaspoon sea salt
2 tablespoons safflower oil
2 tablespoons clover honey
¾ cup boiling water
1 egg
3½ cups (approximately) stone-ground whole-wheat flour

Filling:
⅔ cup cottage cheese
1 teaspoon Brownies Vege-C-Salt (see page 40)
1 teaspoon garlic powder
2 tablespoons diced scallions
2 tablespoons snipped fresh chives
2 tablespoons parsley flakes

In a small bowl combine the first 3 ingredients without stirring. Stir until smooth when mixture starts to increase in volume and set aside. In a mixer with a bread hook (or by hand, using a wooden spoon) blend the next 5 ingredients until lukewarm. Add the yeast mixture and egg and mix until smooth. Gradually add the flour until a ball forms, adding more flour if needed. Remove to a floured board and knead until smooth. Place in a lightly oiled bowl, turning to coat completely. Cover and let rise in a warm place until doubled. Make filling by combining remaining ingredients and set aside. Punch dough down and form into 2 balls. Roll each ball into a rectangle. Divide the filling between the 2 rectangles and roll up tightly. Cut each roll into 12 slices and place in oiled muffin cups. Let rise until doubled. Bake in a preheated 400° F. oven until brown—about 30 minutes.

Yield: 24.

POPPY CRACKED-WHEAT BREAD

2 tablespoons active dry yeast
½ teaspoon clover honey
½ cup warm water
1 cup toasted wheat germ
¼ cup safflower oil
¼ cup clover honey
1 tablespoon sea salt
2 tablespoons poppy seeds
2 tablespoons celery seed

1½ cups boiling water
2 eggs
1 cup cracked wheat
1 cup chickpea flour
1 cup brown-rice flour
4 cups (approximately) stone-ground whole-wheat flour

Combine the first 3 ingredients in a small bowl without stirring. Stir smooth when mixture starts to increase in volume and set aside. Blend the next 7 ingredients in a mixer with a bread hook until lukewarm (or mix by hand, using a wooden spoon). Add the yeast mixture and eggs and mix until smooth. Combine the remaining ingredients and add gradually until dough forms a ball. Add more whole-wheat flour if needed. Remove to a floured board and knead until smooth. Place in a lightly oiled bowl, turning to coat completely. Cover and let rise in a warm place until doubled. Punch down and divide into 2 balls. Form into 2 loaves and place in 2 lightly oiled standard loaf pans. Cover and let rise in a warm place until dough reaches the tops of the pans. Bake in a preheated 400° F. oven until brown—about 45 minutes to 1 hour.

Yield: 2 loaves.

SESAME WHEAT-GERM TWIST

2 tablespoons active dry yeast
½ cup warm water
½ teaspoon clover honey
½ cup toasted wheat germ
1 tablespoon sea salt
¼ cup safflower oil
¼ cup clover honey
1½ cups boiling water
3 eggs
7 cups (approximately) unbleached white–and–wheat-germ flour
1 tablespoon milk
Sesame seeds

Combine the first 3 ingredients in a bowl without stirring for 5 minutes, then stir until smooth and set aside. In a mixer with a bread hook (or by hand, using a wooden spoon) combine the next 5 ingredients until lukewarm. Add the yeast mixture and 2 of the eggs and mix thoroughly. Gradually add the flour until a smooth ball forms and leaves the sides of the bowl. Turn onto a floured board and knead until smooth, adding more flour if necessary. Place in a lightly oiled bowl, turning to coat completely. Cover and let rise in a warm place until doubled. Punch down and divide into 6 smooth balls. Roll each ball into a rope about 18 inches long. Braid 3 ropes together and place on a lightly oiled baking sheet. Repeat with the other 3 balls. Make egg wash by beating together 1 egg and 1 tablespoon milk. Brush loaves with egg wash and sprinkle with sesame seeds. Make a tent out of aluminum foil, cover the bread with the tent, and let rise until doubled. Bake in a preheated 375° F. oven until brown—about 45 minutes to 1 hour.

Yield: 2 twists.

CARAWAY WHOLE-RYE BREAD

2 tablespoons active dry yeast
½ cup warm water
½ teaspoon clover honey
½ cup toasted wheat germ
¼ cup lecithin
½ cup soybean powder
2 tablespoons caraway seeds
2 tablespoons parsley flakes
1 tablespoon sea salt
¼ cup soybean oil
¼ cup Barbados molasses
1½ cups boiling water
5 cups (approximately) whole-rye flour
1 egg white
Caraway seeds

Combine the first 3 ingredients in a small bowl without stirring. Stir until smooth when mixture starts to increase in volume and set aside. In a mixer with a bread hook combine the next 9 ingredients until lukewarm (or mix by hand, using a wooden spoon). Add the yeast mixture and mix 1 minute. Gradually add flour until a ball forms. Remove and knead on a floured board until smooth, adding more flour if necessary. Place in a lightly oiled bowl, turning to coat completely. Cover and let rise in a warm place until almost doubled. Punch down and form into 1 regular loaf and 1 round loaf. Place the first loaf in a lightly oiled standard loaf pan and the round loaf in a lightly oiled 9-inch pie pan. Brush both with lightly beaten egg white and sprinkle with caraway seeds. Cover and let rise until doubled in size. Bake in a preheated 400° F. oven until brown—about 45 minutes to 1 hour.

Yield: 2 loaves.

OATMEAL CHIA BREAD

2 tablespoons active dry yeast
½ cup warm water
½ teaspoon clover honey
½ cup toasted wheat germ
¼ cup sesame oil
¼ cup clover honey
1 tablespoon sea salt

½ cup chia seeds
1½ cups boiling water
2 cups rolled oats
1 cup brown-rice flour
2½ cups (approximately) stone-ground whole-wheat flour

Combine the first 3 ingredients in a small bowl without stirring and let stand for 5 minutes. Stir until smooth when mixture starts to increase in volume and set aside. In a mixer with a bread hook (or by hand, using a wooden spoon) combine the next 6 ingredients at medium speed until lukewarm. Add the yeast mixture and mix until smooth. Gradually add the remaining ingredients, adding more whole-wheat flour if necessary so that a smooth ball forms. Place in a lightly oiled bowl, turning to coat completely. Cover and set in a warm place to rise until almost doubled. Punch down on a floured board and divide in half. Form into 2 loaves and place in 2 oiled standard loaf pans. Cover and let rise to tops of pans. Bake in a preheated 400° F. oven until brown—about 45 minutes to 1 hour.

Yield: 2 loaves.

QUICK BREADS

After they are taken out of the oven, let quick breads sit in their pans for 10 minutes, then remove and finish cooling on a wire rack.

MAPLE WALNUT BANANA BREAD

2 cups sliced bananas
2 eggs
1 cup sour cream
¼ cup safflower oil
¼ cup raw sugar
¼ cup maple syrup
1 teaspoon cinnamon
1 teaspoon maple extract

1½ cups stone-ground whole-wheat flour
1 cup Fearn Soy-O Mix
¼ cup toasted wheat germ
¼ cup whole millet
2 teaspoons tartrate baking powder
1 cup walnut pieces
12 walnut halves

Combine the first 8 ingredients in the blender and mix at high speed for 30 seconds. In a mixing bowl blend the remaining ingredients except for the halved walnuts. Pour in the liquid mixture all at once and stir until just moistened. Turn into an oiled standard loaf pan and top with halved walnuts. Bake for 1 hour in a preheated 350° F. oven or until toothpick inserted in center of loaf comes out clean.

Yield: 1 loaf.

WHOLE-WHEAT BANANA FIG BREAD

2 eggs
¼ cup raw sugar
¼ cup tupelo honey
¼ cup sesame oil
1 ripe banana
½ cup goat-milk yogurt
1 teaspoon orange extract
1 cup stone-ground
   whole-wheat flour
¼ cup Viobin Wheat Germ

2 tablespoons soybean powder
2 tablespoons powdered
   nonfat dry milk
½ teaspoon sea salt
2 teaspoons tartrate baking
   powder
½ teaspoon cinnamon
⅓ cup diced dried
   Calimyrna figs
¼ cup sliced filberts

Beat the first 4 ingredients for 2 minutes in a mixing bowl. Mash the banana with the yogurt and orange extract and set aside. Blend the next 7 ingredients and add half to the first combination, mixing until smooth. Add the banana mixture and blend until smooth. Add the remaining flour mixture and mix until smooth. Mix in the figs. Pour into a lightly oiled standard loaf pan, top with the filberts, and bake in a preheated 350° F. oven for 30 minutes or until toothpick inserted in center of loaf comes out clean.

    Yield: 1 loaf.

PECAN BLUEBERRY BREAD

1 cup stone-ground
   whole-wheat flour
½ cup brown-rice flour
½ cup raw sugar
¼ cup toasted wheat germ
¼ cup soybean powder
2 teaspoons tartrate baking
   powder
½ teaspoon sea salt

½ teaspoon cinnamon
2 eggs
¼ cup soybean oil
½ cup orange juice
½ cup goat-milk yogurt
1 teaspoon orange extract
1 cup blueberries
½ cup pecan pieces

Blend the first 8 ingredients and mix thoroughly. Mix until smooth the next 5 ingredients and add all at once to the dry mixture, stirring till just moistened. Fold in the blueberries and pecans and pour into a lightly oiled standard loaf pan. Bake for 1 hour in a preheated 350° F. oven or until toothpick inserted in center of loaf comes out clean.

Yield: 1 loaf.

PEACH APRICOT WALNUT BREAD

1⅓ cups stone-ground
  whole-wheat flour
½ cup toasted wheat germ
½ cup sesame meal
2 tablespoons powdered
  nonfat dry milk
2 tablespoons lecithin
2 teaspoons tartrate
  baking powder
½ teaspoon sea salt
½ cup chopped walnuts

2 eggs
¼ cup safflower oil
½ cup tupelo honey
½ cup canned unsweetened
  pineapple juice
⅓ cup sour cream
½ cup diced peaches
½ cup diced dried apricots
1 teaspoon orange extract
⅓ cup chopped walnuts

Blend the first 8 ingredients in a bowl and set aside. Combine the remaining ingredients except last in a blender and mix at high speed for 30 seconds. Pour all at once into the dry ingredients and stir till just moistened. Turn into an oiled standard loaf pan and top with chopped walnuts. Bake in a preheated 375° F. oven for 1 hour or until toothpick inserted in center of loaf comes out clean.

Yield: 1 loaf.

CHICKPEA DATE LOAF

½ cup safflower oil
½ cup raw sugar
2 tablespoons clover honey
2 eggs
½ teaspoon cinnamon
1 cup stone-ground
  whole-wheat flour
¼ cup chickpea flour
¼ cup millet meal
2 tablespoons powdered
  nonfat dry milk
2 tablespoons toasted wheat
  germ
2 teaspoons tartrate baking
  powder
½ teaspoon sea salt
½ cup goat-milk yogurt
½ cup buttermilk
½ cup diced dates
⅓ cup chopped pecans

Combine the first 5 ingredients in a mixing bowl and mix with electric mixer at medium speed for 2 minutes (or mix by hand, using a wooden spoon). Blend the next 7 ingredients in a bowl and add half to the first mixture, stirring until smooth. Add the yogurt and buttermilk and mix well. Add the other half of the flour mixture and blend until smooth. Stir in the dates and pecans. Pour into a lightly oiled standard loaf pan and bake in a pre-heated 375° F. oven for 45 minutes or until toothpick inserted in center of loaf comes out clean.

Yield: 1 loaf.

MIXED-UP RICE LOAF

¼ cup safflower oil
½ cup orange-blossom honey
½ cup Barbados molasses
2 eggs
1 teaspoon orange extract
1 cup stone-ground
  whole-wheat flour
½ cup brown-rice flour
½ cup yellow cornmeal
½ cup Viobin Wheat Germ
1 teaspoon sea salt
1 tablespoon tartrate baking
  powder
½ cup orange juice
½ cup dried currants
½ cup Basic Brown Rice
  (see page 150)
¼ cup sunflower seeds

Combine the first 5 ingredients in a mixing bowl and beat for 2 minutes. In another bowl combine the next 6 ingredients and blend together. Add half of this mixture to the first mixture, stirring until smooth. Stir in the orange juice, and mix until smooth. Add the other half of the flour mixture and mix until smooth. Blend in the currants and cooled rice and mix until smooth. Pour into a lightly oiled standard loaf pan, top with the sunflower seeds, and bake in a preheated 400° F. oven for 30 minutes, then in a 350° F. oven until toothpick inserted in center of loaf comes out clean.

    Yield: 1 loaf.

STRAWBERRY CORN BREAD

1 cup yellow cornmeal
½ cup brown-rice flour
½ cup rolled oats
½ cup raw sugar
¼ cup toasted wheat germ
2 tablespoons lecithin
2 teaspoons tartrate baking powder
½ teaspoon sea salt
2 eggs
¼ cup safflower oil
1⅓ cups buttermilk
1 teaspoon orange extract
½ cup sliced strawberries
⅓ cup toasted sliced almonds
Toasted sliced almonds

Blend the first 8 ingredients and mix lightly. Mix the next 4 ingredients until smooth and add all at once to the dry mixture, stirring just until moistened. Fold in the strawberries and ⅓ cup almonds and pour into a lightly oiled loaf pan. Top with some sliced almonds and bake for 30 minutes in a preheated 350° F. oven or until toothpick inserted in center of loaf comes out clean.

    Yield: 1 loaf.

AVOCADO RYE BREAD

1 cup stone-ground whole-rye flour
½ cup stone-ground whole-wheat flour
¼ cup soybean powder
⅓ cup raw sugar
2 teaspoons tartrate baking powder
½ teaspoon sea salt
½ cup mashed avocado
3 eggs
¼ cup Barbados molasses
⅓ cup sesame oil
½ cup goat-milk yogurt
⅓ cup canned unsweetened pineapple juice
1 teaspoon vanilla extract
⅓ cup toasted sunflower seeds

Blend the first 6 ingredients together. Beat the remaining ingredients except for sunflower seeds until smooth and add all at once to the dry ingredients, mixing just until moistened. Pour into a lightly oiled standard loaf pan. Top with sunflower seeds and bake in a preheated 350° F. oven about 1 hour or until toothpick inserted in center of loaf comes out clean.

Yield: 1 loaf.

SUPER SUPPER BREAD SQUARES

1 cup diced Spanish onion
3 cloves garlic, minced
2 tablespoons safflower oil
¼ cup diced pimiento
½ cup alfalfa sprouts
½ cup goat-milk yogurt
½ teaspoon Brownies Vege-C-Salt (see page 40)
2 tablespoons toasted wheat germ
1 cup stone-ground rye flour
½ cup cracked wheat
⅓ cup millet meal
⅓ cup soybean powder
¼ cup toasted wheat germ
1 teaspoon sea salt
1 tablespoon poppy seeds
2 teaspoons tartrate baking powder
½ cup safflower oil
2 eggs
1 cup skim milk

Sauté the onion and garlic in the 2 tablespoons safflower oil until golden. Remove from heat and add the next 5 ingredients. Mix thoroughly and set aside. Combine the remaining ingredients and mix until smooth. Pour into a lightly oiled 9-inch baking pan. Spread the onion mixture carefully on top of the batter. Bake in a preheated 400° F. oven for about 45 minutes or until golden brown. Cool and cut into squares.

Serves 8.

FRUITY NUT BREAD AND MUFFINS

1 cup stone-ground whole-wheat flour
1 cup stone-ground rye flour
½ cup soybean powder
½ cup rolled oats
½ cup toasted wheat germ
1 tablespoon tartrate baking powder
1 teaspoon sea salt
½ teaspoon cinnamon
3 eggs
¼ cup raw sugar
¼ cup Barbados molasses
1½ cups buttermilk
½ cup canned unsweetened pineapple juice
½ cup canned unsweetened crushed pineapple
½ cup filberts
⅓ cup cut-up dried Calimyrna figs
⅓ cup cut-up dried black mission figs
1 teaspoon vanilla extract
½ cup toasted cashew pieces
½ cup dried currants
Whole cashews

Combine the first 8 ingredients in a mixing bowl and set aside. Blend the next 10 ingredients in the blender at high speed for 1 minute. Pour all at once into the dry ingredients and mix together. Add the cashew pieces and currants and mix lightly. Turn part of the batter into 12 lined or lightly oiled muffin cups and top each with a whole cashew. Pour the remaining batter into an oiled standard loaf pan and top with whole cashews. Bake both muffins and bread until brown—about 30 minutes for the muffins, about 45 for the bread—in a preheated 350° F. oven.

Yield: 12 muffins and 1 loaf.

MUFFINS

MEAL IN A MUFFIN

¼ cup safflower oil
¼ cup Barbados molasses
¼ cup raw sugar
2 eggs
½ cup California tomato juice
½ cup buttermilk
1 teaspoon lemon extract
1 cup brown-rice flour
½ cup whole millet

¼ cup chia seeds
¼ cup toasted wheat germ
¼ cup soybean powder
2 tablespoons lecithin
2 teaspoons tartrate baking
powder
½ teaspoon sea salt
Chia seeds

Combine the first 7 ingredients and beat together thoroughly. Blend the remaining ingredients except for the last, add all at once to the first combination, and stir just until moistened. Divide among 12 lined or lightly oiled muffin cups. Sprinkle each with some chia seeds and bake for 30 minutes in a preheated 375° F. oven.

Yield: 12.

SAUERKRAUT CARAWAY MUFFINS

1 cup rye flour
1 cup brown-rice flour
¼ cup soybean powder
2 tablespoons lecithin
2 tablespoons powdered
nonfat dry milk
¼ cup caraway seeds
⅓ cup raw sugar
1 tablespoon tartrate baking
powder
1 teaspoon Brownies
Vege-C-Salt (see page 40)

1 tablespoon snipped fresh
chives
1 teaspoon garlic powder
3 eggs
⅓ cup soybean oil
1 cup goat-milk yogurt
½ cup drained chopped
sauerkraut
½ cup diced Spanish onion
¼ cup diced pimiento
Caraway seeds

Blend the first 11 ingredients in a mixing bowl and set aside. Combine the remaining ingredients except the last and mix thoroughly. Add all at once to the dry combination and mix just until moistened. Turn into lined or lightly oiled muffin cups and 'top with caraway seeds. Bake 30 minutes or until brown in a preheated 350° F. oven.

Yield: 12.

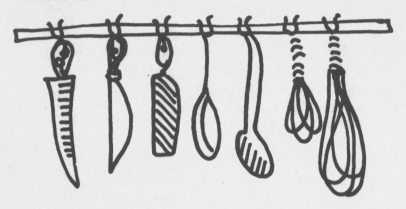

CARAWAY CARROT ALFALFA MUFFINS

2 eggs
¼ cup soybean oil
½ cup skim milk
½ cup buttermilk
1½ cups Fearn Whole Wheat Soy-O Mix
¼ cup toasted wheat germ
¼ cup soybean powder
1 tablespoon snipped fresh chives

1 tablespoon vegetable-broth powder
1 teaspoon Brownies Vege-C-Salt (see page 40)
2 teaspoons Krisp
½ cup shredded carrots
½ cup chopped alfalfa sprouts
Caraway seeds

Combine the first 4 ingredients and beat for 3 minutes. Blend the next 7 ingredients, add all at once to the first mixture, and mix quickly. Stir in the carrots and alfalfa sprouts and stir lightly. Divide among 12 lined or lightly oiled muffin cups and top with caraway seeds. Bake in a preheated 375° F. oven for 35 minutes or until brown.

Yield: 12.

CARROT CHEESE WHEAT RICE MUFFINS

½ cup cottage cheese
2 eggs
½ cup tupelo honey
½ cup goat-milk yogurt
½ cup carrot juice
1 teaspoon vanilla extract
1 cup stone-ground whole-
  wheat flour
½ cup brown-rice flour

¼ cup soybean powder
¼ cup toasted wheat germ
2 teaspoons tartrate baking
  powder
½ teaspoon sea salt
½ cup dried currants
⅓ cup toasted unsweetened
  shredded coconut
Unsweetened shredded coconut

Whip until smooth the first 6 ingredients. Blend the remaining ingredients except last and add all at once to the first mixture, stirring just until moistened. Pour into 12 lined or lightly oiled muffin cups and top with shredded coconut. Bake for 30 minutes in a preheated 350° F. oven.

Yield: 12.

PEANUTTY CORN MUFFINS

1 cup yellow cornmeal
½ cup buckwheat flour
¼ cup Viobin Wheat Germ
¼ cup soybean powder
2 teaspoons tartrate baking
  powder
½ teaspoon sea salt
2 eggs
⅓ cup safflower oil

1 cup goat-milk yogurt
½ cup tupelo honey
½ cup fresh-ground peanut
  butter
2 tablespoons lecithin
1 teaspoon vanilla extract
1 cup toasted peanuts
32 toasted peanuts

Blend the first 6 ingredients in a mixing bowl and set aside. Combine the next 7 ingredients in a blender at high speed for 1 minute. Pour all at once into the dry ingredients and mix just until moistened. Gently stir in the 1 cup peanuts and pour batter into 16 lined or lightly oiled muffin cups. Top each with 2 peanuts and bake for 40 minutes in a preheated 350° F. oven.

Yield: 16.

SOYA BLUEBERRY MUFFINS

3 cups unbleached white–and–wheat-germ flour

½ cup soybean powder

1 tablespoon tartrate baking powder

1 teaspoon sea salt

⅔ cup raw sugar

½ cup toasted wheat germ

½ cup powdered nonfat dry milk

2 teaspoons cinnamon

4 eggs

½ cup soybean oil

2 cups water

1½ cups blueberries, dusted with flour

Blend the first 8 ingredients in a bowl with an electric mixer at low speed. Add the eggs, oil, and water and mix for 1 minute. Lightly stir in the blueberries. Fill 24 lined or lightly oiled muffin cups ¾ full and bake about 30 minutes in a preheated 400° F. oven.

Yield: 24.

APPLE CINNAMON MUFFINS

1 cup stone-ground whole-wheat flour
½ cup brown-rice flour
½ cup toasted wheat germ
¼ cup soybean powder
¼ cup powdered nonfat dry milk
2 tablespoons lecithin
2 teaspoons tartrate baking powder
½ teaspoon sea salt
2 cups diced McIntosh apples with skin
⅔ cup dried currants
1 teaspoon cinnamon
⅓ cup safflower oil
½ cup raw sugar
2 eggs
1 cup goat-milk yogurt
½ cup buttermilk
1 teaspoon vanilla extract
Cinnamon
18 pecan halves

Combine the first 8 ingredients in a mixing bowl and set aside. Toss the next 3 ingredients together and set aside. Whip the next 6 ingredients together and add all at once to the dry ingredients, stirring till moistened. Lightly stir in the apple combination. Turn into 18 lined or lightly oiled muffin cups and sprinkle some cinnamon and 1 pecan half on top of each muffin. Bake for 35 minutes in a preheated 350° F. oven.

Yield: 18.

APPLE CARROT WHOLE-WHEAT MUFFINS

2 eggs
½ cup raw sugar
¼ cup Barbados molasses
¼ cup safflower oil
½ cup canned unsweetened
   pineapple juice
½ cup shredded carrots
½ cup shredded McIntosh
   apple with skin
1 teaspoon orange extract
½ teaspoon lemon extract

1½ cups stone-ground whole-
   wheat flour
½ cup toasted wheat germ
2 tablespoons powdered nonfat
   dry milk
2 teaspoons tartrate baking
   powder
½ teaspoon sea salt
½ cup pumpkin seeds
Pumpkin seeds

Combine the first 9 ingredients and mix together thoroughly. Blend the remaining ingredients except the last together, add all at once to the first mixture, and stir just until moistened. Divide among 12 lined or lightly oiled muffin cups, top with pumpkin seeds, and bake for 30 minutes in a preheated 375° F. oven.
    Yield: 12.

PINEAPPLE CORN RICE MUFFINS

2 eggs
⅓ cup safflower oil
½ cup orange-blossom honey
½ cup canned unsweetened
   pineapple juice
½ cup canned unsweetened
   crushed pineapple
1 teaspoon almond extract
1 cup yellow cornmeal

½ cup brown-rice flour
¼ cup soybean powder
½ cup toasted wheat germ
2 tablespoons lecithin
2 teaspoons tartrate baking
   powder
½ teaspoon sea salt
⅓ cup dried currants
Cinnamon

Beat the first 6 ingredients together. Blend the remaining ingredients except cinnamon and add all at once to the first mixture, stirring just until moistened. Pour into 16 lined or lightly oiled muffin cups and sprinkle with cinnamon. Bake for 30 minutes in a preheated 350° F. oven.
    Yield: 16.

CASHEW BANANA WHEAT OAT MUFFINS

2 eggs
¼ cup tupelo honey
¼ cup Barbados molasses
1 cup mashed bananas
¼ cup safflower oil
½ cup buttermilk
1 cup stone-ground whole-
  wheat flour
1 cup rolled oats
¼ cup sesame meal

¼ cup toasted wheat germ
¼ cup soybean powder
2 teaspoons tartrate baking
  powder
1 teaspoon cinnamon
½ teaspoon sea salt
½ cup toasted cashew pieces
½ cup dried currants
Cashew pieces

Beat until smooth the first 6 ingredients. Blend the remaining ingredients except last and add all at once to the first mixture, mixing just until moistened. Pour into 14 lined or lightly oiled muffin cups, top each with a few cashew pieces, and bake for 30 minutes in a preheated 375° F. oven.
  Yield: 14.

WHOLE-WHEAT DATE MUFFINS

¾ cup raw sugar
½ cup soybean oil
¼ cup clover honey
2 eggs
½ teaspoon sea salt
1 teaspoon cinnamon
1 cup water
¼ cup toasted wheat germ

2 teaspoons tartrate baking
  powder
¼ cup powdered nonfat dry
  milk
2 cups stone-ground whole-
  wheat flour
1 cup diced pitted dates
9 pitted dates, halved

Combine the first 6 ingredients in a bowl and mix with an electric mixer for 2 minutes. Add the water and wheat germ and mix for 1 minute. Add the next 4 ingredients and mix for 2 minutes. Fill 18 lined or lightly oiled muffin cups ⅔ full, top each with a date half, and bake for 30 minutes in a preheated 400° F. oven.
  Yield: 18.

RICE-POLISH MUFFINS

1 cup brown-rice flour
½ cup rice polishings
¼ cup soybean powder
¼ cup powdered nonfat dry
  milk
½ cup raw sugar
2 tablespoons lecithin
2 teaspoons tartrate baking
  powder

½ teaspoon sea salt
2 eggs
¼ cup safflower oil
1½ cups buttermilk
1 teaspoon vanilla extract
½ cup dried currants
⅓ cup unsalted Soy Nuts

Combine the first 8 ingredients and blend together. Whip the next 4 ingredients together and add all at once to the dry mixture, stirring thoroughly. Add the currants and Soy Nuts and mix lightly. Divide among 12 lined or well-oiled muffin cups and bake for 45 minutes in a preheated 375° F. oven.
Yield: 12.

GINGER RYE MUFFINS

1 cup stone-ground rye flour
½ cup rolled oats
½ cup raw sugar
¼ cup toasted wheat germ
¼ cup soybean powder
¼ cup powdered nonfat dry
  milk
2 teaspoons tartrate baking
  powder
½ teaspoon sea salt
½ teaspoon powdered ginger

¼ teaspoon nutmeg
¼ teaspoon cinnamon
2 tablespoons diced preserved
  ginger
2 eggs
⅓ cup sesame oil
⅔ cup buttermilk
⅓ cup canned unsweetened
  pineapple juice
6 dates, halved

Combine the first 12 ingredients in a mixing bowl. Add the remaining ingredients and mix just until moistened. Divide among 12 lined or lightly oiled muffin cups and top each with a date half. Bake in a preheated 400° F. oven for 30 minutes.
Yield: 12.

SWEET EVERYTHINGS
(Pies, Cakes, and Cookies)

Years before everybody became so calorie-conscious, Edith came out with a dessert line that packed a nutritional wallop while weighing in lower calorically. Long before white sugar, "enriched" white flour, and butter began to get such bad names, she had found superior substitutes for these items. You can eat

Edith's cake, so to speak, and have it too—have an enhanced diet, that is.

Quite a few celebrities find their way to our doors. It is no invasion of their privacy to reveal that their sweet tooth is as prominent as yours or ours. We were innocently pleased when Carol Channing, who is so finicky about her diet that she usually carries around her special foods in a cellophane bag, commissioned us to make a cake that she could share backstage with her fellow cast members of *Hello, Dolly!* When he was starring on Broadway in *Two by Two,* our friend Danny Kaye often used to come down around teatime to nibble on a little something hot out of the oven.

Surely no one has been more articulate in his appreciation than actor Robert Cummings. Bob Cummings, as you probably know, is a healthnik who always manages to look pretty fabulous—and about 20 years younger than the date on his passport would make him out to be. Normally all sweets are proscribed from his diet, but the night he dined with us, he broke down and sampled some of Edith's wares. A few days later we had a 2-page single-spaced typewritten rhapsody from him.

Sinful or blameless, the ultimate distinction of Edith's baking is in the tasting. Don't take anyone else's word for it—try it yourself!

PIES

DEEP-DISH APPLE CRANBERRY PIE

½ cup Coconut Sesame Mix (see page 279)
½ cup cranberries
¼ cup water
½ cup raw sugar
6 cups peeled sliced McIntosh apples
½ teaspoon cinnamon
3 tablespoons soybean oil
2 tablespoons ground seeded orange with peel
1 tablespoon fresh lemon juice
½ cup apple juice
1 cup Sesame Streusel (see page 279)
¼ cup sliced filberts

Sprinkle the Coconut Sesame Mix in the bottom of a 10-inch pie pan and set aside. Combine the next 2 ingredients and ¼ cup of the sugar in a saucepan and cook for 5 minutes on a medium fire. Add the next 6 ingredients and the remaining sugar and stir thoroughly. Cover and cook on a low fire for 10 minutes. Pour into the pie pan and cover with the Sesame Streusel and filberts. Bake in a preheated 400° F. oven for 15 minutes, then at 350° F. for 15 minutes.

Serves 10.

SPECIAL-COMPANY APPLE CHEESE PIE

½ recipe Whole-Wheat Walnut
Crust (see page 278)
½ cup clover honey
½ cup raw sugar
¼ cup canned unsweetened
pineapple juice
2 tablespoons safflower oil
¼ teaspoon sea salt
4 large Delicious apples with
skin, cored and sliced
1 orange with peel, seeded and
ground
½ cup dried currants
⅓ cup pecan pieces
⅓ cup toasted wheat germ

1 teaspoon cinnamon

Cheese Topping:
1½ cups cottage cheese
½ cup farmer cheese
2 eggs
⅓ cup goat-milk yogurt
¼ cup raw sugar
¼ cup unsweetened canned
pineapple juice
2 tablespoons clover honey
2 tablespoons sesame meal
1 teaspoon vanilla extract
Toasted sesame seeds

Roll out the Whole-Wheat Walnut Crust and fit into a 10-inch pie pan. Flute the edge and prick all over with a fork. Bake for 25 minutes in a preheated 350° F. oven and set aside. Combine the honey, sugar, pineapple juice, oil, and salt in a saucepan and simmer. Poach the apple slices in 2 batches for 10 minutes each in the honey syrup. Let cool for 10 minutes, then add the next 5 ingredients, stirring lightly. Pour into the cooled pie shell. Make cheese topping by combining the remaining ingredients except for the sesame seeds. Mix in a bowl until smooth. Pour over apple filling and sprinkle with sesame seeds. Bake in a preheated 350° F. oven for 45 minutes.

Serves 12.

"IT'S THE BERRIES" PIE

½ recipe Whole-Wheat Walnut Crust (see page 278)
1½ cups blueberries
½ cup cranberries
1 tablespoon safflower oil
¼ cup raw sugar
¼ cup canned unsweetened pineapple juice
2 tablespoons clover honey

2 tablespoons ground seeded orange with peel
2 tablespoons brown-rice flour
⅓ cup toasted sliced filberts
½ teaspoon orange extract
½ teaspoon almond extract
2 tablespoons toasted sliced filberts

Roll out the Whole-Wheat Walnut Crust and fit into an 8-inch pie pan. Flute the edge, prick all over, and bake until well-browned in a preheated 375° F. oven; set aside. Combine the remaining ingredients except the last in a saucepan and cook on low heat until thickened. Pour into the baked crust and top with the filberts. Serve warm or cold.
    Serves 6.

PINEAPPLE APRICOT PIE

½ recipe Whole-Wheat Walnut Crust (see page 278)
1 cup canned crushed unsweetened pineapple
½ cup sliced canned drained dietetic apricots
⅓ cup dried currants
⅓ cup unsweetened shredded coconut

3 tablespoons raw sugar
1 tablespoon soybean oil
3 tablespoons sesame-sunflower meal
½ teaspoon orange extract
½ teaspoon lemon extract
¼ cup unsweetened shredded coconut

Roll out the Whole-Wheat Walnut Crust and fit into an 8-inch pie pan. Flute the edge, prick all over, and bake for 15 minutes in a preheated 375° F. oven; set aside. Combine the next 9 ingredients and mix thoroughly. Pour into the cooled partially baked crust, top with the coconut, and bake in a preheated 375° F. oven for 30 minutes or until coconut is light brown.
    Serves 6.

DRIED-APRICOT DATE PIE

½ recipe Whole-Wheat Walnut
 Crust (see page 278)
½ cup diced dried apricots
½ cup diced pitted dates
3 tablespoons raw sugar
¾ cup canned unsweetened
 pineapple juice
2 eggs
1 cup goat-milk yogurt
¼ cup Viobin Wheat Germ
1 teaspoon minced candied
 ginger
½ teaspoon almond extract
½ teaspoon vanilla extract
⅓ cup walnut pieces

Roll out the Whole-Wheat Walnut Crust, fit into an 8-inch pie
pan, and flute the edge. Set aside. Combine the next 4 ingredients
in a saucepan and cook on low heat until thick, stirring occasionally. Set aside until cool. Combine the next 6 ingredients in a
bowl and whip thoroughly. Add the cooled fruit mixture and
blend together. Pour into the pie crust and top with the walnut
pieces. Bake in a preheated 350° F. oven for 45 minutes.
 Serves 6.

CHERRY STRAWBERRY CUSTARD PIE

½ recipe Whole-Wheat Walnut
 Crust (see page 278)
2 cups skim milk
¼ cup powdered nonfat dry
 milk
¼ cup raw sugar
Simmering water
2 eggs
½ cup cold water
4 tablespoons brown-rice flour
1 tablespoon soybean powder
1 tablespoon safflower oil

1 teaspoon vanilla extract

Cherry Strawberry Topping:
1½ cups pitted Bing cherries
1 cup sliced strawberries
¾ cup canned unsweetened
 pineapple juice
¼ cup raw sugar
2 tablespoons brown-rice flour
½ teaspoon almond extract
1 cup Coconut Sesame Mix
 (see page 279)

Roll out the Whole-Wheat Walnut Crust and fit into a 10-inch
pie pan. Flute edge, prick all over, and bake in a preheated

375° F. oven for about 25 minutes or until well-browned. Set aside. Combine the skim milk, powdered milk, and sugar in a double boiler over the simmering water until warm. Beat the eggs and add to the warm milk mixture, whipping constantly with a wire whisk. Mix the cold water, the brown-rice flour, and the soybean powder until smooth, then add to the milk-egg mixture. Cook until very thick, stirring occasionally. Remove from fire, add the oil and vanilla, and mix thoroughly. Pour custard into the cooled baked pie shell and refrigerate. In a saucepan combine the cherries, strawberries, ½ cup of the pineapple juice, and sugar and cook on a low fire until hot. Mix the remaining pineapple juice with the brown-rice flour until smooth and add to the fruit mixture, stirring over fire until thickened. Remove from fire and add the almond extract and Coconut Sesame Mix, mixing lightly. Cool to lukewarm and pour on top of the chilled custard pie filling. Refrigerate for several hours before serving.

Serves 12.

FRESH-PLUM YOGURT CUSTARD PIE

½ recipe Whole-Wheat Sour-Cream Dough (see page 278)
4 cups Italian blue plums
½ cup raw sugar
¼ cup sesame-sunflower meal
2 teaspoons cinnamon

3 eggs
1 cup goat-milk yogurt
½ cup sour cream
1 teaspoon vanilla extract
Cinnamon

Roll out the Whole-Wheat Sour-Cream Dough, fit into a 10-inch pie pan, and flute the edges. Cut the plums in half, pit, and place cut side up on the dough. Combine the next 3 ingredients and sprinkle half over the plums. Bake in a preheated 375° F. oven for 25 minutes. Combine the eggs and the remaining sugar mixture and whip together. Add the yogurt, sour cream, and vanilla and stir thoroughly. Lower the oven heat to 325° F. Pour the yogurt mixture over the plums and sprinkle with cinnamon. Bake for 45 minutes. Serve chilled.

Serves 10.

CARROT CUSTARD PIE

½ recipe Whole-Wheat Walnut Crust (see page 278)
2 cups skim milk
⅓ cup powdered nonfat dry milk
⅓ cup raw sugar
Simmering water
2 eggs
½ cup carrot juice
¼ cup brown-rice flour

2 tablespoons soybean powder
1 tablespoon safflower oil
1 teaspoon vanilla extract
⅔ cup shredded carrots
½ cup Coconut Sesame Mix (see page 279)
⅓ cup dried currants
⅓ cup Coconut Sesame Mix (see page 279)

Roll out the Whole-Wheat Walnut Crust and fit into a 9-inch pie pan. Flute edge, prick all over, and bake in a preheated 375° F. oven for about 25 minutes or until well-browned. Set aside. In a double boiler combine the skim milk, powdered milk, and sugar and heat over simmering water until warm. Add the eggs and whip. Combine the next 3 ingredients and mix until smooth. Stir into the milk-egg mixture and blend until smooth. Cook, stirring occasionally, until very thick. Remove from fire and stir in the next 5 ingredients. Pour into the cooled baked pie crust. Make a 1-inch border around the edge of the pie with the remaining Coconut Sesame Mix. Refrigerate and serve chilled. Serves 8.

CASHEW DATE PIE

½ recipe Whole-Wheat Walnut Crust (see page 278)
1 cup safflower-oil margarine
1 cup raw sugar
½ cup clover honey
3 eggs

1 cup sesame-sunflower meal
1 teaspoon maple extract
1 cup diced pitted dates
⅔ cup toasted cashew pieces
⅓ cup Coconut Sesame Mix (see page 279)

Roll out the Whole-Wheat Walnut Crust and fit into a 10-inch pie pan. Flute edge, prick all over, and bake in a preheated 375° F. oven for 15 minutes; set aside. In a bowl, using an elec-

tric mixer, cream the margarine and sugar for 5 minutes. Add the honey and eggs and mix 5 more minutes. Add the next 2 ingredients and mix 2 minutes. Stir in the dates and cashews and mix thoroughly. Pour into the cooled partially baked crust and sprinkle with the Coconut Sesame Mix. Bake in a preheated 350° F. oven for about 45 minutes or until firm to the touch.
Serves 10.

SUGAR-FREE COTTAGE CHEESE PIE

½ cup Coconut Sesame Mix (see page 279)
1 cup cottage cheese
1 tablespoon fresh lemon juice
⅓ cup water
2 teaspoons unflavored gelatin
2 tablespoons powdered nonfat dry milk

1 teaspoon Sweet 'n Low
½ cup powered nonfat dry milk
1 teaspoon fresh lemon juice
½ cup water
1 teaspoon vanilla extract
Coconut Sesame Mix (see page 279) (optional)

Sprinkle the Coconut Sesame Mix in the bottom of a 9-inch pie pan and set aside. Combine the cottage cheese and lemon juice in a bowl and whip with an electric mixer at medium speed for 10 minutes. Blend the water, gelatin, powdered milk, and Sweet 'n Low until smooth in a saucepan on a low fire and stir until the gelatin dissolves. Add to the cottage-cheese mixture and mix thoroughly. Refrigerate until completely jelled. Whip the powdered milk, lemon juice, water, and vanilla at high speed with the electric mixer until as thick as whipped cream and set aside. Whip the jelled cottage-cheese mixture with the electric mixer for 5 minutes at medium speed. Gradually add the whipped powdered milk and mix until incorporated. Pour into the pie pan and sprinkle with a little Coconut Sesame Mix if desired. Refrigerate for 2 hours before serving.
Serves 8.

NEAPOLITAN CHEESE PIE*

½ recipe Whole-Wheat Walnut
  Crust (see page 278)
1 pound part-skim ricotta
  cheese
2 eggs
¼ cup raw sugar

1 teaspoon vanilla extract
½ teaspoon almond extract
½ cup carob bits
¼ cup toasted cashew pieces
¼ cup dried currants
⅓ cup finely cut-up carob bits

Roll out crust and fit into a 9-inch pie pan. Flute edge, prick all over, and bake in a preheated 375° F. oven for 25 minutes or until well-browned. Set aside. In a bowl, using an electric mixer, whip the ricotta at medium speed for 5 minutes. Add the next 4 ingredients and mix 5 minutes more. Lightly stir in the next 3 ingredients and pour into the cooled baked pie crust. Sprinkle the finely cut-up carob bits over the top and refrigerate for several hours before serving.
Serves 8.

CAROB CREAM-CHEESE PIE

2 tablespoons safflower oil
½ cup Coconut Sesame Mix
  (see page 279)
3 eggs
½ cup raw sugar
2 teaspoons vanilla extract
12 ounces cream cheese (at
  room temperature)

Carob Topping:
1 cup sour cream
2 tablespoons raw sugar
½ teaspoon almond extract
¼ cup carob powder
½ teaspoon cinnamon
Coconut Sesame Mix (see page
  279)

Brush the bottom and sides of a 10-inch pie pan with the oil. Sprinkle the Coconut Sesame Mix on bottom and set aside. Using an electric mixer, whip the eggs at high speed for 5 minutes in a mixing bowl. Add the sugar and the vanilla and whip for 5

* If desired, this may be made in individual serving dishes; instead of Whole-Wheat Walnut Crust use Coconut Sesame Mix (see page 279) as a base.

minutes. Gradually add cream cheese in small bits, continuing to whip at medium speed until mixture is very smooth. Pour into pie pan and bake in a preheated 375° F. oven for about 35 minutes or until firm. Cool at room temperature for 30 minutes. Combine the next 5 ingredients and mix until very smooth. Spread carefully on cooled pie and make a 1-inch border of the Coconut Sesame Mix. Return to a preheated 350° F. oven for 5 minutes. Refrigerate for several hours before serving.

Serves 10.

CAKES AND PASTRIES

WHOLE-WHEAT CHOCOLATE SESAME CAKE

1½ cups stone-ground
   whole-wheat flour
1¼ cups raw sugar
½ cup soybean powder
2 teaspoons tartrate baking
   powder
½ teaspoon sea salt
½ teaspoon cinnamon
⅓ cup soybean oil
¼ cup sour cream

1 cup buttermilk
2 eggs
¼ cup clover honey
3 squares unsweetened
   chocolate, melted
1 teaspoon vanilla extract
½ cup date chips
⅓ cup toasted sesame seeds
Toasted sesame seeds

In a mixing bowl, with an electric mixer at low speed, combine the first 6 ingredients. Add the next 3 ingredients and mix for 2 minutes at medium speed. Add the next 4 ingredients and mix for 2 minutes. Blend in the date chips and ⅓ cup sesame seeds and pour into an oiled 9-inch tube pan. Top with sesame seeds and bake in a preheated 300° F. oven for about 1 hour or until toothpick inserted in center of cake comes out clean.

Serves 12.

CAROB HONEY CAKE

1 cup raw sugar
1 cup soybean oil
⅓ cup clover honey
3 eggs
1 cup carob powder
1¼ cups water
2 teaspoons vanilla extract

1¾ cups unbleached
  white–and–wheat-germ flour
2 tablespoons powdered
  nonfat dry milk
¼ cup soybean powder
1 tablespoon tartrate baking
  powder
1 teaspoon sea salt

Combine the first 4 ingredients in a bowl and mix with an electric mixer for 5 minutes. Add the next 3 ingredients and mix for 2 minutes. Add the remaining ingredients and mix for 2 minutes. Pour into an oiled *bundt* pan and bake for 45 minutes in a preheated 350° F. oven or until toothpick inserted in center of cake comes out clean.
Serves 12.

FRESH ORANGE CAKE

1 cup soybean oil
1½ cups raw .sugar
4 eggs
2 teaspoons orange extract
½ teaspoon vanilla extract
¼ cup powdered nonfat
  dry milk

2 tablespoons Viobin
  Wheat Germ
1 cup water
2½ cups Fearn Soy-O Mix
3 tablespoons ground seeded
  orange with peel

Using an electric mixer, combine the oil, sugar, 2 of the eggs, and the next 6 ingredients at low speed in a bowl and then mix at medium speed for 5 minutes. Add the remaining 2 eggs and ground orange and mix 5 minutes more. Pour into 2 oiled standard loaf pans or 1 oiled *bundt* pan and bake in a preheated 300° F. oven about 1 hour or until toothpick inserted in center of cake comes out clean.
Serves 12.

CRUNCHY SOY-NUT PEACH CAKE

¾ cup stone-ground
  whole-wheat pastry flour
1 cup unbleached white–and–
  wheat-germ flour
¼ cup soybean powder
1½ cups raw sugar
2 teaspoons tartrate baking
  powder
2 teaspoons cinnamon
½ teaspoon sea salt
3 eggs

½ cup safflower oil
½ cup goat-milk yogurt
½ cup carrot juice
1 cup diced dried peaches
1 cup shredded carrots

Soy Nut Topping:
¾ cup unsalted Soy Nuts
¾ cup orange-blossom honey
1 teaspoon orange extract

Combine the first 7 ingredients in a mixing bowl and set aside. In small bowl beat together the next 4 ingredients and add all at once to the dry mixture. Stir in the peaches and carrots and pour batter into an oiled 10-inch spring-form pan. Bake in a preheated 350° F. oven for about 1 hour or until brown and toothpick inserted in center of cake comes out clean. Meanwhile combine remaining ingredients to make topping. Remove cake from oven and quickly spread the topping over the top of the cake. Return the cake to the oven and bake for 10 more minutes. Serves 12.

CHERRY PECAN BUTTERMILK CAKE

½ cup soybean oil
1 cup raw sugar
2 eggs
½ teaspoon almond extract
½ teaspoon lemon extract
½ cup stone-ground
  whole-wheat pastry flour
½ cup unbleached
  white–and–wheat-germ flour
¼ cup soybean powder

¼ cup Viobin Wheat Germ
2 teaspoons tartrate baking
  powder
½ teaspoon sea salt
½ cup buttermilk
½ cup halved pitted Bing
  cherries
½ cup pecan pieces
¼ cup unsweetened
  shredded coconut

Combine the first 5 ingredients in a mixing bowl and, with an electric mixer, mix for 2 minutes at medium speed; set aside. Blend the next 6 ingredients in another bowl and add to egg mixture alternately with the buttermilk, making in all 4 additions of the flour mixture and 3 additions of the buttermilk. Mix until smooth after each addition. Stir in the cherries and pecans and pour into an oiled standard loaf pan. Sprinkle with the coconut and bake in a preheated 350° F. oven for 1 hour or until toothpick inserted in center of cake comes out clean.

Serves 8.

CARROT COCONUT CAKE

⅔ cup safflower oil
1½ cups raw sugar
3 eggs
2 teaspoons vanilla extract
1 teaspoon cinnamon
¾ cup cooked pureed
   pumpkin
2¼ cups Fearn Soy-O Mix

¼ cup Viobin Wheat Germ
½ cup buttermilk
¼ cup carrot juice
½ cup shredded carrots
⅓ cup dried currants
¼ cup unsweetened
   shredded coconut

Combine the first 5 ingredients in a bowl, using an electric mixer at medium speed, and mix for 5 minutes. Add the pumpkin, mix for 1 minute, and set aside. Blend the Soy-O Mix and wheat germ in a bowl and set aside. Combine the buttermilk and carrot juice. Add alternately to the pumpkin mixture first the Soy-O mixture and then the buttermilk mixture, making in all 4 additions of the first and 3 additions of the second; after each addition mix until smooth. Stir in the carrots and currants and mix lightly. Pour batter into an oiled *bundt* pan, sprinkle with the coconut, and bake in a preheated 375° F. oven for about 50 minutes or until a toothpick inserted in the center of the cake comes out clean.

Serves 12.

WHOLE-WHEAT SPICE CAKE

1 cup safflower-oil margarine
1 cup raw sugar
½ cup Barbados molasses
4 eggs
½ cup buttermilk
1 teaspoon almond extract
2 cups stone-ground
   whole-wheat flour
½ cup sesame meal
½ cup dried currants
¼ cup toasted wheat germ
¼ cup soybean powder
2 teaspoons tartrate baking
   powder
½ teaspoon sea salt
1 teaspoon cinnamon
½ teaspoon powdered ginger
¼ teaspoon nutmeg
¼ teaspoon mace

Using an electric mixer at medium speed, combine the first 3 ingredients in a mixing bowl for 5 minutes. Add the eggs 1 at a time, mixing until smooth after each addition. Add the buttermilk and almond extract and mix for 3 minutes. Blend together the remaining ingredients in a bowl, add gradually to first mixture, and then mix for 2 more minutes. Pour batter into an oiled 9-inch tube pan and bake in a preheated 325° F. oven for 1 hour and 20 minutes or until toothpick inserted in center of cake comes out clean.

Serves 12.

WHOLE-WHEAT CASHEW CAKE

1 cup raw sugar
½ cup clover honey
1 cup soybean oil
⅔ cup fresh-ground
   cashew butter
3 eggs
1 teaspoon vanilla extract
¾ cup canned unsweetened
   pineapple juice
2 cups stone-ground
   whole-wheat flour
¼ cup soybean powder
2 teaspoons tartrate baking
   powder
½ teaspoon salt
½ cup toasted cashew pieces

Combine the first 6 ingredients in a mixing bowl, using an electric mixer at medium speed, for 3 minutes. Add the pineapple juice and mix for 1 minute. Add the remaining ingredients and mix for 2 minutes. Pour into an oiled 9-inch tube pan and bake in a preheated 300° F. oven for about 1 hour or until a toothpick inserted in center of cake comes out clean.

Serves 12.

MAPLE WALNUT CAKE
(Dennis's Favorite)

1 cup safflower oil
1½ cups raw sugar
4 eggs
2 teaspoons maple extract
¼ cup maple syrup
½ teaspoon vanilla extract
¼ cup powdered nonfat
   dry milk

2 tablespoons Viobin
   Wheat Germ
1 cup water
2 cups Fearn Soy-O Mix
⅔ cup toasted ground
   walnuts
½ cup walnut pieces

Using an electric mixer at low speed, combine in a bowl the oil, sugar, 2 of the eggs, and the next 7 ingredients and then mix at medium speed for 5 minutes. Add the remaining 2 eggs and ground walnuts and mix for 5 more minutes. Pour into 2 oiled standard loaf pans or 1 oiled *bundt* pan and bake in a preheated 325° F. oven for 15 minutes. Top with the walnut pieces, turn oven down to 300° F., and continue baking for about 30 minutes or until cake is brown and a toothpick inserted in the center comes out clean.

Serves 12.

WALNUT YOGURT CAKE

¾ cup safflower oil
1 cup raw sugar
2 eggs
1 cup goat-milk yogurt
1 teaspoon maple extract
1 cup unbleached white–and–
   wheat-germ flour
¾ cup stone-ground
   whole-wheat pastry flour

¼ cup soybean powder
½ teaspoon sea salt
2 teaspoons tartrate baking
   powder
⅓ cup walnut pieces
⅓ cup diced prunes
1 teaspoon cinnamon
2 tablespoons raw sugar
Walnut halves (optional)

Using an electric mixer at medium speed, combine the first 3 ingredients in a mixing bowl for 3 minutes. Add the yogurt and maple extract and mix for 2 minutes. Blend together the next 5 ingredients in a bowl, add to the yogurt mixture, and mix for 2 minutes. Oil a standard loaf pan and pour in half the batter. Combine the next 4 ingredients and sprinkle over the batter. Carefully spoon the remaining batter on top. If desired, sprinkle a few walnut halves over the top of the batter. Bake in a preheated 350° F. oven for about 1 hour and 10 minutes or until a toothpick inserted in the center of the cake comes out clean. Serves 8.

APPLE CHEESE HORSESHOES

Whole-Wheat Sour-Cream Dough (see page 278)
Stone-ground whole-wheat flour
¼ cup safflower oil
1 cup creamed cottage cheese
3 eggs
¾ cup date sugar
⅔ cup dried currants
2 large Delicious apples with skin, shredded
½ cup Coconut Sesame Mix (see page 279)
2 teaspoons vanilla extract
2 teaspoons cinnamon
2 tablespoons water
Sliced almonds

Divide the dough into 2 pieces and roll out each piece on a lightly floured board into a 10 × 14-inch rectangle. Brush the oil evenly over both pieces of dough. Combine the cottage cheese, 2 of the eggs, and the next 6 ingredients and mix thoroughly. Divide mixture between the 2 rectangles, leaving a ½-inch border all around. Roll each rectangle up tightly, place each on an oiled baking pan, and shape into a U. Combine the remaining egg with the water and beat together to make an egg wash. Brush egg wash over horseshoes and sprinkle them with the almonds. Bake in a preheated 375° F. oven for 45 minutes. Serves 12.

WHOLE-WHEAT CREAM PUFFS

½ cup water
¼ cup safflower oil
⅓ cup stone-ground
  whole-wheat flour
2 tablespoons brown-rice flour

2 tablespoons Viobin
  Wheat Germ
⅛ teaspoon sea salt
2 eggs
Carob Custard

Bring the water and oil to a boil in a saucepan. Combine the next 4 ingredients and quickly add them all at once, stirring until a ball forms and leaves the sides of the pan. Remove from heat and cool slightly. Add the eggs 1 at a time, beating until the mixture is smooth and glossy. Drop by rounded tablespoonfuls on a lightly oiled baking sheet. Bake in a preheated 450° F. oven for 15 minutes, then lower the heat to 350° F. and continue baking for 20 minutes more or until puffs are lightly browned. Cool. Slice a small cap from the top of each puff and remove any soft dough that may remain inside. Fill cream puffs with chilled Carob Custard, first stirring it until completely smooth.
Serves 12.

Carob Custard

1 cup skim milk
¼ cup raw sugar
2 tablespoons maple syrup
Pinch of sea salt
3 tablespoons brown-rice flour

3 tablespoons soybean powder
3 tablespoons carob powder
2 eggs, slightly beaten
1 teaspoon vanilla extract

Combine the first 7 ingredients in a saucepan on a low fire, mixing until smooth. Stir constantly until thickened. Quickly stir the eggs into the milk mixture. Remove from heat and add the vanilla, blending until smooth. Refrigerate.

COOKIES

TRIPLE BASIC PROTEIN COOKIES

1¼ cups safflower-oil margarine

1½ cups raw sugar

2 teaspoons vanilla extract

3 eggs

2¼ cups unbleached white–and–wheat-germ flour

½ cup soybean powder

¼ cup powdered nonfat dry milk

¼ cup toasted wheat germ

2 teaspoons tartrate baking powder

½ teaspoon sea salt

1 cup water

½ cup carob bits

⅓ cup sliced almonds

½ cup dried currants

⅓ cup walnut pieces

¾ cup diced dates

¼ cup sliced almonds

Carob bits

Walnut pieces

Sliced almonds

Combine the first 3 ingredients in a mixing bowl, using an electric mixer at medium speed, and mix for 3 minutes. Add the eggs and mix for 2 minutes. Blend the next 6 ingredients together, add half to the egg mixture, and mix for 2 minutes. Pour in the water and mix for 1 minute. Add the remaining half of the flour mixture and mix for 2 minutes. Divide the batter into thirds, with approximately 1½ cups in each. Add the carob bits and almonds to the first third, mixing thoroughly. Add the currants and walnuts to the next third, mixing thoroughly. Add the dates and almonds to the last third, mixing thoroughly. Drop cookie doughs from a tablespoon onto lightly oiled baking sheets. Top each carob cookie with 1 carob bit, each currant cookie with a few walnut pieces, and each date cookie with a few almonds. Bake in a preheated 300° F. oven until brown—about 25 minutes.

Yield: about 90.

WHOLE-WHEAT PROTEIN COOKIES

½ cup safflower-oil margarine
¾ cup raw sugar
½ teaspoon powdered ginger
¼ teaspoon Brownies
  Vege-C-Salt (see page 40)
1 teaspoon tartrate baking
  powder
½ teaspoon orange extract
2 eggs
1 cup stone-ground
  whole-wheat flour

¼ cup toasted wheat germ
¼ cup sesame-sunflower meal
2 tablespoons powdered
  nonfat dry milk
2 tablespoons lecithin
2 tablespoons soybean powder
⅓ cup orange juice
½ cup unsalted Soy Nuts
½ cup dried currants
Unsalted Soy Nuts

Combine the first 6 ingredients in a mixing bowl, using an electric mixer at medium speed, for 3 minutes. Add the eggs and mix for 2 minutes. Blend the next 6 ingredients, add half to the batter, and mix for 2 minutes. Add the orange juice and mix for 1 minute. Add the remaining half of the flour mixture and mix for 2 minutes. Stir in the Soy Nuts and currants and mix well. Drop from a tablespoon onto lightly oiled baking sheets and top each cookie with a few Soy Nuts. Bake in a preheated 300° F. oven until brown—about 25 minutes.

Yield: about 50.

TAHINI WHOLE-WHEAT COOKIES

½ cup tupelo honey
¼ cup raw sugar
½ cup safflower oil
2 eggs
½ cup toasted wheat germ
½ cup toasted sesame seeds
⅓ cup *tahini*
1 cup buttermilk
1 teaspoon maple extract

1 cup Monukka raisins
1 cup rolled oats
1 cup stone-ground
  whole-wheat flour
2 tablespoons lecithin
2 tablespoons powdered
  nonfat dry milk
Toasted sesame seeds

Blend the first 4 ingredients in a mixing bowl, using an electric mixer at medium speed, for 2 minutes. Add the next 5 ingredients and mix for 1 minute. Add the remaining ingredients, except for the last, and mix for 2 minutes. Drop from a tablespoon onto lightly oiled baking sheets and sprinkle each cookie with some sesame seeds. Bake in a preheated 300° F. oven for 30 minutes or until brown.

Yield: about 60.

SALT-FREE WHOLE-WHEAT DATE COOKIES

¾ cup raw sugar
1 cup toasted wheat germ
1 cup soybean oil
2 eggs
¾ cup buttermilk
1 teaspoon vanilla extract

½ teaspoon cinnamon
¾ cup diced dates
1 cup stone-ground
  whole-wheat flour
2 tablespoons soybean powder
Coarsely diced dates

With an electric mixer at medium speed combine in a bowl the first 4 ingredients for 2 minutes. Add the next 3 ingredients and mix for 2 minutes. Add the next 3 ingredients and mix for 2 minutes. Drop batter from a tablespoon onto oiled baking sheets and top each cookie with a date piece. Bake about 25 minutes or until brown in a preheated 300° F. oven.

Yield: about 45.

SALT-FREE WHOLE-WHEAT OATMEAL COOKIES

¾ cup raw sugar
1½ cups rolled oats
1 cup soybean oil
2 eggs
¾ cup buttermilk
1 teaspoon vanilla extract

¼ teaspoon lemon extract
¼ teaspoon cinnamon
½ cup dried currants
1 cup stone-ground
  whole-wheat flour
Oatmeal flakes

Combine the first 4 ingredients in a mixing bowl and mix with an electric mixer at medium speed for 2 minutes. Add the next 4 ingredients and mix for 2 minutes. Blend the next 2 ingredients and mix for 2 minutes. Drop dough from a tablespoon onto lightly oiled baking sheets. Sprinkle a few oatmeal flakes in the center of each cookie. Bake in a preheated 300° F. oven until brown—about 25 minutes.

Yield: about 45.

SALT-FREE WHOLE-WHEAT SUNFLOWER COOKIES

¾ cup raw sugar
1 cup toasted wheat germ
1 cup soybean oil
2 eggs
¾ cup buttermilk
½ cup sunflower seeds
½ teaspoon orange extract

1 teaspoon vanilla extract
2 teaspoons lecithin
2 tablespoons soybean powder
¾ cup stone-ground
  whole-wheat flour
Sunflower seeds

Using an electric mixer, combine the first 4 ingredients in a mixing bowl and mix for 2 minutes at medium speed. Add the next 4 ingredients and mix for 2 minutes. Stir in the next 3 ingredients and mix for 2 minutes. Drop dough from a tablespoon onto ungreased cookie sheets. Top each cookie with a few sunflower seeds and bake in a preheated 300° F. oven for 30 minutes or until brown.

Yield: about 45.

CHOCOLATE NUT BROWNIES
(Gayle's Favorite)

2 squares unsweetened
  chocolate
½ cup soybean oil
2 eggs
¾ cup raw sugar
2 teaspoons vanilla extract
⅔ cup Fearn Soy-O Mix

¼ cup Viobin Wheat Germ
2 tablespoons powdered
  nonfat dry milk
⅓ cup water
½ cup walnut pieces
12 large pecan halves

Combine the chocolate and oil in a saucepan on low heat until chocolate is melted; set aside. Combine the eggs, sugar, and vanilla in a bowl and mix with an electric mixer for 5 minutes. Add the chocolate mixture and blend for 1 minute. Combine the Soy-O Mix, wheat germ, and powdered milk and add half to the batter, mixing for 30 seconds. Add the water and mix for 30 seconds. Add the remaining Soy-O mixture and mix for 1 minute. Stir in the walnut pieces and pour batter into an oiled square baking pan. Top with the pecan halves and bake for about 40 minutes in a preheated 325° F. oven or until a toothpick inserted in the center of the brownies comes out clean. Cool brownies in pan. When cool cut into 12 squares.

Serves 12.

SUNFLOWER DATE STRIPS
(Karen's Favorite)

2 cups raw sugar
1 cup soybean oil
¼ cup powdered nonfat
dry milk
3 eggs
1 teaspoon vanilla extract
1 teaspoon lemon extract
½ teaspoon cinnamon
¼ cup water
¼ cup sunflower meal
1 cup sunflower seeds

1 cup diced pitted dates
½ cup walnut pieces
1 cup soybean powder
1 tablespoon tartrate baking
powder
1 teaspoon sea salt
5 cups unbleached
white–and–wheat-germ flour
2 tablespoons water
Sunflower seeds

With an electric mixer at medium speed, beat the sugar, oil, powdered milk, 2 of the eggs, vanilla, lemon extract, and cinnamon in a bowl for 3 minutes. Add to this mixture the next 3 ingredients and mix for 2 minutes. Add the dates and walnuts and mix for 1 minute. Gradually add the soybean powder, baking powder, salt, and flour at low speed until the dough is thoroughly mixed. Knead dough until smooth on a lightly floured board. Divide dough into 4 balls and roll each ball into an 18-inch rope. Place on oiled baking sheets and flatten each roll to a 4-inch width. Beat together remaining egg and water and brush on the rolls. Sprinkle with sunflower seeds and bake in a preheated 300° F. oven about 30 minutes or until brown. Remove from oven and immediately cut rolls into 2-inch strips.

Yield: 36.

SESAME STRIPS

2 cups raw sugar
1 cup soybean oil
3 tablespoons powdered
   nonfat dry milk
3 eggs
1 teaspoon vanilla extract
1 teaspoon orange extract
½ cup water
¾ cup toasted sesame seeds
¼ cup toasted wheat germ

½ cup soybean powder
1 cup dried currants
½ cup toasted cashew pieces
1 tablespoon tartrate baking
   powder
1 teaspoon sea salt
5½ cups unbleached
   white–and–wheat-germ flour
2 tablespoons water
Toasted sesame seeds

Combine the sugar, oil, powdered milk, 2 of the eggs, vanilla, and orange extract in a bowl and with an electric mixer mix at medium speed for 3 minutes. Add to this mixture the next 4 ingredients and mix for 2 minutes. Add the currants and cashews and mix for 1 minute. Gradually add the next 3 ingredients at low speed until the dough is thoroughly mixed. Knead the dough until smooth on a lightly floured board. Divide into 4 balls, then roll each ball into an 18-inch rope. Place ropes on oiled baking sheets and flatten until each is 4 inches wide. Beat together the remaining egg and water and brush on strips. Sprinkle with sesame seeds and bake in a preheated 300° F. oven about 30 minutes or until brown. Remove from oven and immediately cut into 2-inch strips.

Yield: 36.

DRIED PEACH AND BANANA BARS

3 cups Sesame Streusel
  (see page 279)
½ cup dried peaches
1 cup boiling water
½ cup safflower-oil margarine
½ cup raw sugar
2 eggs
½ cup Barbados molasses
½ cup buttermilk
½ teaspoon cinnamon
1 teaspoon lemon extract

1 cup stone-ground
  whole-wheat flour
¼ cup soybean powder
¼ cup toasted wheat germ
2 teaspoons tartrate baking
  powder
½ teaspoon sea salt
⅓ cup diced dried bananas
⅓ cup chopped macadamia
  nuts

Spread 1½ cups of the Sesame Streusel in the bottom of an oiled 9-inch-square baking pan. Soak the peaches in the water until softened. Drain, discarding water, then dice peaches and set aside. In an electric mixer combine the next 7 ingredients and mix for 3 minutes. Add the next 5 ingredients and mix for 2 minutes. Stir in the peaches, bananas, and macadamia nuts. Pour over the streusel in the baking pan and top with the remaining streusel. Bake in a preheated 350° F. oven about 45 minutes. When cool, cut into 1 × 3-inch bars.
    Yield: 16.

PRUNE APRICOT STREUSEL SQUARES

½ recipe Whole-Wheat
  Walnut Crust (see page 278)
Prune Apricot Mix

½ cup walnut pieces
1½ cups Sesame Streusel
  (see page 279)

Roll out the dough to fit a 9-inch-square baking pan and place in bottom. Fill with the Prune Apricot Mix, top with the walnuts, and sprinkle the Sesame Streusel over all. Bake in a preheated 350° F. oven for 45 minutes. Cool in pan. When cooled slightly, cut into 12 squares.
    Serves 12.

Prune Apricot Mix

1 cup diced pitted prunes
½ cup diced dried apricots
3 cups water
¼ cup raw sugar

¼ cup honey orange
  marmalade
1 teaspoon cinnamon
1 teaspoon orange extract

Combine the first 4 ingredients in a saucepan and cook on a low fire for 30 minutes, stirring occasionally. Remove from heat, add the remaining ingredients, and mix thoroughly. Refrigerate.

PUMPKIN-SEED FRUIT SQUARES

¼ cup toasted wheat germ
½ cup rolled oats
¼ cup powdered nonfat
  dry milk
½ cup raw sugar
⅓ cup Barbados molasses
½ cup soybean oil
2 eggs
½ cup goat-milk yogurt
1 teaspoon vanilla extract

1¼ cups stone-ground
  whole-wheat flour
1 teaspoon tartrate baking
  powder
½ teaspoon sea salt
½ teaspoon cinnamon
½ cup dried currants
½ cup pumpkin seeds
¼ cup chopped pitted dates
¼ cup diced pitted prunes
Pumpkin seeds

Using an electric mixer, combine the first 6 ingredients in a bowl for 1 minute. Add the next 3 ingredients and mix for 2 minutes. Add the remaining ingredients except for the last and mix for 2 minutes. Pour into an oiled 9-inch-square baking pan and top with pumpkin seeds. Bake about 45 minutes in a preheated 350° F. oven. Cool in pan. When cool, cut into 12 squares.
  Serves 12.

WHOLE-WHEAT WALNUT CRUST

2 cups (approximately)
    stone-ground whole-wheat
    flour
½ cup toasted wheat germ

½ cup soybean oil
⅓ cup ground walnuts
1 egg
½ cup cold water

Blend all the ingredients in a bowl until a smooth ball forms, adding a little more flour if needed. Refrigerate well-wrapped in either plastic film or aluminum foil. Will keep in refrigerator for 1 week or can be frozen.

    Yield: dough for 2 8-, 9-, or 10-inch pie crusts.

WHOLE-WHEAT SOUR-CREAM DOUGH

1 cup stone-ground
    whole-wheat flour
1 cup unbleached white–and–
    wheat-germ flour
¼ cup toasted wheat germ

¼ cup soybean powder
½ teaspoon sea salt
¾ cup safflower-oil margarine
1 egg
½ cup sour cream

Blend the first 5 ingredients in a mixing bowl. Add the margarine and stir with a fork until crumbly pieces form. Add the egg and sour cream and mix together until a smooth round ball forms. Wrap well in plastic film or aluminum foil and refrigerate until needed. Will keep in refrigerator for 1 week or can be frozen.

    Yield: dough for 2 8-, 9-, or 10-inch pie crusts.

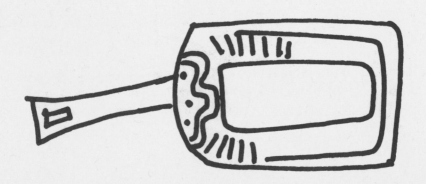

COCONUT SESAME MIX

1 pound unsweetened   2 cups sesame seeds
  shredded coconut

Place coconut on a baking pan in a preheated 300° F. oven and bake until light brown, stirring occasionally. Repeat process, using sesame seeds. When cool, combine in a covered jar or plastic bag and refrigerate. Will keep indefinitely.

Yield: about 6 cups.

SESAME STREUSEL

1 cup raw sugar   3 cups stone-ground
1 cup safflower oil   whole-wheat flour
1 egg   ½ cup toasted wheat germ
2 teaspoons cinnamon   ½ cup toasted sesame seeds

Combine all the ingredients in a mixing bowl, using an electric mixer at medium speed, until crumbs form. Refrigerate in a covered jar.

Yield: about 5 cups.

INDEX